ARKANA

SIMPLE LOVING

Janet Luhrs has studied fine art, commercial art, and photography and has degrees in journalism and law. She has been a newspaper editor and has received numerous writing awards. Janet is the founder, editor, and publisher of *Simple Living*, the journal of voluntary simplicity, which the *Boston Globe* calls "the nation's premier newsletter on voluntary simplification." She is author of the best-selling *The Simple Living Guide* and has hosted her own radio show on public radio. Janet has appeared in nearly all the major media in the United States and Canada, including the *New York Times*, the *Wall Street Journal*, *U.S. News & World Report*, the *Washington Post*, and *Ladies' Home Journal*. When they're not off seeing the world, Janet and h̶e̶r̶ ̶t̶w̶o̶ ̶c̶h̶i̶l̶d̶r̶e̶n̶ ̶l̶i̶v̶e̶ ̶i̶n̶ ̶S̶e̶a̶t̶t̶l̶e̶,̶ ̶W̶a̶s̶h̶i̶n̶g̶t̶o̶n̶.̶

SIMPLE LOVING

A Path to

Deeper, More Sustainable

Relationships

· JANET LUHRS ·

P E N G U I N   A R K A N A

ARKANA
Published by the Penguin Group
Penguin Putnam Inc., 375 Hudson Street,
New York, New York 10014, U.S.A.
Penguin Books Ltd, 27 Wrights Lane,
London W8 5TZ, England
Penguin Books Australia Ltd, Ringwood, Victoria, Australia
Penguin Books Canada Ltd, 10 Alcorn Avenue,
Toronto, Ontario, Canada M4V 3B2
Penguin Books (N.Z.) Ltd, 182–190 Wairau Road,
Auckland 10, New Zealand

Penguin Books Ltd, Registered Offices:
Harmondsworth, Middlesex, England

First published in Arkana 2000

3 5 7 9 10 8 6 4

Illustrations by Dave Albers

LIBRARY OF CONGRESS CATALOGING IN PUBLICATION DATA
Luhrs, Janet.
Simple loving : a path to deeper, more sustainable relationships / Janet Luhrs.
p. cm.
Includes bibliographical references and index.
ISBN 0 14 01.9610 2
1. Marriage.   2. Love.   3. Intimacy (Psychology)
4. Married people—Psychology.   5. Married
people—Conduct of life.   6. Simplicity.   I. Title.
HQ734.L79   2000
646.7´8—dc21   99–087441

Printed in the United States of America
Set in Fairfield Light
Designed by Mia Risberg

Grateful acknowledgment is made for permission to reprint
the following copyrighted works:
"Simple Steps Make a Marriage Sing" by John M.
Gottman. By permission of The Gottman Institute.
Excerpt from To Love and Be Loved by Sam Keen. Copy-
right © 1997 by Sam Keen. Used by permission of Bantam
Books, a division of Random House, Inc.
Selection from The Prophet by Kahlil Gibran. Copyright
1923 by Kahlil Gibran and renewed 1951 by Administrators
CTA of Kahlil Gibran Estate and Mary G. Gibran. Reprinted
by permission of Alfred A. Knopf, a division of Random
House, Inc.
Excerpts from There Is a Season by Joan Chittister. Copy-
right 1995 by Joan Chittister. Published by Orbis Books,
Maryknoll, New York. Used by permission of the publisher.
Excerpt from "Know Deeply, Know Thyself More Deeply"
from Complete Poems by D. H. Lawrence, edited by Vivian de
Sola Pinto and Warren Roberts. Copyright © Angelo Ravagli
and C. M. Weekley, Executors of The Estate of Frieda
Lawrence Ravagli, 1964, 1971. Used by permission of Viking
Penguin, a member of Penguin Putnam Inc.

"The Hard Work of Relationships" and "Keep Track of
Conflict in Order to Avoid It" by Donna Miller. By permission
of the author.
"Learning Humility" by Thich Nhat Hanh, The Mindful-
ness Bell, issue 15, 1995–1996. Reprinted by permission of
Thich Nhat Hanh.
Selections from On the Wings of Eros compiled by Alicia
Alvrez. Copyright © 1995 by Alicia Alvrez. Used by permis-
sion of Conari Press.
"Four Key Qualities to Turn an Ordinary Home into a Per-
sonal Haven" and "6 Special Ways to Enhance Your Sanctu-
ary" by Tricia Clark-McDowell and Forrest McDowell. By
permission of the authors.
Excerpt from Simply Organized! by Connie Cox and Cris
Evatt. Copyright © The Simply Organized Woman, 1986.
Used by permission of The Berkley Publishing Group, a
member of Penguin Putnam Inc.
Excerpt from True Love by Daphne Rose Kingma. Copy-
right © 1994 by Daphne Rose Kingma. Used by permission
of Conari Press.
Excerpts from 1001 Ways to Be Romantic and Love—The
Course They Forgot to Teach You in School by Gregory Godek.
Copyright © 1997, 2000 by Gregory Godek. Reprinted by
permission of the publisher, Sourcebooks, Inc.
Excerpt from How to Stay Lovers for Life by Sharyn Wolf.
Copyright © Sharyn Wolf, 1997. Used by permission of Dut-
ton, a member of Penguin Putnam Inc.
Excerpts from Simple Pleasures by Robert Taylor, Susannah
Seton, and David Greer. Copyright © 1996 by Robert Taylor,
Susannah Seton, and David Greer. Used by permission of
Conari Press.
Excerpts from Goddess in the Kitchen by Margie Lapanja.
Copyright © 1998 by Margie Lapanja. Used by permission of
Conari Press.
Excerpt from The Spell of the Sensuous by David Abram.
Copyright © 1996 by David Abram. Used by permission of
Random House, Inc.
"A Third Body" from Loving a Woman in Two Worlds by
Robert Bly. Copyright © 1985 by Robert Bly. Used by permis-
sion of Doubleday, a division of Random House, Inc.
Excerpt from "Marriage: What's the Point?" by Susan
Dixon, Context, no. 10. Reprinted by permission of Context
Institute.
"Inexpensive Ideas for Keeping the Romance Alive" by
Michael Webb, The RoMANtic Newsletter. By permission of
the author.
"Balancing Rituals for Couples" from Living in Balance by
Joel Levey and Michelle Levey (Conari Press, 1998). By per-
mission of the authors.
"Are There Wedding Bells in Your Future?" by Juliette Fair-
ley, Investor's Business Daily. By permission of Investor's Busi-
ness Daily, Inc.
"Team Safer" by Marilyn Meyer. By permission of the au-
thor.
"The Need to Give and Receive Affection" by Lloyd J.
Thomas. By permission of the author.
Selections from Wedding Alternatives, published by Alter-
natives for Simple Living. Used by permission of the pub-
lisher.
"Creating a Marriage Contract" by Peter Sugarman and
Kirstie Lewis. By permission of the authors.
"Green Weddings" by Carol Reed-Jones. By permission of
the author.

Photograph credits:
Page 12: photo by Valari Jack. 39: Eugene Gal. 63: Renee
Nelson. 90: Sarah Wall. 113: Gail Moulton. 141: Janet Luhrs.
165: Phil Schofield. 189: Marilyn Phillis. 210: Yuen Lui Stu-
dios, Seattle, Washington. 228: Jim Bammert. 229: Janet
Luhrs.

To the loves and delights of my life, Patrick and Jessica.
And to those who taught me about love by being there:
Mom, Dad, Karen, and Don, and Auntie Pat, too.
And how could I forget: In loving memory of Gram.

THANK-YOU PAGE

Thank you to my wonderful literary agent, Theresa Park, and to the best editor, Janet Goldstein, for their inspiration and support in creating this book. And thank you to Associate Editor Susan Hans O'Connor for her work as my "personal editorial trainer," in helping to get the manuscript into shape! Thank you Marilyn Meyer, for your time, comments, and friendship. Finally, thank you to all of the individuals and couples who shared their intimate lives with me, so we could all learn to love deeply. And for helping to keep those home fires burning at my journal, *Simple Living*, thank you to a very devoted staff: Patty Lowry, Heidi Wolf, Nancy Reifler, and Marin Bjork, and to Lynn Pruzan and Michelle Hall.

CONTENTS

INTRODUCTION

W e teach what we have to learn. After the emotional fallout from my divorce, I decided what I needed to do was learn what it takes to have a lasting intimate relationship. But I wanted more than what had been written about in the typical "how-to" relationship books—something deeper, that spoke of the soul, and the heart of intimacy. I wanted to be inspired. Then I remembered. I had interviewed many, many people involved in the simplicity movement in some way, large or small, over the seven years I'd published my newsletter, *Simple Living*, and more for my book, *The Simple Living Guide*. What stayed with me was the special closeness of the couples. I wondered why I was so much more affected by these people I interviewed than by most other couples I knew. What was the link? What were these people doing, or how were they different, from couples who had not simplified their lives in some way?

I knew that the concept of simplicity was painted broadly—it didn't mean just one thing, or have one set of rules that applied to everybody. I had met people who had simplified their lives in a variety of ways—some lived in the city and held professional jobs and careers, others lived in small towns, and still others on twenty-five acres, generating their own light and heat. Some had children; some did not. Their ages and incomes ranged all over the spectrum. So what was the common theme?

The first thing I realized was that all these people have very high levels of self-awareness. They have taken the time to know themselves as individual human beings—and to know themselves deeply. They are also fully aware that this journey of inner knowledge is an ongoing one, and they make room for that in their relationships. I also noticed that they are very conscious about the way they design and live their lives. Those lives don't necessarily follow what society says are the right and proper routes—no, they are lifestyles specifically created by and for these people. They know what they are doing; they do not live on autopilot. There are a few other common threads: none of them carry consumer debt, all of them know what "enough" is for them, none compare themselves to the Joneses, and all have a more wide-ranging picture of life than simply going to work, paying the bills, and dropping exhausted at night in front of the TV. Some have always lived this way, and others came to it after years of frustration trying to keep up and get ahead.

But what exactly was this splendid closeness I perceived in the couples? I interviewed more couples and then sat quietly with my thoughts, ultimately creating a list of critical traits, beginning with *who they are as human beings,* moving into *how they relate to each other,* and ending with *how they interact in the world.* I explored these traits and turned each one into a chapter. I was so inspired that I wanted to share what I'd learned with other people who wondered the same thing: *What's missing in our lives and how can we create whatever that is?*

The closeness that I witnessed in these couples is brought on not just by *living,* but by *loving* consciously, and loving from the depths of their souls. The couples connect at their essence, rather than on the surface. It was also refreshing to discover that these people are not perfect. They argue and disagree like anyone else, but the difference is they are able to ultimately stand back from the argument and see it for what it is. They are able to see past daily irritations to the big picture of their lives. They are able to see that whatever disappointment is going on in the moment is not worth losing their precious relationship over. But they are also clear, as one husband said, that their marriage is not a set of murky compromises. Instead, it is an evolution of two defined people who can stand on their own as well as together. Most of them also live under a common umbrella of values. Something bigger than themselves keeps them together and thriving. This, I discovered, is the heart and soul of loving simply . . . the examined life, the examined relationship.

These are the stories about couples with open space, open time; about two people focusing within and on one another, and not on who is busier and whose career is more important. These are the stories of the husband who brushes his wife's hair every night as she reads to him; of the couple who celebrates the coming of Christmas not by shopping frantically, but by turning the lights off in the evening, lying side by side near the fire, not speaking, and noticing the lines around each other's eyes as if for the first time. This is about the couples who celebrate, not ignore, the simple pleasures of life . . . like making love on the screened porch during thunderstorms. A husband writes:

> For six months of the year we sleep on a screened porch in the woods, on the floor, on a thin foam pad. Last midnight's thunderstorm was a miracle: the faraway rumblings, then the hot hurried winds and first huge drops breaking on the screens into a million tiny droplets of life. We laughed, and we made love to the beat of nature's greatest sound-and-light show . . .
>
> Come, be with us. Any day, any night. Each moment is truly a miracle, but this can only be so if we humans are willing to slow down, to turn off the lights, to be silent, to listen, to see, to wonder.

These are couples who live in the modern world, yet still make time for each other, time for themselves, and time for their children. They are couples who say that when all else is stripped away, a life lived with love is what matters.

This book is about creating that open space, open time, letting go of some of the busyness and demands of everyday life, and in exchange, going deeper within ourselves, and with our partners.

• *Part One* •

IT STARTS WITH ME

Chapter *I*

The Soul of a
Simple Loving Relationship

The soul should always stand ajar ready
to welcome the ecstatic experience.
—EMILY DICKINSON

A Buddhist nun asked my meditation group to describe our souls. We sat looking at her, a sea of blank faces struggling with the concept. Then she asked us to imagine that we, as human beings, were laid out in parts—the arms, legs, toes, noses, and so on. Was that "us," she asked? We could easily describe and see a leg, an arm, skin, teeth. So, was that a human being? Was that what made me different from you? Well, on one level, yes. My eyes and my legs are different from yours. But what about the bad jokes I tell? Where do those come from? What about the twinkle in your eye? What is that all about?

We squirmed. What *is* that all about? Where does it come from? What is this soul, anyway? It's so much easier to live in the concrete world where we can categorize, label, describe, and be certain. But we all know the soul is there. If we took the soul out, we'd be lifeless . . . no twinkles, no tears, no bad jokes, . . . just the legs, arms, and noses, covered with a new

· 3

outfit, maybe a briefcase in the hand, maybe beautiful hair, maybe fingers on the wheel of a red sports car. But no twinkles.

Once I had a partner complain to me that I never danced with him. He didn't mean literally dance—he meant stop and listen to his soul. It was a plea to go deeper, past his skin and into his essence, past talking about what he did for a living, what he thought about the latest events in the news, past all that, and into the music of his heart.

The music of the heart is Simple Loving—connecting two people at that mysterious level underneath the outfit, briefcase, car, legs, and hair. Connecting at the poetry—the drama and magnificence—of each of us. It is not about the dulling of our existence or leading lives of quiet desperation, as Henry David Thoreau put it. If the soul is nourished, it takes us beyond the torpid ache that continually whispers, "There must be more than this." It reaches for the absolute height of our splendor, yet also allows for the depths of our despair. It is not shallow. It is both the mystery and the madness.

Simple Loving calls us to unearth the soul that we have masked with our outward lives. We've covered our souls with jobs, new cars, more clothes, tools, gadgets, and toys. Many of us have become so adept at masking that we're hardly aware of our souls being in there: in a blur we go to college, get a job, earn money, rise up the corporate ladder, get married, buy a house, raise families, watch TV. Day after day we're out of the house at seven-thirty, going to a meeting at three, convening for drinks at five, skiing on Saturday, fixing the car on Tuesday, meeting the deadline at the end of the week, taking the kids to soccer after school, reveling in the promotion, shopping to allay our tears, eating to feel nourished. Who's in there? No time to think about it. As James Hillman, author of *The Soul's Code*, says, "We're living in the shallows of meaningless. We are not put here on earth to simply do the daily rounds."

Indeed, the more we've got going on the outside, the more successful and important we seem. Being soulful doesn't mean turning away from worldly pleasures and successes; rather, it means balancing those things with our inner selves, and not defining who we are and where we stand in

THE PRACTICE OF ATTENTION

by Sam Keen

The discipline of attention begins with meta-attention. Cultivate the habit of inter- rupting yourself to take note of what you habitually notice and what you ignore. Spy on your own consciousness. Meditate on how you invest your consciousness.

✧ Do you habitually lavish your attention on ideas? Things? Persons? Col- leagues? Clients? Customers? Friends? A lover? Family? On your body, mind, spirit? The goings-on in your community? God? The enemy? Money? Sports?

✧ If you were to chart the changing foci of your attention during the course of a day, what would the graph look like? And if, to paraphrase Jesus, "where your at- tention is, there will your heart be also," what would your pattern of attention say about you? What priority would love have in the hierarchy of your days? How would you like to change your investments of attention, time, and concern?

✧ Think back to the first time you made contact with a person whom you have come to love. Remember the moment in detail, and reconstruct it as a film pro- ducer or novelist would. How was the scene lit? What caught your attention? What did you feel? Were you attracted or repulsed by your first impression? How close or distant were you from the center of the scene? What other persons were present? As you reconsider this first contact in light of what you have since come to know and love about the person, were the first impressions that you had accu- rate or inaccurate?

—From *To Love and Be Loved*

the universe by those outward manifestations. On the outside, those things make us look as though we're fulfilled. On the inside, it can be another story.

Often we remain on the surface because it's safer and easier than revealing our depth. Sooner or later we notice that we are lonely, because those whom we most want to be intimate with—our partners—have only our top layer to love or even exist with. How many people have we all met (including ourselves) who tell us how alone they feel in their marriages? They connect with their partners over the kids, the chores, perhaps the vacations and the plans, but not with their souls.

You can tell when people connect with each other's souls, rather than merely on the outside. The soul connections say things like "She touches my heart" before they mention what she does for a living. The soul connections place more emphasis on sharing similar values, rather than sharing similar activities. Someone who shares your soul is more concerned with your well-being than with what

> *Ah, I remember well (and how can I*
> *But evermore remember well) when first*
> *Our flame began, when scarce we knew what was*
> *The flame we felt.*
>
> —ETHAN CANIN

outfit you are wearing tonight. The soul connections live fully in the world, as much as anybody, but they've added another dimension, and that is the core of who we are as human beings.

Simple Loving is all about that unexplainable whistle—the connection that is soul to soul, rather than career to career or ego to ego. James Hillman likens our soul to an acorn: we are all born with our destiny written into the acorn. "It's already there," he says, "[but] we dull our lives by the way we conceive them. We have stopped imagining them with any sort of romance, any fictional flair."

We could say we are leading pseudo lives—plenty on the surface, but not much underneath. The *Wall Street Journal* carried an article that described this style of living: "Achieving balance isn't easy. By the time most people acquire a casual chic wardrobe, a vacation home with rustic country decor, get married, have children, get them into private schools, buy a utility vehicle, work out, master the Internet, and climb a mountain, they are exhausted. That may be why the antidepressant Prozac is also quite hip."

There we are. Busy covering all the surface bases of our lives, with no time left over to nourish the spirit. Perhaps Prozac is "hip" because we can only deny our souls for so long: Something has to give.

Thomas Moore, author of *Care of the Soul*, says:

> The emotional complaints of our time, complaints we therapists hear every day in our practice, include:
>
> > *emptiness*
> > *meaninglessness*
> > *vague depression*
> > *disillusionment about marriage, family, and relationships*
> > *a loss of values*
> > *yearning for personal fulfillment*
> > *a hunger for spirituality*
>
> All of these symptoms reflect a loss of soul and let us know what the soul craves. We yearn excessively for entertainment, power, intimacy, sexual fulfillment, and material things, and we think we can find these things if we discover the right relationship or job, the right church or therapy. But without soul, whatever we find will be unsatisfying, for what we truly long for is the soul in each of these areas.

We may deny our soul in the way we conduct our individual lives, and perhaps also in the way we relate to each other. Most of us forget that at some level all of our intimate pairings are soul mates—drawn to each other to fulfill some destiny or other of the soul, and not simply to go to the movies together. Relating at a soul level allows for the full range of our imperfect humanness—which, underneath it all, is what we all crave so much. "I just want to be understood and be allowed to be myself," we all

SIMPLE STEPS MAKE A MARRIAGE SING

by John Gottman, Ph.D.

There are simple steps you can take to keep your marriage alive and healthy. Here are some ideas that have been gleaned from years of research with couples:

1. Seek help early. The average couple waits six years before seeking help for marital problems (and half of all marriages that end do so in the first seven years). Meaning the average couple lives with unhappiness for far too long.

2. Edit yourself. Couples who avoid saying every angry thought when discussing touchy topics are consistently the happiest.

3. Be careful how you "start up" a conversation. Arguments first "start up" because a spouse sometimes escalates the conflict from the get-go by making a dramatic, or angry, or upsetting remark in a confrontational tone.

4. A marriage succeeds to the extent that the husband can accept influence from his wife. If a woman says, "Do you have to work Thursday night? My mother is coming that weekend, and I need your help getting ready," a husband who replies "My plans are set, and I'm not changing them" is a guy in a shaky marriage.

A husband's ability to be persuaded by his wife is so critical because, research shows, women are already well practiced at accepting influence from men, and a true partnership only occurs when a husband is able to do so as well.

5. *Happy couples had high standards for each other even as newlyweds.* The most successful couples are those who, even as newlyweds, refused to accept hurtful behavior from each other. The lower the level of tolerance for bad behavior in the beginning of a relationship, the happier the couple is down the road.

6. *Successful couples know how to exit an argument.* Happy couples know how to repair the situation before an argument gets completely out of control. Successful repair attempts include: gossiping about other people together (very useful); changing the topic to something completely unrelated; throwing in some humor; stroking your partner with a caring remark ("I understand that this is hard for you"); making it clear you're on common ground ("This is our problem"); backing down (in marriage, as in the martial art Aikido, you have to yield to win); and, in general, offering signs of appreciation for your partner and his or her feelings along the way ("I really appreciate and want to thank you for . . .")

7. *Focus on the bright side.* In a happy marriage, couples make five times as many positive statements to and about each other and their relationship ("We laugh a lot" as opposed to "We never have fun") as negative ones. A good marriage must have a rich climate of positivity. Make deposits to your emotional bank account.

John Gottman is director of the Gottman Institute and author of *Why Marriages Succeed or Fail* (New York: Simon & Schuster, 1994). For information, call 888-523-9042 or contact www.gottman.com.

say. "Why can't I be loved for being me? Why do I always feel that who I am is not enough?"

Loving the full range of our humanness is not living a life swept under the carpet. Stephen Levine, profiled on page 11, says: "If we can't share our suffering and can't swim in the reservoir of each other's grief, we have a shallow relationship. Most people withdraw when their partner's grief comes out. That's the time to grow, not leave."

Tricia Clark-McDowell, profiled on page 62, said of her marriage: "We've come to accept all of our moods, including melancholy, which is a very delicious, bittersweet sadness. It's not depression. We honor it in each other—we know we're in this together, and so we accept each other's ups and downs. Usually people who are depressed go into an escapist mode by eating ice cream, or watching a video. If it's their partner who is depressed, they'll think, 'if so and so is in a funky mood, I'm out of here.' I used to do that, too."

Simple loving, soul loving, is really no more than loving first ourselves and then each other at the core. We may still have our briefcases and cars, but we can't stop there.

Our core selves are so much more than our outer personas and worldly labels . . . accountant, college graduate, chef, homemaker, or farmer. We are more than the books we have read or not read, the sports we play, the exotic destinations we have visited, the facts and figures we can rattle off at parties. We initially connect at those levels, but Simple Loving does not stop there. After all, what are all the boats, degrees, club memberships, and clothes if we are not cherished at our depth?

Loving simply takes time, and loving simply gives time. The couples who live and love simply have given more priority to their compassionate, open, cooperative, loving souls than to their outer, commercial layers of success. "We're not poor," they often say. "We just measure wealth and happiness in a different way—by our level of intimacy, our personal and family growth, and by the fact that we live in harmony."

Loving simply nourishes our souls—after all, our souls aren't so concerned with wearing the right watch, driving the right car, going to the right places. That nourishment comes instead from connection, intimacy, and authenticity. When the desire for intimacy and authenticity is stronger than the desire for worldly applause, many changes occur within a relationship: we toss out the focus on power and status, we stop the competition with each other. And when we feel so secure within ourselves that we have no need to control and dominate others, we open ourselves to loving cooperation.

A woman quoted in Duane Elgin's book, *Voluntary Simplicity*, said it well: "Voluntary simplicity is an individual thing . . . It has to be something that springs from the heart because it was always there, not something you can be talked into by persuasive people, or something that is brought on by financial necessity . . . This is not something we do because we want to be different, or because we're rebellious to convention, but because our souls find a need for it."

A Conscious Marriage

Stephen Levine says that nearly every morning when he wakes up, he's grateful his wife of twenty years, Ondrea, is next to him. Ondrea feels the same way. Both of them are conscious about this—they don't just wake up to the scream of an alarm clock, mindlessly race out of bed, inhale a piece of toast, and fly out the door to another life. Instead, after years of learning to be mindful, they awaken consciously, noticing their beloved next to them and feeling joy.

At the same time, the Levines are just as aware that their marriage has been a challenging vehicle for their greatest growth. Stephen says: "Relationship is one of the ways we come to know ourselves, because it's a fierce mirror. It's so fierce that's why people get out. They can't stand the pain. We're in pain because we can't stand the wretchedness. Relationships confront us with our fears, our desire for control, distrust, anger, abusiveness. It's all right there, in a relationship. That's why 35,000 children are dying from hunger today. It's from greed, fear, distrust, seeing people as 'other.' If we didn't see people as 'other,' including our partners, then how would we let a child die for lack of food when we have pancakes we're throwing away? That sense of 'me' and 'other' is the basis of all difficulties, and at the same time, a remarkable potential for healing all relationships."

Stephen Levine is a poet and teacher of Buddhist meditation. He's written many books, including *A Gradual Awakening*, *Who Dies?*, *Healing into Life and Death*, and *A Year to Live*. He and Ondrea wrote *Embracing the Beloved* about their relationship. Together, they work with the terminally ill and travel around the country giving workshops.

"Deeper love is about healing together," says Stephen Levine of his relationship with Ondrea. "It happens when your heart is open and your mind is clear."

"I can't imagine being with someone else," Stephen says. "I looked for Ondrea in everyone I met, and when we finally did meet, I knew instantly it was her. I was looking for a true heart . . . a mystical union. When love really happens, it's like meeting a teacher. It's gravity. You don't decide to fall, but the ground is no longer beneath you."

This is Stephen's third marriage and Ondrea's second. She came to the marriage with one child, and he came with two. They raised all of them together. He admits that merging the families was "a shakedown at first" but they evolved over the years to the point where Ondrea's son is as close to Stephen as anyone, and vice versa. There was a period when Stephen and Ondrea's son did not get along. Stephen says, "At one moment I turned to him and said, 'James, are we going to be like this forever? What a shame. What a loss for both of us.' Our relationship changed from that moment on."

Stephen says this about their philosophy of intimate relationships: "Ondrea and I are the most important *people* in each other's lives, but we're not the most important *thing* in each other's lives. The most important *thing* to us is growth, insight, love, evolution, and spirit. If you're in a relationship with someone and she is the most important *thing* to you, you're in big trouble because you've got no frame of reference for when the heart is not open. When she's gone, all you feel is abandoned and angry, but if you have mindfulness, insight, a sense of connection to the divine, no matter what is taken away, you always have that connection. From there come understanding, compassion, and forgiveness."

There is no single way to open your consciousness, and what works for one person does not necessarily work for someone else. It can be a meditation practice, a service practice . . . anything that focuses you on something bigger than yourself. Stephen says, "I know nurses who come to their shift two and a half hours early just so they can sit and cradle the dying children who will never be taken home. In that two and a half hours you could ask them, 'Are you meditating?' and they'd say, 'No, I'm just holding this child.' It's the same thing—they have connected to something larger than themselves."

For Stephen and Ondrea, the connection is through service as well as a regular practice of meditating. He says, "I've taught with the Dalai Lama and Zen masters, and *nothing* has taught me more than simply sitting quietly with merciful awareness, watching what arises in my mind when it arises . . . the insight comes and I see that nothing is worth the heart being closed, even for a moment longer. The more your heart opens, the further it has to go to close."

৵ *Regular Meditation*

Once you follow a regular practice of meditation, you take that same awareness with you as you go through your day. You begin to pay attention to your thoughts and sensations, and become more attuned to your partner's subtle shifts as well. Stephen says, "The Buddha taught that you can learn as much insight into state of mind by watching another as you can by watching yourself; so to the degree that I'm familiar with my own fear, I can meet Ondrea's state of fear with love rather than judgment.

"I love Ondrea, but that doesn't mean that there aren't times when our hearts don't meet. The mark of growth for us is not that those things don't happen, but that they drop away sooner and sooner and sooner.

"We all have bad days, bad periods," he says. "All of us. In fact, once I asked the Dalai Lama, 'do you have fear?' He said, 'Not only do I have fear, but I have anxiety, too.' If he has these, then everybody does, but it doesn't mean that in the next millisecond he can't enter into a more loving space.

"Insights in relationships can come at any time. You can be together twenty-three and a half hours a day just being, helping, smiling, nothing special, then in that last half hour of the day something happens between you that triggers an old childhood pain. That's where real healing is possible. When you're in a relationship you'll have to accept that you'll swim in the reservoir of your partner's grief. That means, not swimming in circles, but swimming across the lake, across that sea of sorrow to get to the other side together. For most people, as soon as the other person's grief comes up they withdraw and say, 'she's too neurotic,' or 'he's too negative,' and so on.

"These things that draw people apart in an unconscious relationship are the gems that draw them together in a conscious relationship."

৵ *A Conscious Relationship*

Stephen says: "A relationship doesn't really start until those states of mind arise. The love and chemicals go on for six months, a year, two years, but

FOCUS ON WHAT YOU HAVE

If your relationship isn't bringing you the joy and passion you wish for and the focus is more and more on what you don't have as a couple, try an experiment for two weeks: focus on what you do have instead. This can be difficult in the midst of a low ebb in a relationship, so start out just getting through one day with a positive focus, then the next day, and so on, until you get to two weeks. If your partner won't try this with you, then do it alone, remembering that when you behave differently, your partner will be affected—most likely in a positive way.

During these two weeks, it can help to keep a daily list of these positives, just to remind you that they do indeed exist. By completing this exercise, you will find that your attitude will have changed for the better, and that will surely have an impact on your partner. If not, at least you will feel better on the inside, which is a magnificent gift to yourself.

real love doesn't start until disappointment arises. If you have no room for disappointment, you have no room for a relationship and no room for enlightenment, because a relationship is one insult after another, in the sense that the other person does not agree with you.

"In the beginning, it's great. You want the red one, and I want the red one. You want blue, and I want blue. Then your partner wakes up and says, 'I want yellow, and you want blue.' If that person is the most important *thing* to you, your relationship is over. But if becoming whole is the most important thing to you, you'll see this as a challenge, not a defeat.

"My advice is to pay attention. Watch your judging mind and your communication. And recognize that projection is a really important part of a relationship. The person into whose eyes you're looking is in as much pain as anybody. When your awareness gets deeper, you go more and more to love. The deeper you go, the less definable you are, and the more real you become. The more shallow you are, the more your partner is an object of your mind, instead of the subject of your heart, and the less likely you are to connect on a deeper and deeper level.

"Deeper love is about healing together and finding someone you can work with on an even keel—sometimes you're the helper, and sometimes you're the helped. You switch roles. It happens when you can really trust somebody; when you can love without needing to be loved. It happens when your heart is open and your mind is clear."

ↂ   ↂ   ↂ

Resources

BOOKS

Awakening Intuition, by Frances E. Vaughan (New York: Anchor, 1979).

Care of the Soul: A Guide for Cultivating Depth and Sacredness in Everyday Life, by Thomas Moore (New York: HarperPerennial, 1994).

Finding Your Way Home: A Soul Survival Kit, by Melody Beattie (San Francisco: HarperSanFrancisco, 1998).

Handbook for the Soul, edited by Richard Carlson and Benjamin Shield (Boston: Little, Brown, 1997).

Inner Knowing: Consciousness, Creativity, Insight, and Intuition, edited by Helen Palmer (New York: Putnam, 1999).

Karmic Relationships, by Martin Schulman (York Beach, Maine: Samuel Weiser, 1987).

Living in Process: Basic Truths for Living the Path of the Soul, by Anne Wilson Schaef (New York: Ballantine, 1998).

The Marriage of Sense and Soul, by Ken Wilber (New York: Broadway Books, 1999).

The Scientific Evidence for Past Lives of Old Souls, by Tom Shroder (New York: Simon & Schuster, 1999).

The Seat of the Soul, by Gary Zukav (New York: Fireside, 1990).

Seven Steps to Developing Your Intuitive Powers, by Betty Bethards (Rockport, Mass.: Element, 1998).

The Soul Bird, by Mikhal Senuit (New York: Hyperion, 1999).

Soul Healing, by Dr. Bruce Goldberg (St. Paul, Minn.: Llewellyn, 1996).

Soul Mates, by Thomas Moore (New York: HarperPerennial, 1994).

Soul Play: Turning Your Daily Dramas into Divine Comedies, by Vivian King, Ph.D. (Georgetown, Mass.: Ant Hill Press, 1998).

Soul Psychology: How to Clear Your Negative Emotions and Spiritualize Your Life, by Joshua David Stone, Ph.D. (New York: Ballantine Wellspring, 1999).

Soul Purpose: Discovering and Fulfilling Your Destiny, by Mark Thurston, Ph.D. (New York: St. Martin's, 1989).

Soul Therapy, by Joy Manne (Berkeley, Calif.: North Atlantic Books, 1997).

Soulful Living: The Process of Personal Transformation, edited by Rick Nurrie-Stearns, Mary NurrieStearns, and Melissa West (Deerfield Park, Fla.: Health Communications, 1999).

The Soul's Code, by James Hillman (New York: Warner, 1997).

Soulwork: Clearing the Mind, Opening the Heart, and Replenishing the Spirit, by BettyClare Moffatt (Berkeley, Calif.: Wildcat Canyon Press and New World Library, 1994).

A Soulworker's Companion: A Year of Spiritual Discovery, by BettyClare Moffatt (Berkeley, Calif.: Wildcat Canyon Press, 1996).

Spirit Called My Name: A Journey of Deepening into Soul, by Sally M. O'Neil (Freeland, Wash.: Soaring Eagle Publishing, 1997).

Chapter 2

Loving Authentically

When love beckons to you, follow him
Though his ways are hard and steep.
And when his wings enfold you yield to him,
Though the sword hidden among his pinions may wound you.
And when he speaks to you believe in him,
Though his voice may shatter your dreams as the north wind lays
   waste the garden.
For even as love crowns you so shall he crucify you.
Even as he is for your growth so he is for your pruning.
Even as he ascends to your height and caresses your tenderest
   branches that quiver in the sun,
So shall he descend to your roots and shake them in their clinging to
   the earth.

—FROM *The Prophet*, BY KAHLIL GIBRAN

I read this poem a few times until I understood it with my heart. It's about not hiding from love—but instead, fully committing to it and learning. Love is the greatest of teachers in that *if we stay conscious and open*, sooner or later, we *will* learn our lessons. But in order to learn those lessons, *we need to be as real and authentic as we possibly can*. We can learn nothing if we wear masks, we can learn very little if we do not look within ourselves and use love's lessons for our growth, and we can learn even less if we don't listen to our hearts and souls. We can only pay attention to our core when we are authentic—because it takes great authenticity in order to know ourselves that well.

I have learned my greatest lessons when I have paid attention to my soul—even if it didn't seem like the most "intelligent" idea at the time, and even if it caused me some amount of pain. One of Tennyson's most famous lines is " 'Tis better to have loved and lost than never to have loved at all." I couldn't agree more. Love has broken my heart, and love has elevated my heart to the heights of passion and delight. I am thankful that I have bared my soul in order to have lived and loved deeply. I cherish this aspect of simplicity, which is living an authentic, vital life.

It is for this reason that I never look back on my life and regret the past by saying things such as "If only" or "Why was I so stupid" or "I wish I hadn't done it that way" . . . That's because I know that all the decisions I've made in my life led me to a particular lesson—a lesson I needed to learn. I've been able to move forward like this only because I do look upon past relationships as lessons that benefited me, rather than focusing either blame or longing on the other person. This doesn't mean that during the process I am not angry at that person, or that I don't grieve or feel any other emotion—it simply means that as soon as I am able to, I sit back and look at the big picture of my life and ask myself what my soul needed to learn. I can do that when I follow the words of the poem and realize that even as love crowns me, "So shall he crucify you. Even as he is for your growth so he is for your pruning . . ."

Joan Chittister says in *There Is a Season*: "Life is not a drama made up of scenes around a common theme leading to resolution. No, . . . life is a series of experiences, all of them important, all of them here to be plumbed and squeezed and sucked dry, not for their own sake but so that we may come to know ourselves. Life is not what we see happening on the outside. Life is what goes on inside in the quiet, murky waters of our souls."

Loving authentically—that is, without masks—is the nuts and bolts of loving from our souls. After all, the soul is the absolute core of who we are—no masks, no facades, no saying all is well when it isn't, no smiles covering tears, no following pursuits that don't nourish our hearts, and no defensiveness layered on top of vulnerability.

Loving authentically takes guts; yet it is also deeply, passionately, and incredibly satisfying. When I think of loving authentically, I imagine that I am a beautiful, strong willow tree—able to stand in my ground knowing full well who I am—yet also able to bend in the breeze. Being authentic means knowing myself down to my roots and letting the world see me as I am. But it can also be frightening, standing out there in the world, emotionally naked.

When I am a willow tree, I can be with another and can still stand my ground—I don't change and become a different kind of tree just to please the other. I stand as myself even when the other pushes up against me. But I can bend when I want to, and I can grow when I need to.

If I am not this willow tree, then I'm not sure who I am inside. I hold out my mirror to everyone who walks by and ask them to reflect back to me who I am. If they say I'm lovable, then I feel lovable. If they say I'm not appealing, then I don't feel appealing. If they want me to be a certain way, then I'll try to become that way hoping they will like me.

There is no depth, no fire, no honest-to-goodness passion in living a facade. It's also exhausting because we're always questioning, shifting to suit the circumstances, and molding to avoid confrontation. Being authentic takes courage, because we lay bare our deepest selves and hope that when our partners catch a glimpse, they won't walk away in search of someone who appears to have it more together. But when we are authentic, we give our partners space to be authentic, too, and then we both find out that neither of us has it all together. We are authentic and we are vitally alive.

Donna Miller is a therapist in Portland, Oregon, and knows how complex it can be to maintain an image and a life that isn't truly your own. She says, "It takes time—your life—and tremendous effort to figure out how to please or how to fool everyone around you. It's a way of selling yourself

Two Pots

ಌ

A water bearer in India had two large pots, each hung on each end of a pole which he carried across his neck. One of the pots had a crack in it, and while the other pot was perfect and always delivered a full portion of water at the end of the long walk from the stream to the master's house, the cracked pot arrived only half full. For a full two years this went on daily, with the bearer delivering only one and a half potfuls of water in his master's house. Of course, the perfect pot was proud of its accomplishments, perfect for the end for which it was made. But the poor cracked pot was ashamed of its own imperfection, and miserable that it was able to accomplish only half of what it had been made to do.

After two years of what it perceived to be a bitter failure, it spoke to the water bearer one day by the stream: "I am ashamed of myself, and I want to apologize to you." "Why?" asked the bearer. "What are you ashamed of?" "I have been able, for these past two years, to deliver only half my load because this crack in my side causes water to leak out all the way back to your master's house. Because of my flaws, you have to do all of this work, and you don't get full value from your efforts," the pot said. The water bearer felt sorry for the old cracked pot, and in his compassion he said, "As we return to the master's house, I want you to notice the beautiful flowers along the path." Indeed, as they went up the hill, the old cracked pot took notice of the sun warming the beautiful wild flowers on the side of the path, and this cheered it some. But at the end of the trail, it still felt bad because it had leaked out half its load, and so again it apologized to the bearer for its failure. The bearer said to the pot, "Did you notice that there were flowers only on your side of the path, but not on the other pot's side? That's because I have always known about your flaw, and I took advantage of it. I planted flower seeds on your side of the path, and every day while we walk back from the stream, you've watered them. For two years I have been able to pick these beautiful flowers to decorate my master's table. Without you being just the way you are, he would not have this beauty to grace his house."

Each of us has our own unique flaws. We're all cracked pots. So don't be afraid of your flaws. Acknowledge them, take advantage of them, and you, too, can be the cause of beauty.

—AUTHOR UNKNOWN

out, ending up in a Gordian knot of blame, resentment, double binds, dilemmas, and divorces until you quiet down and get to know yourself.

"To show up in a relationship as authentically who you are, you have to know yourself. Every one of us has heard that phrase so often that we barely even bother to give it anything but superficial lip service. To know yourself, you have to slow down and pay attention. Getting real is a slow discovery. It is a slow and sometimes painful revealing of yourself to yourself and others. It cannot be done in the fast lane.

"Becoming who you are reminds me of the children's classic *The Velveteen Rabbit*, where the stuffed animal becomes real by being loved and played with and pummeled by a live little boy. It is the daily wear and tear and nurturing of love that turns it into something deep. If we allow it, *life* becomes the teacher, *love* is the subject, and long-term intimate relationship is the authenticity boot camp."

Donna has been inspired by the work of Dr. David Schnarch, author of *Passionate Marriage*. His focus is on helping partners in intimate relationships to become what he calls "differentiated": capable of being close and intimate with their partner, while also being fully authentic and able to hold on to themselves—that's the willow tree analogy. It requires speaking and living who you really are, even without the support and validation of your partner, and the ability to take care of yourself emotionally and stand on your own two feet.

Simple loving is authentic loving—it goes way, way past the kind of furniture you pick out together . . . the kind of vacations you take . . . what you do for a living . . . who takes out the garbage. It goes to the guts and soul of who you are. It takes great courage, and expansive, loving, open space to provide the kind of environment in which two souls can become known to each other at this level. And when this happens, simple loving can begin.

Too often, when unattached people talk about a new romantic interest, they excitedly relate all the surface details that signal common interests: they like the same food, the same books, the same activities. We all need these elements to get started, but many couples never go deeper than this level. I know, because I've been there, afraid to get to know the core of myself and, even when I began getting to know that core, afraid to share it with a partner. No wonder so many of us feel lonely in our relationships—

we haven't gotten to know our deepest selves and haven't let ourselves be known to our partners.

I once attended a personal-growth workshop that focused on finding the courage to be authentic. Hanging over the speaker's podium was a huge banner that said TELL THE TRUTH. Every day, the speaker would ask us to leave our images at the door. It was not easy, but those who did break through their fears and insecurities felt the joy of being totally accepted by a roomful of people—accepted as the real, inside person. There is even greater joy in being totally accepted as our real self by our partners. That can only happen when each of us takes the time to discover who we are, and then finds the courage to throw away the masks and be ourselves.

Through the years, I've gained more and more courage to be a strong willow tree rather than a chameleon, changing colors to fit with a certain person so he or she would like me better. At one point in my life, I was unsure of my level of intelligence. I met a man who was more educated than I, and so I assumed that as soon as he discovered the "real, not-as-intelligent-as-he-was-me" that he'd leave. To compensate, I engaged in verbal contests and tried to throw around any intellectual banter I could muster. How surprised I was to have him tell me later that it was sometimes exhausting trying to keep up with me, and that mostly what he wanted to do when we were together was relax and enjoy each other's company. Oops!

Years later, after my divorce, and after I began editing my *Simple Living* newsletter, I experienced chameleon behavior in reverse. I met a nice, well-meaning man who was very interested in me. Before he knew what I did for a living, he told me that he was working very hard to earn as much money as possible. Then, after I told him about my simplicity connection, he very subtly changed his tune and told me that money wasn't all that important to him. I lost all respect for him. Whether he agreed with my philosophy or not (and at that point he didn't even *know* my whole philosophy about money), I would have much preferred that he'd been honest about who he was. Then I could have decided whether I wanted to know him further based on the real, not chameleonlike him.

So often couples live in constant frustration and disappointment because they don't behave in ways each other expects. Part of that problem comes from people not being totally honest about who they are. When we misread a potential partner's identity, we expect from him what he can't provide. Then we complicate our lives by trying to change him, and both people are frustrated. If "who he is" isn't what we need or can accept, then we simplify our lives immensely by moving on and finding someone who is more in line with what we need.

Still, there is a fine balance. Simple loving is very much about living in reality. Reality is never, ever perfect. Simple loving is not about running away from imperfection, but instead, deciding early on during the dating process whether you and your potential partner share core values. You'll only know that once you've gotten to know yourself, and are open to really knowing your partner.

There is also the problem of having other people misunderstand us when we aren't real. I remember that many years ago, in the early stages of my personal-growth quest, I visited a counselor who asked me how I was feeling about a particular incident. I sat there and thought and thought and finally said, "I don't know. I really don't know." I honestly didn't have a clue how I was feeling. That lack of awareness, of course, wasn't confined to just one incident. I realized that if I didn't know myself and how I was feeling, I could not possibly expect my partner to respond to me in the way that I needed.

I still need to stay focused on this every day. There are times when someone will do or say something that bothers me, and it may take a day or two before I am conscious enough to realize exactly how I'm feeling. When I have awareness, I can go to the person in a calm and authentic way and tell him how I feel. Then I'm letting him know the real me. The more self-aware I become, the sooner I can respond to these kinds of situations. I also appreciate it immensely when a friend or partner takes the risk and lets me know if I've done something that annoyed or disappointed him, so long as he does so in a nonattacking way (Let's hear it for "I" statements!). When I don't hear about the problem until weeks or months later,

I'm left with the realization that this person has been harboring some level of ill feeling toward me all that time and I didn't know about it, or I was left to wonder why there seemed to be some distance between us.

THE FREEDOM OF AUTHENTICITY

Author, investment advisor, and Libertarian candidate for president of the United States Harry Browne says he cannot imagine that he will find anyone he admires more or feels more at home with than Pamela, his wife of fourteen years. He knows she feels the same about him. But it took his being absolutely true to himself to attract such a mate.

He's been so acutely aware of the benefits of being authentic that he wrote a book about it titled *How I Found Freedom in an Unfree World*. The freedom he talks about in the book is the freedom that comes from defining who you are and living an authentic, truthful life.

"I think the key is being yourself and advertising yourself as you are, so people who are like you will be attracted to you. I certainly did that," he says. "First, make sure you don't fall prey to the temptation to act in a way you normally wouldn't act and, second, wherever appropriate in a conversation, subtly define a point that is unique about yourself. It's something that practice improves upon so you can do it without being awkward or aggressive.

"If you know yourself well you can define your needs better than if you haven't really given a thought to who you are, what's good about you, and what may be considered weaknesses.

"I was always an individualist, definitely by high school, and possibly in grammar school. It was a process over the years that caused me to look at myself more and realize what I wanted. There were things that it seemed I ought to want but didn't. There were things about me that seemed unattractive, but were a part of me; so rather than try to overcome them or hide them, I decided it was more important to be myself. It was a long and steady process, but there is a point where you're able to grow into this, and are able to enjoy the fruits of that growth.

"By the time I was about thirty years old, I was able to begin profiting from it, by making decisions that were good for me—for example, getting out of a marriage that was not right for me, gearing my professional life to things I liked to do and did well, rather than doing things that seemed at first glance more remunerative, such as being a salesman. I knew I could make a decent living in sales, and didn't know if I could make it writing. Despite that, I chose writing because it was more in line with who I was."

Harry coined a phrase to describe the situation people find themselves in when they don't present their authentic selves to the world (or to themselves). It's called the "identity trap." He writes: "You're in the *identity trap* when you try to be interested in something because it's expected of you, or when you try to do the things that others have said you should do, or when you try to live up to an image that others say is the only legitimate, valid image you're allowed to have.

"You're in the *identity trap* if you buy a Cadillac to prove you're successful, or a small foreign car because your friends are anti-Detroit. In any of these ways, you allow someone else to determine what you should think and be."

He says the way to determine your own identity is to look inside yourself. "Look at the world and decide what you can have that would ignite your nature into real happiness. And then figure out how you can make it happen."

One of Harry's most cherished "against the grain" beliefs that has served him well in his personal relationships is the idea that all human beings are selfish. "Everyone is naturally selfish," he says. "And everyone is doing what he believes will make himself happier. For example, somebody like the late Mother Teresa would have been very unhappy if you prevented her from doing what she wanted to do with her life. She would have felt very uncomfortable if she had been unable to follow her calling. In fact, Irving Wallace once said, 'Poke any saint deeply enough, and you touch self-interest.' "

The Hard Work of Relationships

by Donna Miller

In 1997 my partner Peter and I were traveling in New Zealand. I was supposed to be the expert from afar, giving a workshop to a group of therapists and lay people on relationships. The day before my talk we nearly broke up. I walked into the session, Peter was with me, and I thought, "People want me to speak on relationships?" So I started by saying "Yeah, I'd like to speak about relationships because I'm right in the middle of both the ecstasy and agony of relationships." Then I told them very simply that my partner and I were in the process of breaking up and here I am, standing before them, telling them how to have a successful relationship. Hands shot up all over the room, saying how much they appreciated my being real, and how they faced this same kind of dilemma in their own lives and practices. I went on to speak for a couple of hours, but my real learning happened after my talk.

The woman who owned the center where I was speaking was a therapist and body worker. She told me about a previous ten-year marriage of hers in which her ex-husband seemed to her to be very needy and emotional, always wanting time and attention from her. She got tired of it and left him. Sometime later she got into a relationship with her present partner who was from India, and had been a yogi for twenty years. This man practiced detachment in all parts of his life. Within a very few months, she found herself needy, demanding, emotional, and jealous . . . just like her first husband had been.

She couldn't stand herself at this point, so she got herself together and went to visit the only three couples she could think of whom she considered extremely healthy and committed to each other. They were like the Rock of Gibraltar in her eyes. She asked every one of them, "How do you create a healthy, satisfying, long-term committed relationship?"

After she finished interviewing them for several hours each, she condensed the essence of what each couple told her. She said, "The first 3–10 years were absolute hell. And after those years? It got easier, but it still takes grit and determination nearly every day."

That was the end of her story. It touched me very deeply. I've shared it with a lot of clients who are demoralized at how hard it can be. Peter and I began the process of healing after that. It was going to the brink of disaster and then out of nowhere shines the light of awareness.

Donna Miller is a therapist in Portland, Oregon, and teaches couples workshops. For information, see page 41.

He is careful to note, however, that "selfish" drawn out to its logical conclusion does not mean ignoring the needs and desires of others. The difference is that you have figured out that the more loving you are to those who are important to you, the better your own life will be. People often make the mistake of thinking they should get their own needs met at the expense of others. If they do, those others will be unhappy. If people around you are unhappy, you will be unhappy because they won't be kind and loving toward you.

By giving to your spouse and others, you increase your own chances of being happy. By ignoring or being unkind to your spouse, you will pay the price. So, if you truly believe that we are all selfish, then you'll want to increase your happiness at all costs. Harry says, "If my wife is unhappy, I'm unhappy, so it's in my best interest to figure out what to do for her. That removes my discomfort. In fact, I want to do everything possible so that nothing ever gets in the way of Pamela and me."

USE MEDITATION TO KNOW YOURSELF

There are many ways to know yourself, from attending personal-growth workshops, seeing therapists, following some spiritual disciplines, and through the regular practice of meditation.

Many of the couples you'll meet in this book have reached high levels of awareness through the regular practice of meditation. When we meditate, we slow down and spend quiet, focused time on ourselves, and we begin to pay attention to what goes on in our minds. Without this time to ourselves, we find that one day flows into the next in a continual blur of activity. From morning until night, we're either busy with activities or busy focusing outside ourselves. We can't get to know who is inside unless we deliberately stop and set aside time for some kind of regular inner practice.

Henry Ajayan Borys has spent years meditating and says meditation is a way to fill ourselves so we have something to give to others. He says: "Literally, gaining clarity of your inner experience is the ultimate solution because no matter how many seminars you take, they'll only *modify* the way you find fulfillment in relationships. You have to get *inside* yourself first."

Ajayan, as he prefers to be called, suggests people sit for twenty minutes in the morning and twenty minutes in the late afternoon before dinner. He also recommends attending regular retreats as another form of spiritual nourishment. He says, "There is a parallel to simplicity because the very nature of meditation is to come more into simplicity. Our awareness is outer-directed through the senses. It adapts to whatever it is applied to. Usually it's completely identified with our thoughts, emotions, and different boundaries of experiences, so the mind becomes very complicated.

"With meditation you melt those boundaries of experience that hold and grip the awareness. You develop a sense of inner fullness. You come out of meditation and your mind remains calmer, your emotions are more well ordered and not as shaken by so many ripples and thoughts, so your whole being becomes more orderly and subtle. The agitated emotions that can get stirred up in relationships can be nipped in the bud because you're operating from a more subtle level.

"A lot of times people go into relationship workshops and they learn tools. For a while, they'll be giving more attention to the marriage, but if there's some internal deficit, sooner or later, probably sooner, there's a kind of reversion to old patterns, and they don't have the awareness to keep giving for a sustained period of time."

GO ON A VISION QUEST

If Jesus, Buddha, and Mohammed could do it, we can too. A Vision Quest is a period of time that you spend in nature, with just yourself and the great outdoors as company. The goal during a Quest, like the goal of these three masters, is some kind of enlightenment. While our illumination may or may not save the world, it will help us to get to know ourselves better, and move a little closer to understanding the meaning of our lives.

Modern-day Vision Quests in America are generally based on the Native American tradition of rites of passage. Nowadays, people embark on Quests for their own personal-growth journey as well as for major life transitions. A Quest can last for a few hours to several days, with the typical one being three to four days. People are advised to go with an organized group both for safety as well as inspiration. Organized groups have at least one leader, depending on the size of the group, and spend a month or so preparing for the Quest. Preparation includes answering a series of questions having to do with your life's purpose, such as "What are your gifts and fears?" "What's going well?" "What relationships need mending?" "On what values is your life based and why are you embarking on this Quest?"

On the day of the Quest, the group goes to a remote location in the wilderness where they will not be disturbed by anyone, and are removed from the noise and lights of a city. Quest members bring nothing but a tent, sleeping bag, bottle for water, and perhaps an empty journal to write in. No books, phones, or other items to distract. Each person goes off to find his or her own spot, which needs to be far enough from other participants that they can neither hear nor see one another. They use sticks or stones to set up a circle around their tent, symbolizing the four directions—north, east, south, and west. The goal is to be completely, totally alone for the entire period of the Quest. To ensure safety, group leaders periodically come around and refill water bottles, which are left out at designated spots. This lets the Questers know that they are cared for and the leaders know that the Questers are okay. Most people, though not all, fast during a Quest. And often Questers are encouraged to spend the final night of the Quest awake.

Stan Crow, a program leader at the Institute of Cultural Affairs, says: "You're experiencing the gift of the dark as well as the light. There are amazing things that happen in the dark that you don't usually think about—it's probably about as awesome an experience as you can have because it's a sacred, spiritual, awe-filled gift of the mystery of the dark."

There are three phases to a Quest:

1. Severance: a chance to say goodbye to the past and look at the things that entangle your life and keep you from moving on.
2. Liminal space: the no-longer and the not-yet phase, when the Quester spends a lot of time meditating, praying, thinking, or journaling.
3. Incorporation: how Questers can incorporate what they've learned into their lives. In traditional Native American culture that can take a number of years, as these can be deep changes. A Quest is the beginning of a continual reflection on the participant's life, and often, Quests are embarked upon more than once.

Stan says it is most important that Questers be out in nature. "This is not something you do in a bedroom or boardroom," he says. "You need to be able to get in touch with that distance that most of us have traveled from our natural selves. And you also want to be away from the familiar because you don't want to be reminded of your past, such as photos and artifacts around your home.

"There is a gift in being in nature. You encounter 'the other'—the mysteries of nature and of life, when animals come to visit your site, or that you simply have the awareness of being in the elements that you are normally protected from. I think it is important to remember that being comfortable is a detriment to doing this—you want to rid yourself of the commonplace, the things you are accustomed to.

"People are usually higher than a kite when they return from their Quests. And their changes run the gamut. There are people who find they have new resolve and go back and work on their relationships. Some people go in thinking they want to change jobs and come out wanting to keep the job but change their relationship to it. You discover things about yourself that you hadn't realized, because you've had time to bring up many of the things you've been repressing or were struggling with. It's a time to ask serious questions about the meaning of your life."

LEARN TO RESPECT YOURSELF

A natural by-product of knowing yourself is often a renewed respect for yourself—it's like getting to know a friend at a deep level and loving him more as you get to know him more. The same applies to ourselves: if we don't pay attention to who we are inside, it's difficult to love and respect ourselves. If we're going to be in an intimate relationship, we absolutely need to respect ourselves first, before we can possibly respect our partners or anybody else.

There are two analogies that illustrate this point for me. The first is the oxygen mask routine on airplanes. We all know it: if there is an emergency, the parents should put the mask on first before helping their children. After all, a parent who has passed out from lack of oxygen won't be of much help to a child. The second is the stew pot analogy from author and psychologist Virginia Satir who says, "Nothing is more wonderful on a cold day than dishing out bowls of hot stew. It's nurturing, it's love, it's friendship. But at some point, you have to stop dipping and fill up the stew pot. Nurture yourself, so you can then nurture others."

Once you've made sure your own pot is full, you'll then have something to give to your partner. You can't give anything if you yourself are deprived. And you can't respect your partner if you don't respect yourself. How much do you value yourself as a human being? How well do you treat yourself? Focus awareness on this as you go through the day. How do you let others treat you—not just your partner, but co-workers, friends, family members? If you're letting them walk all over you or, worse yet, abuse you, take note and do some personal work around respecting yourself.

People with high self-esteem (those who respect themselves) tend to treat others well, while those with low self-esteem do their best (usually subconsciously) to bring others down with them. They attempt to build their own self-esteem at the expense of their partner's by belittling, using sarcasm, put-downs, threats, or other forms of disrespectful behavior. A friend put it this way: You need to prepare your own runway so the right plane can land. All of this is about doing what it takes to like and respect yourself.

Sylvan Henoch was married to an abusive alcoholic for sixteen years when she'd had enough and began the process of learning to respect herself.

"Before that, I wanted to get love and respect from my husband, even though I didn't love and respect myself," she says. "For all of those years I kept thinking he was going to change and everything would be fine. One day I woke up and realized he was never going to change, and that we were never going to be a family (we had three children). He clearly did not want to have a loving relationship. I thought, 'what am I going to do?' When I married him, I assumed I'd be with him forever."

Sylvan discovered a workshop called Loving Relationships and asked her husband if he'd go with her. He refused, but still she had hope. She assumed she could bring back the information and her husband would see the light. She attended the training alone and began her transformation, realizing she was the one who needed to see the light and change, and it was time to start loving herself. She says, "I had to give to myself what I couldn't get from him, which was self-respect, gentleness, and the sense that I deserved to have a loving relationship. I knew that it had to come from inside me."

Sylvan discovered the power of affirmations. Every day she repeated: *"I deserve to have a loving relationship." "I deserve to have people in my life who love and care for me."* She changed her negative thinking to thinking positively about herself and others. She also did a lot of soul-searching and imagining what her life would look like. An overriding theme was that she wanted love in her life.

"It was amazing that within about a month I started to feel differently about myself," she says, and within the year she made the decision to end her marriage. She had little support and not enough money for professional therapy, yet she didn't give up.

Sylvan's love for herself is evident in many ways today. After divorcing her first husband, she later married a loving man who has her best interests at heart. "We have good communication, we share our feelings with each other, and we tell each other through words and actions that we love each other on a daily basis," she says. On the inside, she feels much more connected to herself: "I love myself. I pay attention to what my body and emotions are telling me. If I'm tired, I rest, rather than pushing further. I stay current with my emotions. If I'm angry about something, I try to share it with the person I'm angry with. If I'm sad or happy I share that, too."

Since Sylvan's metamorphosis twenty years ago, she has incorporated many disciplines into her work as a healer. She believes anything that helps clear blocked energy on any level is vital to learning to be present in one's life. She works with traditional massage as well as shamanic soul retrievals, Akashic record readings, Reiki, chakra clearing, and energetic ancestral clearing.

"The more I do this clearing work, the more present I am in my life," she says. "I'm not off in the future worrying about things. I'm not off in the past. It keeps expanding the more I do this work, the more I feel present.

"I've noticed that most patterns are about low self-esteem, low self-worth, fear of abandonment, feeling unworthy. They're all essentially the same thing. Those are the ones that come up most often for people, or some variation of that, or feeling disconnected from life, feeling isolated, feeling like they're not connected to their full potential, their full creativity. This work is constantly taking me deeper into my own creativity and my own connection to God."

Sylvan's esoteric work connects her to the wealth of experience that exists in the nonconcrete world. "Life for me isn't just about driving to the store to pick up groceries and doing my nine-to-five job every day," she says. "When people can tap into these more subtle energies, it helps them to live more richly and fully. It's like tapping into the poetry of life."

BOUNDARIES AND RESPECT

Respect is also about setting boundaries for yourself and respecting your partner's boundaries. Take time in your own quiet company to discern where your boundaries are before attempting to discuss boundary setting with your partner. You need to find out what's true for you and be very clear, coming from a place of strength, rather than as a reaction to whatever your partner might say.

One of the areas of frequent contention in marriages is in how partners use their time. Both people need to set and respect boundaries around this issue.

Here is an example of how a husband and wife worked through those conflicting needs by respecting each other. The wife is an artist, and she was very much looking forward to spending the upcoming Sunday painting in her studio. She hadn't gotten around to verbalizing this to her partner, however. On Sunday morning her husband came to her and said, "It's a beautiful day, let's go take a hike in the woods!" This is the juncture at which respect and boundaries play a role. At this point, if the wife hadn't respected her own need to paint, she could have agreed to go for a hike and then silently or verbally resented her partner for taking her away from her planned solitude. Or, she could have showed little respect for her partner's need to have her companionship and told him no, she wanted to spend the day painting. But instead, this couple talked about how to meet their conflicting needs. They worked out that they would go for a walk for an hour, then the wife would have the house to herself for the rest of the afternoon. They both had their needs met.

Linda Kavelin Popov, profiled on page 48, has thought a lot about the way boundaries play a role in creating a respectful marriage. She says, "One boundary I have is that I spend my free time the way I choose. If that means going off with a friend for a two-week retreat, I don't feel guilty about it and I expect Dan [Linda's husband] to respect that. I also respect his need to take time for himself. You need to balance being together and being alone. It's one of the questions couples need to answer in a very personal way. Dan and I have our time engineered so we have a lot of intimate experience together, and we also need time apart from each other. Most couples need that but are afraid to take it. Men often call this 'cave time,' and women call it 'retreat time.' I need time with feminine energy, with

DEFINING AND LIVING BY YOUR VALUES

Here is my plan of action for using your values as your guide for life.

1. Assess. To know yourself, take some time to assess your values. That's important because if you're not living your values, you won't be happy; and if you're not happy, you can't be a good partner. Get yourself a little notebook to keep with you, and as you go throughout your day, jot down what's important to you. Certain situations and people will trigger both positive and negative reactions—write them down. After a few weeks of keeping this notebook, you can take time to think about what values these notations represent.

2. Prioritize. Once you've come up with a list of values, the next step is to prioritize. List them in order of importance. For example, being there for my children is more important than, say, earning a huge salary, so I'd list being there for my kids before earning a higher salary. On the other hand, make sure your value list is truly yours from your heart. Just because it sounds better to say you value helping others over making lots of money, if it isn't from your heart, listing it this way won't do you any good. Be honest!

3. Vote with your time. Life isn't worth living if there is no joy in it for you. If the things you are currently spending time on in your life don't bring you joy, then figure out how to eliminate them. If you can't eliminate them, then make sure you have lots of joy to make up for the list of "have-to's" that you don't enjoy.

4. Give the very best to the people and things that are the most important in your life. To make sure this happens, start out with a daily to-do list that expresses your values. For example, back to my list: If being there for my children really is a high-priority value, then, when faced with a conflict, I can remember what my value list looks like and make a more clear, values-based decision.

friends of the same sex, and Dan needs to pound nails with his friend David, which he often does. We all need to fill our cups this way.

"Another boundary I have is that we share the housework. It's not my

> *Go deeper than love, for the goal has greater depths,*
> *love is like the grass, but the heart is deep wild rock*
> *molten, yet dense and permanent.*
>
> *Go down to your old deep heart,*
> *and lose sight of yourself.*
> *And lose sight of me, the me whom you*
> *turbulently loved.*
>
> *Let us lose sight of ourselves, and break the mirrors.*
> *For the fierce curve of our lives is moving again to*
> *the depths*
> *out of sight, in the deep living heart.*
>
> —D. H. LAWRENCE,
> FROM *Know Deeply, Know Thyself More Deeply*

job—it's our house. I couldn't live with anyone who treated me like a maid. For instance, whoever cooks, the other cleans up. We share all of it. We have boundaries about keeping the common areas tidy, and we're free to do as we wish in our own offices. Mine looks just the way I want it and his looks the way he wants it.

"One of Dan's boundaries is that he doesn't want me to talk to him about his physical health, because it was a source of a lot of conflict between us for many years. I have very different ideas about health and nutrition. For example, he eats meat seven days a week. It's not my choice for him, but he has a right to determine what he's going to eat. Because I love to cook, I prepare it for him, even though in my heart I wish he were a vegetarian."

ᴥ *Becoming Real* ᴥ

*I*t wasn't until *Basha Kaplan* became real that she met her husband, her spiritual partner and soul mate. Before that, she tried her best to be what she thought her dates wanted. She was an expert chameleon. Only trouble was, they kept dropping her after they figured out she was not what she had presented herself to be. For a long time she was angry with them, until finally she figured it out: she had betrayed these men by pretending she was someone else. No matter that she pretended in an effort to make them like her—she still pretended. No wonder they left.

"It was an extremely painful period of my life," she remembers. "I was depressed, I went through a lot of mood swings, I vacillated between dating and not dating. I didn't know what to do. Then I stopped, and started therapy. I also moved across the country to California and started a doctorate in psychology. For the first time I was alone in a new city with no one to call. Being that alone forced me to stop and look at myself. I went through an existential crisis that I call my Dark Night of the Soul."

Once Basha Kaplan began living authentically, she was concerned about the "who" of her dates rather than the "what": "the externals were no longer as important." Of husband Jeff she says, "He touched my essence in a way that no one had before."

That was the beginning of Basha's discovering who she was, realizing that she was likeable and lovable, and that it was safe to reveal her true self to the world. She remembers the night that was a turning point: "I had always been the giver to other people . . . the caretaker, the clown . . . but I never really let people be there for me. I also had an eating disorder but never told anyone about it. I was ashamed and embarrassed, and I was terrified. I knew I was eating like that because I was lonely and wouldn't let people see the real me.

"One night I took a chance and asked myself who was the safest person I knew whom I could share this with and probably wouldn't reject me. I thought of my friend Leslie. She and I went to dinner and I decided to tell her who I really was. I said, 'This is hard for me, but I need to tell you something, and I'm afraid you'll reject me.' Then I told her about my binge eating. We both started crying. I'll never forget what she said: 'Basha, I wanted to reach out to you all of this time, but you wouldn't let me in.' That night I went home and, for the first time, I didn't have to binge.

"For me, that was the beginning of being able to tell the truth about who I was and letting people be there for me authentically. When I started examining some of my belief systems, I realized I no longer needed to be perfect. When I accepted my limitations as a human being, life became easier for me."

Once Basha recognized that she didn't need to be perfect, she could finally accept that others didn't need to be perfect, either. She says, "What helped me heal was that I accepted people and events as they were, and didn't try to change anything or take it personally. You can't choose your parents, but you can certainly choose people around you as friends and lovers who are much more nurturing."

Once she became more authentic, Basha also placed far more importance on the "who" of her dates rather than the "what." "All of a sudden I was more concerned with the importance of emotional safety—the externals were no longer as important as they used to be. Not the 'what's' of life, but 'Who is this person?' Is he kind, considerate, loving, nonjudgmental? Has he done work on himself? If I question him, will he get defensive?"

She had also made a list of her non-negotiables—things she knew she needed in a life partner and wasn't going to settle for less. It was then, at age forty-eight after Basha was really open and ready, that a friend insisted she meet her widowed friend Jeff. Even though Basha lived in Chicago and Jeff in New York, the friend thought it would be a strong enough connection that they should make arrangements. It wasn't what Jeff did that inspired Basha to meet him; it was who he was. Her friend said, "Jeff stopped working to take care of his wife, who was dying of cancer." And the second statement was: "He's different from all the other men you dated who wanted you to take care of them. Jeff will be there for you, and he understands how to be in a partnership. He knows how to be married. If you're serious about getting married, you have to meet this man."

They arranged a date for Basha to fly to New York and meet Jeff. Despite the fact that she had a 102-degree fever, she wanted to keep her commitment and went anyway. After one of their subsequent dates Basha says, "We were open and not at all defensive. Truth was paramount. We both let our hair down and bared our souls to each other. Somehow we knew we were in safe hands, with God directing behind the scenes, a true spiritual partnership. He saw me at my worst and loved me for it. That must be the reason that I was sick coming to New York because I needed to really believe that someone could love me with all my imperfections.

"Suddenly I was able to see his soul. He had touched my essence in a way that no one had before."

They had connected on such a soul level that when they arranged to meet again ten days later in Chicago, Jeff was concerned that he wouldn't even recognize Basha. She says, "He knew my soul but could not remember my face. I realized that I felt the same way. What a relief it was when we finally faced each other at the airport and reconnected on the physical level as well.

"We were married six months later on October 1, 1995. The most amazing part of our relationship is how easy and smooth it has been, and we feel more connected each day."

Basha and co-author Gail Prince wrote a book about their experiences and insights titled *Soul Dating to Soul Mating: On the Path Toward Spiritual Partnership* (New York: Perigee, 1999).

છ૭ છ૭ છ૭

Resources

TEACHERS

Donna J. Miller offers a series of three workshops: The Couples Workshop . . . Love, Sex and Conflict; Dealing with Differences and Conflict; and Transforming Your Sexual Relationship. She can be reached on the Internet at www.DonnaJMiller.com; by E-mail, at donnam@SpiritOne.com; or by phone, at (503) 293-1757.

Sylvan Henoch: (206) 523-5317.

VISION QUESTS

1. Wilderness Guides Council
   P.O. Box 482
   Ross, CA 94957
   E-mail: rileymr@earthlink.net.
2. Institute for Cultural Affairs
   www.icajourneys.org
   E-mail: icaric@icg.org.
3. School of Lost Borders
   E-mail: lostbrdrs@telis.org.

A Guide for Creating Your Own Vision Quest, by Denise Linn (New York: Ballantine Wellspring, 1999).

BOOKS

Creative Visualization, by Shakti Gawain (Novato, Calif.: Nataraj Publishing, 1978, 1995).

Edgar Cayce on the Akashic Records, by Kevin J. Todeschi (Virginia Beach, Va.: A.R.E. Press, 1998).

Essential Reiki, by Diane Stein (Freedom, Calif.: The Crossing Press, 1995, 800-777-1048).

The Evolving Self: A Psychology for the Third Millennium, by Mihaly Csikszentmihaly (New York: HarperPerennial, 1994).

Finding Flow: The Psychology of Engagement with Everyday Life, by Mihaly Csikszentmihaly (New York: Basic Books, 1998).

Guided Meditations, Explorations and Healing, by Stephen Levine (New York: Anchor Books, 1991).

Hands of Light, by Barbara Brennan (New York: Bantam, 1993).

Heart Self and Soul: The Sufi Psychology of Growth, Balance and Harmony, by Robert Frazer, Ph.D. (Wheaton, Ill.: Quest Books, 1999).

I Deserve Love, by Sondra Ray (Berkeley, Calif.: Celestial Arts, 1993).

If the Buddha Dated: A Handbook for Finding Love on a Spiritual Path, by Charlotte Kasl, Ph.D. (New York: Penguin Arkana, 1999).

It's a Meaningful Life, by Bo Lozoff (New York: Viking, 2000).

Love 101: To Love Oneself Is the Beginning of a Lifelong Romance, by Peter McWilliams (Los Angeles: Prelude Press, 1995).

Mindfulness in Plain English, by Venerable Henepola Gunaratana (Boston: Wisdom Publications, 1993).

Past Lives, Present Dreams, by Denise Linn (New York: Ballantine, 1997).

The Path to Tranquility, by His Holiness The Dalai Lama (New York: Viking Arkana, 1999).

The Power of Meditation and Prayer, edited by Larry Dossey et al. (Carlsbad, Calif.: New Dimensions Foundation, Hay House Publishing, 1997).

Shamanism, Archaic Techniques of Ecstasy, by Mircea Eliade (Princeton, N.J.: Princeton University Press, 1972).

Solitude: A Return to the Self, by Anthony Storr (New York: Ballantine, 1989).

Something More: Excavating Your Authentic Self, by Sarah Ban Breathnach (New York: Warner, 1998).

Soul Dating to Soul Mating: On the Path Toward Spiritual Partnership, by Basha Kaplan, Psy.D., and Gail Prince, M.Ed. (New York: Perigee, 1999).

Soul Retrieval, by Sandra Ingerman (San Francisco: HarperSanFrancisco, 1991).

The Tao of Abundance: Eight Ancient Principles for Abundant Living, by Laurence G. Boldt (New York: Penguin Arkana, 1999).

Voices of Insight: Teachers of Buddhism in the West Share Their Wisdom, Stories and Experience of Insight Meditation, edited by Sharon Salzberg (Boston: Shambhala, 1999).

The Way of the Shaman, by Michael Harner (San Francisco: HarperSanFrancisco, 1990).

A Year of Living Consciously: 365 Daily Inspirations for Creating a Life of Passion and Purpose, by Gay Hendricks (San Francisco: HarperSanFrancisco, 1999).

Your Book of Life: Accessing the Akashic Records, by Gary Bonnell (Atlanta: Richmond Rose Publishing, 1998).

Chapter 3

Loving from Your Essence

*In the final analysis, we count for something only
because of the essential we embody,
and if we do not embody that, life is wasted.*

—C. G. JUNG

*E*ssence is the innate goodness of our souls. A workshop leader helped me to understand the concept of essence by holding up a bowl that was filled with cornmeal. She dug under the surface and pulled out a little glass gem that had been buried in the meal. That gem, she said, was our essence. The cornmeal—i.e., our divisiveness, little lies, selfishness, and the rest—is what buries our essence. Our true essence, she said, is like the gem; even though it's buried sometimes, it's always there. It is our center.

Marianne Williamson speaks of this essence in her book *A Return to Love*. She says:

*Our deepest fear is not that we are inadequate.
Our deepest fear is that we are powerful beyond measure.
It is our light, not our darkness that most frightens us.*

We ask ourselves, Who am I to be brilliant,
gorgeous, talented and fabulous?

Actually, who are you not to be?
You are a child of God.
Your playing small doesn't serve the world.
There is nothing enlightened about
shrinking so that other people
won't feel insecure around you.

We are born to make manifest the
glory of God that is within us.

It's not just in some of us,
it's in everyone.

And as we let our own light shine,
we unconsciously give other people
permission to do the same.

As we are liberated from our own fear,
our presence automatically liberates others.

This is living from our essence—living as if we truly believe we are re-markable human beings. Naturally, when we feel magnificent inside, we can't help but treat others well.

Nonetheless, this sort of philosophy is very often easier to think about than to do. We may wake up in the morning, read Marianne Williamson's words, and no sooner finish the last line when an argument erupts with our spouse. Our best intentions go right out the window and there we are, groveling in the mud. So much for philosophy.

What then? We need a framework—a daily framework that gives us

A Lesson on Love

by Joan Chittister

A rabbi disappeared every Shabat Eve "to commune with God in the forest," his congregation thought. So one Sabbath night they sent one of their cantors to follow the rabbi and observe the holy encounter. Deeper and deeper into the woods the rabbi went until he came to the small cottage of an old Gentile woman, sick to death and crippled into a painful posture. Once there, the rabbi cooked for her and carried her firewood and swept the floor. Then when the chores were finished, he returned immediately to his little house next to the synagogue.

Back in the village, the people demanded of the one they'd sent to follow him, "Did our rabbi go up to heaven as we thought?"

"Oh no," the cantor answered after a thoughtful pause, "our rabbi went much, much higher than that."

The rabbi's message sears the soul: Love is not for our own sakes. Love frees us to see others as God sees them.

To love is to come to see beyond and despite good taste, good sense, and good judgment. Love sees us as we are, as we really are, and as we can be, as well.

Love sees little but good in us and forgives everything that is not. We watch it happen every day and, from a dry and loveless perch in our desiccated souls, pronounce it ridiculous when, perhaps, we should proclaim it holy. Foolish love, in fact, may be all we ever know of the love of God on earth and, in the end, it will be everything that each of us needs. In the end it will indeed be "the bridge, the survival, the meaning."

—From *There Is a Season*

guidelines to call forth when we forget our essence. One word for this framework is *virtues*. Virtues—such as compassion, kindness, honesty, tact, generosity, and so on—are something we can all relate to. As opposed to pure philosophy, each one of these words means something concrete, so we can call them forth when we need to. Let's say our partner comes home in a bad mood because he's just gotten upbraided by his boss. He walks in the door snarling at the world, us included. If we have no framework with which to remember our essence, then we can easily get caught up in the drama of the moment and snarl back (been there, done that!). If we have something concrete to ring up, we may feel like snarling back, but we may also be able to take a breath and remember the virtue of compassion. If we were compassionate, how would we respond to this situation?

My friend Linda Kavelin Popov, author of *The Family Virtues Guide* and *Sacred Moments*, says: "Virtues are the gifts within your soul. Virtues are the essence of soulfulness. They are described by all cultures and religions as both the qualities of the Divinity and the simple elements of the human soul, the qualities of character which reflect the "image and likeness" of God. An act of love, or justice, or creativity or any of our other virtues is essentially an expression of our spirituality.

"One of the clearest definitions of virtue I have ever heard was from a six-year-old girl who said, 'Virtues are what's good about us.' "

Linda and her husband, Dan Popov, not only write about the virtues but also live them every day. They started the Virtues Project* because they felt called to do something to counteract the rising violence by and toward children. They were moved to explore the sacred texts of the world's religions for some keys to transformation and discovered that the virtues were a common thread running through all sacred traditions. Linda says, "I had children from my previous marriage, but Dan and I didn't have children together. The Virtues Project was the fruit of our marriage—our child. We conceived the idea for something that would help humanity and then supported each other in making that dream come true."

Together, Linda and Dan have brought their message all over the world, to South Pacific Islanders, Australians, New Zealanders, Russians, Malaysians, as well as to prisons, schools, corporations, and organizations throughout North America. Their work is being used in more than eighty-five countries.

There are many ways that Linda and Dan rely on the virtues to make

*For information on the Virtues Project, see page 67.

their marriage stronger. Linda says: "Virtues are at the heart of our marriage. We were attracted by the core of overarching virtues, but it's the little daily practice that keeps our love alive.

"We connect through the big virtues in our lives, such as service, idealism, and faith in the creator. We both have a feeling that life is very short and we have a spiritual purpose that comes from God. But what makes our marriage joyful are the little daily expressions of virtues, the daily kindnesses and considerations. For example, we both work at home but have very different schedules. Dan works from seven P.M. until three A.M. and I work from six A.M. till noon. He goes to bed at three-thirty A.M. and I get up at four-thirty A.M. In between we have lunch together, go for walks, and spend time in each other's company until seven. We tend to make love in the daytime.

"It's a strange schedule, but part of what works for us is the virtue of acceptance—acceptance of our unique needs and idiosyncratic styles. I remember when we were first married, I told a friend that Dan didn't come to bed with me. He tried for a month, but it didn't work—that's not the way his body works. This friend got furious and said, 'I would never allow that in my marriage!' Well, because I honor Dan's being different in that way, we have peace around that issue. It works perfectly fine and, as a matter of fact, works even better for us because we both need a lot of solitude. I have my mornings alone, and Dan has his evenings alone.

"My acceptance of Dan's unusual hours makes for a very peaceful life."

Dan is also accepting and forgiving of the ways Linda is different from him. He has a more naturally easygoing attitude, while Linda's way is to respond to life with more intensity. "He accepts that in me," she says. "He doesn't criticize me for it. We have found that criticism is like poison in our relationship. Mutual acceptance is a very important virtue for us, so we have unity in diversity. In fact, someone once came up to us after a presentation and said, 'I never met a couple who are so different from each other, and who make such a great team!' "

The couple also relies on humor to keep their love alive. They laugh off problems, or each try to say things that will make the other one laugh.

"Every single day we laugh together," Linda says. "Today, we've been laughing all day.

"We always try to think of little kindnesses for each other, and we like to surprise each other all the time. For example, I hosted a women's circle at our house recently and Dan baked for two days for it. He also left a note for the water man to leave an extra bottle of water for the circle. I didn't ask him for that—he thought about what I'd need during my women's circle. If he thinks I'm blue, he'll bake homemade chocolate chip cookies and pour me a glass of milk. At night, because we don't go to bed at the same hour, he'll turn the covers down for me."

Linda says what is equally important to keeping their marriage thriving is practicing the art of spiritual companioning.* She says: "We really listen to each other and hear the other person's point of view. Instead of getting defensive, we ask 'cup-emptying' questions that start with 'what' and 'how.' If he's really upset, I'll ask, 'What's upsetting you?' or 'What are you angry about?' I'm not just giving lip service—I really want to know.

"We also use ACT with Tact. ACT stands for Acknowledge, Correct, and Thank. Say something positive, then tell them what you would like changed, and then thank them for something. We use the virtue of tact a lot in this marriage.

"One of the things I enjoy about our relationship is that we're still in love after eighteen years. There's a lot of passion for each other as well as affection, and a real sense of being cherished by each other. We came to that through a lot of stages . . . there have been times in the past when I've wondered if I made another mistake by marrying Dan (this is my second marriage)—we've had our crisis points, but I think what has gotten us through is the commitment that this is the love of our lives and we don't want to let it go easily."

*For more information on spiritual companioning, see page 180.

ESSENTIAL VIRTUES FOR
COUPLES TO REMEMBER

Forgiveness

Like almost everyone, I've had a more difficult time with this virtue than with practically any other one. When someone wrongs me, the last thing I want to do is release him. There is also my concern that forgiving someone means condoning his behavior.

Over the years, however, I've decided I like living a free life better than holding grudges. I am not free when I've got chains of anger wrapped around me. To maintain my freedom, I make sure that I'm not associating with people who continually disrespect my boundaries. Everyone screws up now and again, myself included, but when it becomes a pattern, I make the choice not to have that person in my life. Luckily I have rarely had to make that choice.

So, given that I have chosen to associate with respectful people, I find that I am not continually trying to wrestle with the forgiveness issue. When an issue does arise, it is usually minor enough that I am able to work past it fairly easily. In those cases, my theory is that the relationship is far more important than this particular transgression. I am also acutely aware that I have erred myself at one time or another.

But what happens when we just can't seem to let go? If freedom is ultimately a more important value than holding grudges, the process will be faster. One way is to sit quietly and conduct a "Forgiveness Meditation." I learned about this in Stephen Levine's book, *A Year to Live*. (Take note of the title. Would you be more quick to forgive if you knew you had only a year left?) Here is how it works: Take some time alone and sit in a comfortable position. After doing some deep breathing to relax, close your eyes and bring to mind someone toward whom you feel resentment. It is easier to think of someone who is the least transgressor, and start with her, then very gradually expand that mercy to include all those whose time has come for forgiveness. Say to each person, "I forgive you." In your heart repeat, "I forgive you." You can even imagine that you are speaking to that person, telling her how you feel. Listen to your heart. Let her image float in your consciousness surrounded by intentions for her well-being. Stephen says that forgiveness is an act of self-compassion: "As this ability to invite them into your heart to be touched by the possibility of forgiveness increases with repetition, there seems more space for them and, quite noticeably, more space for yourself as well."

You can also visualize people who may be holding resentment toward you—people whom you have wronged. In the same way, imagine a conversation with them, and imagine them forgiving you. Stephen says: "As this process of sending and receiving forgiveness matures, we eventually come to the point where we can turn and say, 'I forgive you' to ourselves. It is a radical departure from the hells to which we have become so accustomed."

Finally, say an imaginary good-bye to these people and expand the boundaries of your forgiveness and care to include everyone. You can say: "May all beings everywhere, seen and unseen, be free from suffering. May they know the absolute joy of their absolute nature.

"May all beings take the opportunity of existence to become free.

"May all beings overcome suffering and discover the ever-uninjured essence of their true heart."

Every time we release a resentment, we get that much closer to our "uninjured," or pure, essence. The closer we are to that purity, the more we are able to love not only others but also ourselves.

Responsibility and Justice

It is no accident that the virtues of "responsibility" and "justice" come right after forgiveness. We can't control others, but we can control our own behavior. If we have wronged someone, the best thing we can do is take responsibility for our actions and make reparations to the person we have wronged. Nothing is worse than having a partner screw up and not take responsibility or try to put the blame on the other person. Haven't we all heard the lines "Well, I wouldn't have done such and such if you hadn't done so and so." Puhleeze! Let's not blame other people, especially our partners, for our bad behavior. Conversely, nothing will open a wronged heart more than having an errant partner honestly and truly take responsibility and do what he or she can to rectify the situation. What an act of humility and love! Making heartfelt amends means we really understand what we have done and are not just giving lip service. An example of lip service is bringing flowers or candy to someone whom we have injured. Anyone can bring flowers or candy for any situation. That hardly shows that we truly understand the nature of our grievance. Did you totally blow an important engagement? Beyond apologizing to your partner, do everything in your power to ensure that you don't blow another one. Call everyone involved and apologize to them as well. Don't make excuses. If it is something you can schedule again, organize it and do it now. Did you say something insensitive? Apologize and then tell your partner why you understand how your words were insensitive.

As parents, we're encouraged to discipline our children using natural consequences. The job is to figure out what the most natural consequence of any misbehavior might be, and to discipline our children accordingly. That way, they learn life's real lessons. We need to do the same for ourselves. What can we do in this situation that will help us learn our lesson and show our partner that we are earnestly trying to make amends? Part of the pact of agreeing to be in a committed relationship is an unspoken (or spoken) contract that we take full responsibility to do our own growth work.

Consideration

This is the golden rule in action. Before making any major or even minor decision, ask yourself how or if it will affect your partner. If it will have even the least impact, then consult with him or her first. If you want to take a job in another city, what will your partner think? If you want to go

Learning Humility

ᘓᘐ

by Thich Nhat Hanh

There is a story that is well known in my country about a husband who had to go off to war, and he left his wife behind, pregnant. Three years later, when he was released from the army, he returned home. His wife came to the village gate to welcome him, and she brought along their little boy. When husband and wife saw each other, they could not hold back their tears of joy. They were so thankful to their ancestors for protecting them that the young man asked his wife to go to the marketplace to buy some fruit, flowers, and other offerings to place on the ancestors' altar.

While she was shopping, the young father asked his son to call him "Daddy," but the little boy refused. "Sir, you are not my daddy! My daddy used to come every night, and my mother would talk to him and cry. When Mother sat down, Daddy also sat down. When Mother lay down, he also lay down." Hearing these words, the young father's heart turned to stone.

When his wife came home, he couldn't even look at her. The young man offered fruit, flowers, and incense to the ancestors, made prostrations, and then rolled up the bowing mat and did not allow his wife to do the same. He believed that she was not worthy to present herself in front of the ancestors. His wife was deeply hurt. She could not understand why he was acting like that. He did not stay home. He spent his days at the liquor shop in the village and did not come back until very late at night. Finally, after three days, she could no longer bear it, and she jumped into the river and drowned.

out to jog every morning at 5 A.M., don't simply make a unilateral decision—talk it over and make any adjustments necessary so that everyone's needs get met. I don't know what the percentages are, but I'd guess an equally high number of marriages break up over a continual pattern of inconsiderateness as do over finances. One wife, now an ex-wife, complained for years that her husband regularly made plans without ever consulting with her. He frequently would sail into the house after work, for example, and simply announce that he was going off to the movies—leaving her at home alone with their children. What kind of partnership is that? This kind of inconsiderate behavior eventually takes its toll. Consid-

That evening after the funeral, when the young father lit the kerosene lamp, his little boy shouted, "There's my daddy." He pointed to his father's shadow projected on the wall and said, "My daddy used to come every night like that and my mother would talk to him and cry a lot. When my mother sat down, he sat down. When my mother lay down, he lay down. 'Darling, you have been away for too long. How can I raise our child alone?' she cried to her shadow." One night the child asked her who and where his father was. She pointed to her shadow on the wall and said, "This is your father." She missed him so much.

Suddenly the young father understood, but it was too late. If he had gone to his wife even yesterday and said, "Darling, I suffer so much. Our little boy said a man used to come every night and you would talk to him and cry with him, and every time you sat down, he also sat down. Who is that person?" she would have had an opportunity to explain and avert the tragedy. But he did not because of the pride in him.

The lady behaved the same. She was deeply hurt because of her husband's behavior, but she did not ask for help. She should have gone to him and said, "Darling, I suffer so much. Please help. I do not understand why you will not look at me or talk with me. Why didn't you allow me to prostrate before the ancestors? Have I done anything wrong?" If she had done that, her husband could have told her what the little boy had said. But she did not, because she was also caught in pride.

This story illustrates that in true love, there is no place for pride. When we are hurt by the person we love, when we suffer most, remember this story. Do not let pride stand in our way. Instead, practice humility.

Thich Nhat Hanh is a well-known author and highly respected Buddhist monk.

eration doesn't mean already having your mind made up and *then* asking your partner what she or he thinks; it means being totally open and considerate of his or her point of view. I've known other partners who have already decided in their minds that they're going to make a major purchase like a new car or boat, and put on a show of asking for the partner's opinion, but in actuality, aren't interested. If the spouse is against it, they then pull out the "hitting-below-the-belt" strategies, such as using guilt, threats, whining, and so on—none of which show the least bit of consideration for their partner's point of view.

Consideration extends to every single area of an intimate relationship.

If you'll be more than ten minutes late, call your partner. If you see your partner could use some help, step up and offer it. If your partner has been working a lot, either at home with children or at a paid job, consideration means not waiting for him to ask for a break—it means you offer to give him one.

I fully grasped the importance of consideration after talking to a husband who is in a successful marriage. We were discussing the subject of power struggles. His response made clear to me why his marriage thrived—he couldn't imagine getting into a power struggle with his wife and said, "Why would anyone be in a marriage where their partner wasn't considerate of their needs?"

Need I say more?

Loyalty and Faithfulness

Another bottom-line team of virtues. If we aren't faithful and loyal to each other, we'll never have deep, long-lasting passion. The equation is easy: If you're devoting your energy to someone else, you're not devoting it to your partner. Whether it's been stated or not, your partner knows at some level that he or she isn't getting your full attention, and cannot fully open to you—thus, you are missing out on your partner's full essence. It is only when we know that our partner is and will be absolutely there for us that we can relax, be vulnerable, really loving and open—all the things that breed passion.

Faithfulness and monogamy create safety and contentment in the marriage. It is essential that you not have any question in your mind that your partner would go with anyone else for any reason, fling or not. If your partner is unfaithful, you need to decide what your bottom line is that can't be crossed. If you are the one having or contemplating having an affair, there is simply no excuse to have one. None. If things are so bad around your house that you're tempted to have one, then take care of the problem with your partner. Do whatever you need to do to work on it. Give it everything you have before making the decision to leave. People don't have affairs because someone else drove them to it; they have affairs because they do not have the courage and inner fortitude to stand up and deal with what is at hand.

Compassion

One of the best things you can do for your relationship is to develop true, honest, and deep compassion for your partner. This real kind of compassion enables you to step out of yourself as if you were watching a movie, and "be" inside your partner to really understand what life is like for her or him. We all know how truly wonderful and heavenly it is when someone we care about seems to really understand us—even if they don't agree. And we also know how isolating it is when our partners don't seem to know or care what our world is like.

True compassion is rare in most relationships because it is very difficult to cultivate and maintain. That's because we're so caught up in our own stuff and we want to be understood so desperately that we are unable to rise up out of ourselves, or put our own needs aside and focus 100 percent on our partner's needs and wants. In conversations we spend more time focusing on our response to what our partner is saying than we do to what he is actually saying and feeling. When we have a disagreement, so often we have our agenda and our partner has his, and our thoughts are about how to get him to agree with us. This is not compassion. Or if our partner is experiencing difficulty, we want to dive in and "fix" the problem as if we know what is best for him.

If we want our relationships to move beyond the mundane, and beyond these parallel lives, we need to cultivate compassion.

This true kind of compassion is not pity. Pity involves arrogance—putting yourself above someone with a smug thought that "I'm glad it's not me." Compassion is simply stepping out of yourself and seeing your partner as a whole human being, just like you are—no better and no worse. Perhaps your partner is experiencing difficulty during this period of her life and you're not—but we all know that sooner or later we'll be in the diffi-

THE PRACTICE OF INCREASING LOVE AND COMPASSION IN THE WORLD

from the Dalai Lama

1. Spend five minutes at the beginning of each day remembering we all want the same things (to be happy and be loved) and that we all are connected to one another.

2. Spend five minutes—breathing in—cherishing yourself; and, breathing out—cherishing others. If you think about people you have difficulty cherishing, extend your cherishing to them anyway.

3. During the day, extend that attitude to everyone you meet. Practice cherishing the simplest person (clerks, attendants, etc.), as well as "important" people in your life; cherish the people you love and the people you dislike.

4. Continue this practice no matter what happens or what anyone does to you.

cult boat and we'll want compassion. What goes around comes around because we're all human—every one of us.

How can we develop it? One way is to follow the program developed by Marshall Rosenberg, called Nonviolent or Compassionate Communication. See page 183 for a more complete discussion of his work. Another is to spend time meditating on compassion. To really, deeply develop compassion, it is best to do both—follow a program like Dr. Rosenberg's *and* meditate every day. Eventually your awareness will broaden and you'll begin to see people in a more compassionate way. Here are two meditations on compassion:

1. Sit quietly and visualize and feel a love that someone gave you when you were a child. Try to think of a specific incident when you felt that love and kindness very deeply. It could be a parent, grandparent, teacher, or

anyone significant in your life. Spend time with that feeling, remember it, and let it infuse your whole being. Stay with it for as long as you can until you really feel it in your heart. Be as clear with the details as you can. Now visualize your partner (or anyone else) and open your heart. Let that love you feel flow out to him, infusing his whole being. Stay with this image for as long as you can. Fill him with your love. If you do this every day, you'll find that compassion naturally emerges, since love and compassion are really the same thing.

2. During your meditation, think of your partner (or anyone else) as exactly the same as you. The Dalai Lama says, "All human beings are the same—made of human flesh, bones, and blood. We all want happiness and want to avoid suffering. Further, we have an equal right to be happy. In other words, it is important to recognize our sameness as human beings." What this means is to think of your partner, or whomever you want to develop compassion for, as a human being, and not as a role or label. See this person not as your husband, wife, father, mother, boss, ex-husband, ex-wife, and so on, but as a person, just like you, with the same needs and wants as you have. Visualize her that way for as long as you can, recognizing that she is a human being wanting love and happiness—just like you.

Trustworthiness

Do what you say you're going to do. If you say you'll be home at 6:00, then be there. If you say you'll spend Saturday working on the yard together, then don't accept an offer to go out with your friends that day, even if it would be more fun. When one partner doesn't follow through on promises, the other partner is relegated to the role of parent or nag—neither of which is fair and neither of which is the stuff of healthy partnerships. And when people consistently break promises, eventually no one takes them seriously.

Trustworthiness isn't just about keeping promises. It also means being honest about how you are feeling or what you are needing at any given

THE FIVE STRATEGIES OF LOVING FROM YOUR ESSENCE

by Linda Kavelin Popov

Strategy 1 • *Speak the Language of the Virtues*
The language of virtues is a language of appreciation: "Thanks, that was kind" or "It was really helpful when you . . ." or "I see your courage in facing . . ." It is specific and empowering. It is also a way to gently remind each other of what's important when we are not acting from the best within us: "I need you to say that tactfully," "Please be patient with me," and "I need to count on your reliability" are all helpful phrases to keep in mind.

Strategy 2 • *Recognize Teachable Moments*
Viewing life as an opportunity to learn our lessons gives meaning to the annoying and frustrating "stuff" that happens every day. When there is conflict in a relationship, that's a time to pause and reflect: "What lesson do I need to be learning here? What virtue do I need to call upon?"

time. If you aren't honest in this way, then your partner can't rely on you, can't trust what you say. If you're upset about something, don't say "nothing's wrong" and expect your partner to know what's going on. Be candid, and do so in a tactful way. At least this way your partner knows where you stand and can then respond accordingly.

Appreciation

This is the floral part of a relationship; it's not as fundamental as trust or faithfulness, but it's what makes a connection extra special, intimate, and joyful. We all love to hear words of appreciation about what we've done, such as "I appreciate that you've made me such a beautiful dinner," "The

Strategy 3 • *Set Clear Boundaries*

It's essential to set clear guidelines and ground rules in order to achieve respect in our relationships and in our family life. We all have "house rules," whether spoken or unspoken. It's best to make them clear and reach agreement on how we share responsibility, what is acceptable and unacceptable for each of us, and what our bottom line in the relationship is, meaning what we will not tolerate.

Strategy 4 • *Honor the Spirit*

Make time for your spiritual needs, from creating routines of reverence to telling your family stories, to creating ceremony for significant life events and establishing a faith practice that fits your beliefs.

Strategy 5 • *Offer the Art of Spiritual Companioning*

The art of presence and listening is a way to help each other get to the heart of the matter. So many couples try to fix each other when what they really need is simply a listening ear and a compassionate heart.

Linda Kavelin Popov is codirector of the Virtues Project. Reprinted with permission of Linda Kavelin Popov.

house really looks clean," "I admire the excellent job you did when you painted the bathroom," "I appreciate the way you are so generous with your friends," "I love the way you are so gentle with me," or "I'm so thankful that you work hard to provide money for this family," and so on.

Showing appreciation is especially important in situations where you see the people every day, such as in a marriage or at work. In these instances, it is so easy to feel taken for granted because, every day, we do the same things: cook meals, clean the house, repair appliances, weed the garden, go to work, pick up children, pay the bills. After a while, we can begin to feel like machines. The last time I checked, machines weren't exactly fun to live with. They don't inspire me to come home and open my heart and be joyful. So, if our partners aren't delighted when they see us coming through the door, we might ask ourselves just how much we're showing that we appreciate them. When was the last time you thanked her for one of those mundane tasks she performs every day? When was the last time you acknowledged him for something he does so often it's become rote even to him?

If you are the one feeling unappreciated, refer to the virtues of assertiveness and tact, and tell your partner you'd like to be acknowledged more often. Feeling taken for granted can ultimately be deadly in a marriage—like one of those homes built on a hill that eventually slides into the sea after the soil has eroded away.

Appreciation is, however, distinguished from the word *differentiated*. You might remember that word from chapter 2, "Loving Authentically." It was coined by Dr. David Schnarch, author of *Passionate Marriage*. A differentiated person does not need validation from a partner in order to feel whole and fulfilled. Thus, if your partner isn't appreciative of the things you do, don't let that stand in the way of your own fulfillment and self-esteem. You can and should appreciate yourself, with or without validation from anyone else. Appreciation from others ought to be the icing on your cake, not the foundation. Differentiation or not, however, appreciation is simply one of the niceties of life that takes a partnership past the mundane into the beautiful.

❧ *A Commitment to Loving* ❧

*T*ricia Clark-McDowell and Forrest McDowell are committed not only to each other; they are equally committed to living from their essence and to being as loving as they possibly can be.

They leave very little of this mission to happenstance: all around the house are icons—reminders of their shared ethic to rise above mundane behavior and reach for their absolute best.

A three-foot statue of Kwan Yin sits in their living room, serving as a constant reminder to practice compassion. (Kwan Yin is the Chinese goddess of loving compassion.) At the base of the statute they keep a candle burning twenty-four hours a day. "It's our way of affirming that we have welcomed the spirit of love and compassion into our home and our marriage in a much more conscious way," Forrest says.

All throughout the house, they also display pictures of a spiritual leader named Parmahansa Yogananda. His portrait is tucked away in the most surprising places, even the bathroom. Forrest says: "It's not him, but what he stands for—the message of consciousness. The images are very good reminders of the way we can conduct our behavior, and that, of course, affects our relationship all of the time. That's why we have so many reminders all over our house and work spaces."

Tricia adds: "Many times a day we are reminded of our goal of how we want to be with each other, how we want to behave. It offers us an ethic that we really want to be true to. The first thing I do when I go downstairs in the morning, and the last thing before I go to sleep, is bow to Kwan Yin and say a little prayer about compassion. It's not the statue, but the spirit of Kwan Yin that lives inside each of us if we pay attention."

Tricia and Forrest live on a twenty-two-acre retreat they named the Cortesia Sanctuary and Center for Natural Gardening and Healing. They teach various subjects ranging from natural fertilizers and pest control to seed saving, herbal home remedies, and nutrition. A day-long workshop,

Tricia Clark-McDowell and Forrest McDowell occasionally retreat to their individual yurts on their 22-acre "sanctuary" for some time alone—a vital component of staying attuned to their essence: "By taking time alone you start seeing the larger picture."

"Creating a Sanctuary Garden," draws throngs of visitors. They coauthored a book titled *The Sanctuary Garden*.

The term *sanctuary* applies not only to their garden and home but also to taking time to be alone—a vital component of staying attuned to their essence. Both Tricia and Forrest have a small yurt on the property—his and hers—where they go to work or take refuge. Forrest's yurt is more traditionally masculine, with a computer and boxes of books. Tricia's is more classically feminine, with tabletop water fountains, soft colors, spiritual reminders, and low light. If they get into an intense disagreement, they often go to their yurts to be alone and think things through.

"Even if we have a fight or an argument, when I take sanctuary time in my yurt, I'll see these pictures and icons all around me," Tricia says. "There is no way I can hang on to the fight. We have filled our environment with so many soulful reminders that we can't go astray very far or for very long. We naturally right ourselves because of all of these influences around us."

Tricia adds: "By taking time alone you start seeing the larger picture. Sometimes I'll stay up half the night in order to find a place of peace within myself, and from that place will come new insight on how to resolve the issue. It's not just about compromise, biding my time, or giving up my ground; it's not some intellectual decision I come to. It's coming more to my soul, and I intuitively know what has to happen. If I'm wrong, I admit it. If I have to stand my ground, I will. Even if there is some little compromise—by taking time to care for myself, I can leave my yurt with the tools I need to come to a much easier solution."

Forrest and Tricia also have an agreement that when they have intense issues-related discussions, they need to talk in the appropriate yurt. They use Forrest's yurt for "very loaded" money disagreements because that is the place where they conduct business. "We have had very fruitful conversations because we've picked the right place to talk about the topic," Forrest says. "We don't talk about money in Tricia's yurt, but we're very likely to talk about our relationship or do some real heartfelt, creative writing there because her yurt is so spiritually dense and peaceful.

You can't go in there and have an argument because there is a lot of receptivity there, which allows us to express ourselves without feeling threatened."

♣ Respecting Each Other

Tricia and Forrest place a very high value on showing respect for each other, and that respect extends to all areas of their life together—even arguments. To that end, they give each other plenty of time to prepare for intense discussions.

"We set it up in advance so each person gets to be ready," Tricia says. "Sometimes I'll approach him and say, 'I really need some time to talk to you.' It may take him a little while, but he'll come out to my yurt when he's ready."

They also allow each other time to talk with no interruptions. "If it's a more loaded kind of thing, one talks first and the other listens and says nothing," Tricia explains. "Then it's the other person's turn . . . no talking and no responding. It's hard, but it's good. Otherwise you can yell back and forth and never get anywhere. We realized we needed to do something that was more honoring of each other."

"We also acknowledge each other's different styles of communication," Forrest says. "I try to accept Tricia's more emotional response and she my more rational response. These are classic male-female roles, and we decided to look at them as ingredients in the stew, and attempt to resolve our differences by a good mix of the two."

The "stew theory" has allowed Forrest and Tricia to learn from each other, too. Forrest says he is more comfortable with the emotional realm and Tricia says she is more reasonable—thus they enable themselves to respond more broadly.

"One of the principles we try to live by is that if you change yourself, you've done your part to change the world; so by taking time away from each other, we can really look at ourselves and ask what is it about ourselves that we can change," Forrest says. "It doesn't mean kowtowing, because we're both fiercely strong people."

Tricia adds: "Change is a very important part of my life. I know I don't want to be stuck. I can have a certain behavior that I've had for years and suddenly I get insight into why it isn't working, and I drop it. On the other hand, there are things about myself that I really value, and I'm not changing."

Forrest sees their willingness to change as a willingness to take risks: "Tricia is more willing to invest in a new form of behavior for the betterment of our relationship, and I'm much the same way," he says. "One example is that Tricia requests to have more time alone because our family has been pretty close—working together at home, and until four years ago, home-schooling our fourteen-year-old daughter, Sonji. But for me, family is my main thing, and I used to resent her needing alone time. Now that I see Tricia's need, I risk my usual ways of thinking to make sure we both have time alone."

❧ Nurturing and Romance

Tricia and Forrest are also very deliberate about caring for each other. Nearly every night for the past twenty years, Tricia has massaged Forrest to sleep. No matter what her mood, no matter how distant they have been feeling during a particular time, no matter what—she has given him a back rub most every night. "In doing something for that long, there were times when I was really mad at him, or feeling very sad or in various emotional spaces, and even then I would do it. It wasn't always easy."

Forrest says: "Tricia works very hard at loving. This is her commitment to move past anger or holding resentment. That's a great teaching quality I get from her. She teaches me devotion and that she's going to be there, no matter what."

Tricia and Forrest are also very conscious of showing their love through romance. They often wear nice clothes for dinner and have dinner by candlelight. They have made a commitment to take advantage of the times when Sonji is away, always making sure that they have a nice meal—sometimes going out and sometimes staying at home. "We do a lot of sensual things, like I'll serenade her by playing guitar and lighting candles, or we'll read poetry together," Forrest says. "Ultimately this moves into love-making."

Tricia regularly puts flowers on Forrest's desk or brings him little treats. Forrest says, "Those little spontaneous gifts are very important. And often, I'll tell both of my ladies (Tricia and Sonji) that I'm taking them out to dinner and a movie. Sometimes I love being one on one with just Sonji because she and I do special little treat things for each other, too."

A regular practice of meditation has been a relationship mainstay as well. Every morning and evening, they take time alone to meditate. Tricia says, "Meditation is a great healer and simplifier because it soothes away the cares of the world, and that above all has allowed us to come into a deeper sense of peace."

෴ ෴ ෴

Resources

The Virtues Project, Box 240, Ganges Station, Salt Spring Island, B.C., Canada V8K 2V9. Phone: (250) 537-1978. Internet: www.virtuesproject.com. E-mail: virtues@saltspring.com.

BOOKS

Do Unto Others: How Good Deeds Can Change Your Life, by Rabbi Abraham J. Twerski, M.D. (Kansas City, Mo.: Andrews McMeel, 1997).

The Choosing to Forgive Workbook: Discover Contentment and Peace by Letting Go of Harmful Anger, by Les Carter, Ph.D., and Frank Minirth, M.D. (Nashville: Thomas Nelson, 1997).

The Daily Journal of Kindness: A Year Long Guide to Creating Your Own Kindness Revolution, by Meladee McCarty and Hanoch McCarty (Deerfield Park, Fla.: Health Communications, Inc., 1996).

Exploring Forgiveness, edited by Robert D. Enright and Joanna North (Madison: University of Wisconsin Press, 1998).

The Family Virtues Guide: Simple Ways to Bring Out the Best in Our Children and Ourselves, by Linda Kavelin Popov (New York: Plume, 1997).

Forgiveness: A Bold Choice for a Peaceful Heart, by Robin Casarjian (New York: Bantam, 1992).

Handbook for the Heart: Original Writings on Love, edited by Richard Carlson and Benjamin Shield (Boston: Little, Brown, 1996).

Jealousy, by Nancy Friday (New York: M. Evans, 1997).

The Path to Love: Spiritual Strategies for Healing, by Deepak Chopra (New York: Three Rivers Press, 1997).

The Practice of Kindness: Meditations for Bringing More Peace, Love and Compassion into Daily Life, edited by Harold Kushner (Berkeley, Calif.: Conari Press, 1996).

Sacred Moments: Daily Meditations on the Virtues, by Linda Kavelin Popov (New York: Plume, 1997).

The Simple Abundance Journal of Gratitude, by Sarah Ban Breathnach (New York: Warner, 1996).

What Really Matters: Searching for Wisdom in America, by Tony Schwartz (New York: Bantam, 1996).

· *Part Two* ·

BEING TOGETHER

Chapter *4*

Make Your Home a Sanctuary

O ne would think that a hurricane was wild and heaving all the way through—that it hurled and gyrated in conflicting, angry motions from one end to the other, with no break in between. But the truth is, at the very center, there is the still point . . . the middle . . . the eye . . . where all is calm. No noise. No racket. No heaving. The eye is a place of repose, of serenity, of refuge.

The eye cradles and embraces the calm in the same way our homes can shelter our loving relationships from the outside world.

It is easier to open our hearts when we provide a safe refuge in which to do so. We ought to make our living spaces not so much places to display knickknacks and exotic paraphernalia, but rather, a sanctuary, a place to embrace relationships. We may not have much control over the cacophony of modern life, but we do have absolute, total control over what we allow to come inside our own lives and homes. Indeed, the more intense the whirlwind outside, the more we need to provide a respite inside.

I had this feeling walking into Denise Linn's home—like I was walking into an embrace.

Denise is the author of ten books on spirituality and home, including her most recent ones, *Feng Shui for the Soul*, *Denise Linn's Altars*, and *Denise Linn's Space Clearing*. She has thought a lot about the effect of environment on well-being. Denise's house sits on a fairly busy arterial in the midst of a big city, yet the moment you pass through the garden gate you are drawn into a place of refuge and serenity. I felt drawn in because Denise has very consciously created it that way—the walkway is lined with plants, flowers, a birdbath, and whimsical garden art. Two ceramic Egyptian cats stand guard at the foot of the stairs. The porch is not simply a place to stand under the weather; it's a welcoming room with a bent willow settee surrounded by wind chimes, plants, and statutes—Quan Yin, the Chinese goddess of compassion, and the Buddha—that invite a guest to rest.

Even the doorknob is significant. Denise says: "That's the first thing you touch in someone's home—it's like a handshake—you get an instant sense and feeling. And the front entrance sets the energy for the rest of the house. It's like when you meet somebody, the first impression is important."

The living room is small, but the couches are large and plush—the kind you sink into, forgetting your cares for just that moment, feeling like you're enveloped in a womb. Every room feels the same—beckoning you to linger and be cared for.

Denise takes me up the stairs to the bedroom she shares with David, her husband of twenty-five years. It is the most important room in the whole house, she tells me, because that's where people spend most of their time. All cream, muted hues of beige, simple, and serene. She's chosen skin tones for a subconscious sense of comfort, of being held in a mother's arms. "Better than cold blue," she says. "And avoid really excitable colors in the bedroom unless you want to be excited, but above all, forget the rules and do what feels good to you. There was a time when I was a teenager when I painted my bedroom walls black because I needed to go into a cave."

Then she asks me, "Did you know that one-quarter of blind people, with some training, have the ability to feel colors? That says that our skin absorbs the environment whether we are awake or asleep."

There's more thought given to this bedroom—the arrangement of furniture, pictures, and lighting. A profile of a girl is framed near the entryway, and the girl faces into, rather than out of, the room. "That draws you in," Denise says, and then points to the bed: "Make sure both sides of the bed are equal. When I go into people's homes and find that only one side of the bed has a lamp or there is more furniture on one side, I find that the relationship is unequal—that person tends to be in control of the relationship."

In placing objects in the room, Denise also thinks about the first thing she sees when waking up in the morning and the last thing at night. Where once a utilitarian lamp stood, now stands a statute of the Buddha. "All of the things around you will have a subconscious effect," Denise says. "I think environments are more powerful than affirmations because your environment becomes a living affirmation. My home reflects my current interests and also what and who I want to be in the future. My environment affirms that, and I believe that in no small way do our environments dictate consciousness.

"I also think my home needs to be serene because I have such a hectic life—I teach in nineteen countries, so when I come home I need a refuge. I notice that when I'm in an environment that feels more comfortable to me, I am more in balance. Every night I am home we light all of the candles, close the drapes in the living room, light a fire, and have a glass of wine together. Sometimes we watch a movie. My environment feels very sensuous—it supports the kind of relationship I like to have."

Alexandra Stoddard also spends a lot of time thinking about the effect that environment has on intimate relationships. She is a professional interior designer and has written many books on the subject, including her most recent, *Feeling at Home . . . Defining Who You Are and How You Want to Live*. She and her husband, Peter, have been married for over twenty-five years and loved each other for over forty-five years. "We met in 1954," Alexandra says. "I was thirteen years old and played tennis with his sister. We each married other people but remained friends. Twenty years later his wife died, I was divorced, and we got married.

"We came together late in life and were determined to live a beautiful life together. I find that most people put their lives on hold. They feel very stressed out, come home, grab something to eat, and go to bed. We feel that our home is a very sacred place where we come to celebrate ourselves and our love of life.

"My husband is also a sensualist who loves beauty and loves to live in a very civilized way," she says. "Our home is a haven because we light candles, always have fresh flowers, we play music, and when we have our breakfast, lunch, tea, and dinner, we dine. We don't just eat. We create a beautiful table setting.

"This is an everyday thing—we don't just do this for special events like birthdays. It's every day; we have tea and light a fire, we have meaningful conversation and eye contact. We like being together. Every day is like this."

Alexandra says it's also important to have only what you love and use in the home. "Everything we have in our home has a soul," she says. "They're not decorations—the paintings are by friends—we know the artists. All of our books we've read. Each piece of antique furniture, we picked out together. And we don't have clutter—clutter is indecision. If there are piles or collections of things you love or use, put them in beautiful matching boxes.

"Our grown daughters and their children like to come here. We've created a place for children and dogs and grown-ups. Our home is full of spirit and really good energy.

"The happiest couples are the ones who both share a strong love of home. If both people are not equally concerned about the way their house or apartment functions, looks, and feels, it is usually a danger sign in the relationship. When a spouse is too busy to be in on the decisions, it usually indicates he or she has tuned out and psychologically lives elsewhere. What greater use of our time can there be than to build a home with someone with whom we have made a commitment of love?"

A Place of Energy

Most of us don't think of our homes as having energy, but they do. Every item in your home has its own energy, and the energy from the people who live in the home is always present. Notice how you can feel that some homes are filled with love, and others make you want to leave. Homes take on the persona of their occupants—they are reflections of who we really are. One woman, who purposely designed her home to be a refuge, said that she noticed when people came to visit, they seemed to open up and spill their souls to her. Another quote I read one time said that a particular home felt like "walking into a lover's outstretched arms."

How does your home feel? Not, how does it *look* and does the furniture show off your elegant tastes, but how does it *feel*? There are at least two schools of thought with regard to the way our environment affects our inner selves. One thought is that when you change your inner self, your outer environment will naturally change. That is true, no doubt. But the other thought, advanced by Denise Linn, is that if you change your outer environment, your inner environment will change. Denise first became aware of this phenomenon after continually noticing during her seminars that people behaved in different ways depending on where they were seated in the room. Then she took it a step further and began working with her clients in the same way, asking them to change certain things in their homes that she felt reflected what was going on in their lives. She finally became convinced that environment does, indeed, make a difference.

CLEAR YOUR CLUTTER WITH FENG SHUI

Take a look at your surroundings. An open, clear, and sensual environment provides the space needed for intimacy. A cluttered, jumbled one leaves no room. Ilse Crawford said in *Sensual Home*:

"Many homes are so weighted down by clutter that those who live in them seem to be crowded out by the furniture. Yet we, rather than the decoration, should take center stage: the home is a backdrop to our lives and not the other way around. Simplify, and embrace the irrational, the beautiful, and exciting."

If we think of our homes as having energy, then it makes sense that each item we bring into our homes also has energy—both positive and negative. The feng shui method of clearing clutter focuses on that energy.

A form of feng shui exists in every traditional culture in the world. Its purpose is to balance and harmonize the flow of energy in buildings and, in so doing, create beneficial effects in people's lives. Even today, people in Bali make daily offerings at their household shrines to the unseen, invisible energies that coexist with the physical world. They do this to ensure that balance and harmony flow between both worlds.

Charlene Weaver is a feng shui practitioner and advises that you look carefully at each object in your home or office and ask yourself: "What does this mean to me?" "Does it take me into the past (pleasant or unpleasant?)?" "Does it keep me in the now, or take me into the future?" If it takes you back to an unpleasant past, get rid of it because it will drain your energy. If it keeps you in the now, ask yourself if that is a place in which you want to stay. Examples of items that keep us in the past are crib and infant paraphernalia that people often store in garages. While that particular past may be very pleasant, if you know you're not going to have more children, release yourself from the past and get rid of it. On the other hand, if you have a wonderful antique bed that you're saving for your daughter, hang on to it because it brings you into the future. Or if you're ready to move on from a particular line of work, you can let go of manuals and items that you needed for that work. The goal is to lift the energy in your home by having just the right objects properly placed. Once you have cleared your clutter this way, be sure to ask yourself the same questions when considering a new purchase. How will it affect the harmony and energy of your home or office?

Karen Kingston is also a feng shui practitioner and author of *Creating Sacred Space with Feng Shui* and *Clear Your Clutter with Feng Shui*. Karen's approach to feng shui is to work directly with the energy of each space. She writes: "Over a twenty-year period, I have developed the ability to see, hear, smell, taste, and sense energy in enhanced ways . . . The his-

Thoughts About Possessions

Ꮬ

by Cris Evatt

Riches prick us with a thousand troubles in getting them, as many cares in preserving them, and yet more anxiety in spending them, and with grief in losing them.

—SAINT FRANCIS

Possessions clutter. Possessions weigh you down emotionally, cluttering your mind. Casually placed possessions clutter tabletops, closets, counters, and garages. Putting stuff away can take all day.

Possessions cost more than the original price. You spend additional money storing, repairing, protecting, and cleaning goods.

Possessions need cleaning. Do you enjoy washing, dusting, polishing, soaking, scouring, and scraping? Even minimal cleaning is time-consuming.

Possessions create errands. How many miles a year do you drive to buy, repair, and clean your things? How many hours do you spend waiting in store lines and looking for parking? Shopping centers thrive on commercialism.

Possessions are worrisome. Fretting about breakage, loss, theft, fire, repairs, and insurance premiums clutters our minds. Every item let go of is one less worry.

Possessions need organizing. Things need to be alphabetized, color-coded, sorted, and grouped, for sanity's sake. Woe to people who do not know how to organize their things.

Possessions get lost. The less you have, the less you have to lose.

Possessions depreciate. Things that spot, rust, crumble, dent, fray, and come unglued lose value. Invest in yourself, not in things.

Possessions are climbed over, hidden, apologized for, and argued over. How much more do you need to know?

Possessions encourage greed. Materialistic people tend to compete with their neighbors, brag, hoard, and constantly desire more. They are seldom satisfied with what they've got.

—From *Simply Organized!*

tory of events is recorded in the walls and furniture in the form of subtle electromagnetic imprints, and through reading and interpreting these, I can detect pretty much everything of significance that has ever happened there. Traumatic or repetitive events are embedded the most deeply and have a correspondingly greater effect on present-day occupants. I am also able to find areas where the energy in the building has become stuck and determine what needs to be done to improve its flow.

"Whenever I come across clutter, its energy field is unmistakable. It presents an obstacle to the flow of energy and has an unpleasant, sticky, unclean feel to it, as if I'm moving my hands through unseen cobwebs. This is what first made me realize that clutter causes problems in people's lives. . . .

"The good news is that after clearing clutter, this unwholesome, stagnant energy and accompanying odor quickly disappear."

There are many different schools of feng shui, but one thing they all agree on is that if there is a lot of clutter in a space, the energy cannot flow smoothly. Karen says that when this happens, it's far more difficult to create a harmonious relationship within the space. She says, "If you find that as you're walking about your home, you're constantly bumping into pieces of furniture, or the layout is such that you keep having to go around corners to get from A to B, then your relationships will be similarly convoluted. Feng shui offers help to homes which are awkwardly designed, to create more harmony and prosperity for the occupants."

One example of clutter in the home is unwanted gifts. People have great difficulty getting rid of gifts that were given to them by loved ones, even though they may feel the gift is ghastly or, at the very least, not what they want. In order not to reject the friend's love, they'll keep the gift forever. Karen says: "My suggestion is that they get rid of the item because whenever they see it, their energy drops. I suggest that they deeply accept the love that came with the gift and allow themselves to let the item go. It is, after all, the thought that counts. If possible, pass it on to someone who will really appreciate it."

The Bedroom and Feng Shui

Like Denise Linn, Karen believes that the bedroom is an important room. She says: "If you're focusing on your relationship, it's most important to 'space clear' your bedroom. [*Space clearing is explained in the next section.*] Our everyday life creates housework, but it also creates housework that needs to be done at an energy level. Most people live with psychic debris which gets deposited on walls and furniture in the home and never gets cleaned out. Bedrooms, in particular, need to be as energetically clear as possible. I get a lot of feedback from people telling me that when they do a space clearing ceremony, their love life improves."

When Karen provides consultations in people's homes, she's amazed to find that people expect their bedrooms to double as a home office, entertainment center, exercise room, beauty parlor, meditation space, and so on. She says: "Bedrooms are supposed to be a place to sleep, rest, and recover when we're sick, and spend our most intimate moments with our partner, but these days, we're expecting all of these kinds of multifunctional things to happen there too.

"The computer not only generates an electromagnetic field which can cause fatigue and chronic health problems if you sleep with one plugged in and close to your bed, but people also switch to their more mental capacity when a computer is present—whether they're using it or not. Having a computer in the bedroom is not advisable if you're trying to generate an atmosphere of love and romance there."

Karen also checks the mattress. "If you're looking for intimacy, one of the key factors is to examine the mattress on the bed," she says. "When I do a consultation in someone's home, I go around and sense the energy in the walls to give me a greater insight into what's happening with people and I will usually energy-sense the bed, too. People leave a total energy imprint on their bed space, so ask yourself what happens if you had a relationship with somebody for ten years, slept with them in a bed for that length of time, then the relationship ends and a new one begins. If you're sleeping with the new partner in the same bed, my question is, How many people are in that bed?

"If you want the new relationship to have the best possibility of success, it's ideal if you can treat yourself to a new mattress. The mattress is the most important item to replace because it's the most absorbent and soaks up the most energy. If your finances won't allow a new mattress, then you can literally fibrate the old frequencies out with, say, a baseball bat. It's kind of wild, but it works. Do one side, flip it over, do the other side and get on with your life. While you're at it, go around and space-clear the energy in your whole bedroom."

It's also beneficial to look at the color and patterns in your bedroom. Karen suggests flowing, rather than geometric or straight, designs; and go for warm, rather than cool, colors. Look for reddish- (though not a red bedroom), orange- and yellow-spectrum colors, including skin tones and earth colors. "You want to create a nest for yourself," Karen says, "and these colors are reminiscent of the womb. They make you feel safe and protected."

Check the emotional clutter in your bedroom, too. Karen lives in Bali for half of each year and is married to a Balinese man. She says the Balinese people place great emphasis on their families and marriages. One

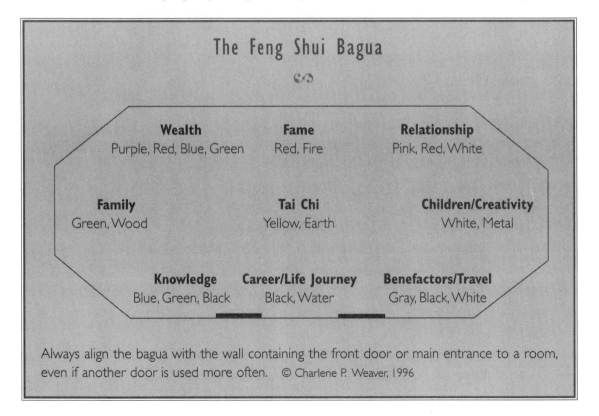

The Feng Shui Bagua

Wealth	**Fame**	**Relationship**
Purple, Red, Blue, Green	Red, Fire	Pink, Red, White
Family	**Tai Chi**	**Children/Creativity**
Green, Wood	Yellow, Earth	White, Metal
Knowledge	**Career/Life Journey**	**Benefactors/Travel**
Blue, Green, Black	Black, Water	Gray, Black, White

Always align the bagua with the wall containing the front door or main entrance to a room, even if another door is used more often. © Charlene P. Weaver, 1996

Make Your Bedroom a Retreat

&

It's worth your while if you want great sex, to create a bedroom that's ideally conducive to intimacy. It doesn't need to be expensively furnished, but it should be clean and uncluttered, have pleasing colors, and not be merely utilitarian; it should inspire a sense of beauty. The bed you use for sex ought to have a special, exotic, otherworldly feeling, almost evocative of an altar. There should be an air of reverence. Some people enjoy making love under a canopy, and you may want to construct one. Soft lighting is immensely helpful, and so is quietly pulsating music. When the whole room feels like a retreat from the hustle and bustle of everyday life, won't you relish the thought of spending time there with your beloved?

—WILLIAM ASHOKA ROSS
(from *On the Wings of Eros*)

practice they have in order to ensure a happy marriage is that a couple will never, ever discuss problems or argue in bed. They'll move to another place to talk over any difficulties.

"In the West, this often doesn't happen," Karen says. "Women in particular are most prone to catch their husbands as they're drifting off to sleep, and bring up an issue that's been bothering them all day. This can be very destructive in a relationship. It's far better that the bed space be treated as a place of sanctuary from life's problems, a place of peace, intimacy, and fun. That will help keep alive the love, friendship, and passion in a marriage."

A feng shui practitioner dealing with relationship issues will look at the bedroom and also the layout of your home in relation to the feng shui bagua. (A bagua is a map.*) As you stand at the front door looking into your home, the relationships corner is located in the farthest right corner of the building. Similarly, on a smaller scale, there is a relationships area in the farthest right corner of every room. Karen often finds that if the rela-

*See page 80.

tionship area in a home is a utility room, relationships can become functional, and if it is a junk room, the relationship can feel clogged. She also finds that when people have a lot of junk in the relationship area of their home, they have a lot of emotional issues buried in the junk as well. Thus, in order to improve your relationship, it is essential to clear clutter in these areas.

"Western people often complain that they don't have energy for relationships because they're so tired from the demands of modern life," Karen says. "Having a clock radio next to the bed is a definite no-no. Sleeping in the electromagnetic field of one of these devices causes most people to wake up feeling like they still need a good night's sleep. Even though the radiation is very weak, there is mounting evidence that electrical equipment such as this impairs the ability of our immune system to regenerate our cell tissues as we sleep." She suggests switching to operating the clock radio on batteries rather than on power or, at the very least, keeping your electric clock radio and its cable a minimum of eight feet away from your body.

Karen says: "We spend one-third of our lives in bed, and the effect of that environment upon our waking life is immense. How you feel during those nighttime hours directly affects what is possible for you during the day, professionally, personally, and every other way."

HAVE A SPACE-CLEARING CEREMONY

Once you have removed the clutter from your home, you can also clear the general energy in the rooms through a process called space clearing. There are three main areas of stuck energy, according to Karen Kingston:

1. *Physical grime.* This includes all types of dirt, dust, grease, and general yuck. Low-level energy always accumulates around dirt. Doing a good cleanup is an essential part of space clearing.

2. *Predecessor energy.* Everything that happens in a building is recorded in the walls, floors, furniture, and objects in the space. This builds up in layers, in much the same way as grime does, except we cannot see it.

3. *Any kind of clutter* creates an obstacle to the smooth flow of energy around a space. This in turn creates stuckness and/or confusion in the lives of the occupants.

Indeed, a large real estate firm in New York now hires a team of space-clearing specialists. They discovered that after a clearing, many of the houses that were not selling sold soon after the clearing ceremony. The owner of the real estate firm said, "I really don't believe in this, but I have to admit, it works." Residual energy is a real-enough phenomenon that, in some states, there is a law that says you must indicate in the deed of sale whether someone has committed suicide on the property. And there is some research that shows that when one business goes bankrupt in a particular location, the next ones that follow often go bankrupt as well.

If you would like to do a space-clearing ceremony in your home, you can pick up Karen Kingston's book *Creating Sacred Space with Feng Shui* or Denise Linn's *Sacred Space.*

Even if you think a space-clearing ceremony is out of your realm, by going through the process, you may develop a new awareness about your home. It will take on a personality of its own and will no longer be a lifeless entity called a "house." Many people who follow these space-clearing ideas also suggest giving your home a name. Again, you are personalizing your home this way and, thus, begin to see it as a real place of nurture and refuge—like your lover's arms.

Whether you perform a space-clearing ceremony or not, the more you can think of your place as a vessel for your loving relationship, the better off you'll be. That kind of awareness will also help you to maintain a clutter-free environment. After all, why would you want to "junk up" such a special place?

Denise Linn lists four steps to space clearing: 1. Preparation, 2. Purification, 3. Invocation, and 4. Preservation.

Step One: Preparation

There are many methods for house clearing, all listed in *Sacred Space*. Choose one and lay out all the tools you'll need prior to your ceremony. The day before, Denise recommends that you clean your house thor-

3. *Inviting.* How to create a setting that is inviting to you each time you enter (and of course, just as inviting to a visitor!)? This should be given special thought. Perhaps it is the way furniture is arranged, how color and lighting are used, the opportunity to listen to inspiring music, a scent in the air, a relaxing chair or pillow, or even the display of nature objects, personal mementos, and inspiring quotes. All this (and more!) should give you or a visitor a feeling that you can relax and be one with yourself or a companion. A thoughtfully designed sanctuary space should feel inviting, not haphazardly cluttered or sterile.

4. *Enfolding.* One of the primary qualities of any sanctuary should be the opportunity for interiorization: to go within oneself and sip from the contemplative well for peace. A home or setting, by the way, if it is consciously stewarded, should feel as if one can easily claim sanctuary, i.e., sacred time and sacred place, within it, even for brief periods of time. Thoughtful effort to create an inviting heartfelt entrance, to maintain a personal or family altar that honors and celebrates life, to embrace and show tribute to the many aspects of nature, and to uphold the spiritual presence of a preferred deity—those are key in helping to peacefully restore and regenerate one's spirit.

—From a pamphlet titled
How to Make Your Home a Sanctuary

For more information on Forrest and Tricia's work, call (541) 343-9544 or E-mail sanctuary@ cortesia.org.

oughly. Before you can even do a thorough cleaning, however, you'll need to get rid of all clutter and paraphernalia that you don't use or love. That will make house clearing easier and deeper.

When you rise on the morning of your ceremony (best to do it in the early morning), consider meditating and visualizing yourself going from room to room, cleansing and clearing each room. Then imagine that the ceremony is complete and your home radiates with sparkling energy. Next, take a salt bath by adding one pound of salt to your water and soak for at

SIX SPECIAL WAYS TO ENHANCE
YOUR SANCTUARY

by Tricia Clark-McDowell and Forrest McDowell

1. An Inviting Entrance. Make the routine of merely entering a room or your home more inviting. Hang an inspiring quote or piece of artwork; place nearby a bowl of polished pebbles, blessing cards, or quotes from which one may be selected; hang a whimsical wind chime; place a statue or objects from nature. Set a tone for entering your sanctuary—it will do much to make one feel enfolded and honored.

2. Create Focal Points. Purposely create places that draw one's attention. A well-placed and -designed altar is always magnetic. A creatively decorated window with a view, an especially fine piece of art, a unique object from nature, a vase of seasonal flowers, even that overstuffed chair with a lap blanket and an open book—each of these beckons the wandering spirit to come, relax, celebrate, and honor.

3. Integrate Nature. Always find ways to honor nature. Maintain plants and flowers you are attracted to, seek furniture and crafts explicitly made from nature, panel a wall with wood, hang art that depicts nature, even consider an indoor fountain gently dripping water.

4. Create an Altar. An altar is a sacred hearth that one approaches with humility and honor. Here one can pray, find peace, sit in communion with someone, celebrate nature, even honor the lives of family members, friends, or some deity. A home may have a family or public altar as well as a personal one, per-

least twenty minutes. Put on clothes you have chosen specifically for this ceremony. Now you're ready to Purify.

Next, define what specific results you want to achieve from your house-clearing ceremony. Denise says: "You might want to think of your overall intention as being like an aerial picture taken from a plane. Your haps in a private space. The altar surface may be a specific piece of furniture such as an antique, bookshelf, chest, table, mantel, even the floor. Always be creative and open to change with your altar. Let it reflect the true spirit of you or family members—decorate it with nature objects, personal items, pictures, a deity, candles, incense, whatever moves you deeper to your soul's core of serenity and self-empowerment.

5. *Effectively Use Color and Lighting.* Colors have a powerful influence on vital energy, affecting feelings and thought processes. By understanding basic effects of color tones, you can decorate and furnish your setting to evoke certain states of mind. Green, for example, is very healing and emits growth, balance, and abundance. Blue emits peace and spiritual enfolding. Purple promotes intuition and inner awareness. White suggests transformation, while black suggests mystery. Red is very energizing, orange is happy and social, and yellow promotes communication, mental stimulation, and positive thinking. Through experimentation, you will find color variations that stir your soul.

Lighting is also important in setting a mood. Soft, ambient light from a window, a tinted lightbulb, stained glass, even from candles or a lantern is much more preferred to create intimacy than harsh bright light from overhead.

6. *Heal and Soothe with Scents.* Aromatherapy has been used for centuries to salve the soul and human emotions. Herbal sachets, a bowl of dried crushed leaves and flowers, scented candles, and especially essential oils are vital to setting a mood. The latter are concentrates of flowers, plants, and woods that, when released in specific combinations or individually, have a definite therapeutic effect on one's psyche. An excellent book is *Complete Aromatherapy Handbook: Essential Oils for Radiant Health* by Suzanne Fischer-rizzi (Sterling Publishing, 1990).

specific intentions would then be coming to earth and bringing into focus the street you live on, your house, the rooms inside, the furniture, the books on the table, the flowers in a vase—all the details which will bring your overall goals to life."

Once you have recorded your specific objectives, ask yourself what long-term results you expect to achieve from your Intent. In *Creating Sacred Space*, Denise provides the following example:

> *Overall Intention.* A home conducive to art and creativity.
>
> *Specific Intentions.* Empty out seldom-used spare bedroom, install appropriate lighting for a studio, make time in schedule every week for painting.
>
> *Long-Term Results.* The creation and sale of the paintings, the exploration of my creative potential.

Step Two: Purification

Denise writes: "Energy in a room can be compared to water in a mountain stream. Imagine that there is a bend in the stream and that in this bend leaves and sticks and debris have collected over time, partially clogging the little stream of clear cold water. You can reach down and clear it out, yet after a while, as more leaves wash downstream, the leaves will begin to collect again. Room purification is similar to removing debris from the little stream, in that you can energize the places in the room where energy tends to go dormant or stagnant, but you may need to repeat the purification periodically."

Begin by standing at the front door to your home, keeping in mind your intention for the clearing. Stretch your body, offer prayers if you like, then sensitize your hands by holding them a few inches apart with the palms facing each other. Slowly move them together and apart. You should feel as if there is a magnet in each hand. Now circle the room using your left hand to feel and perceive places where the energy feels "sticky" or erratic. Use your right hand to do the clearing with something like a bell or water mister. According to Denise, there are four ways to tell when the room has been cleared of stagnant energy: 1. Colors will look brighter; 2. sounds will be crisper and clearer; 3. you will feel you can breathe more deeply; and 4. you will feel lighter and more free.

Step Three: Invocation

After you have cleared the stagnant energies in a home, you want to fill it with clear energy. This simply means that you call forth a higher power (whatever that means to you) for assistance. Return to your Intent and ask to dedicate the energy of your home to, say, romance, intimacy, or something general like the emotional well-being of the family. For example, you might say, "I dedicate this home to love and joy. May the Creator within all things fill this home with harmony and inner peace."

Step Four: Preservation

Finally, you'll want to preserve the energy you have just called in. There are many ways to do this—one is to write down the overall Intention for the entire home, and then buy a houseplant for the sole purpose of helping to preserve the energy that you have created. Fold the paper with your Intention and place it in the soil near the roots. Every time you water the plant, reaffirm your intention for your home.

❧ *Simple Surroundings Help Keep the Peace* ❧

Simplicity, a steady focus on the big picture, and a nonattachment to material things have enabled Cris and Dave Williams to continually live their dreams and have a fluid life—one not heavily weighted down either by their physical realm or by issues between them. Their dream has manifested itself in different ways over the years: once it was a three-year sailing trip to the South Pacific, next it was living in a quaint coastal town, and now they've moved to five acres on a tropical island.

Both Cris and Dave have a natural tendency to let go of things easily and center on what's really important, on the bigger scheme of things,

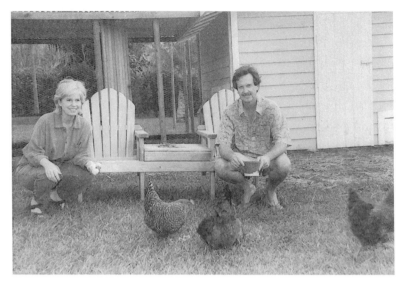

Cris and Dave Williams
tend their chickens at
their home in Hawaii.
Dave says: "By having a
spare, simple home,
we're creating space for
wonderful things to
come into our life."

rather than get bogged down by the minutiae of life. That plays out in both their emotional and material worlds. If Dave hasn't put the closet doors on for four years, Cris consciously decides not to nag him but, rather, to direct her attention to something she appreciates, such as remembering that he's created a beautiful garden and brings her fresh vegetables. "So the closet doors don't function—he has a gorgeous garden. I don't give him a big honey-do list," she says. "He's pretty good about fixing things, so I give him a lot of slack even if it's something important to me. With the closet doors, even though I'd rather have them, I just relax. Besides, he does more around the house than the average person, so when I look at the big picture it doesn't really matter that one or two areas aren't handled. I'd rather hire a handyman than nag.

"Luckily, neither of us is a packrat, but if Dave was, I would find a way to work with him, rather than against him. I would probably create places for him to group his stuff. I might have various-sized baskets for his belongings. Or maybe I would designate a closet or room for his stuff.

"Keeping the peace between us is the same as me keeping peace everywhere I go. I'm one of those people who doesn't like to rock the boat unless it's really important."

Dave is able to look at the positive when Cris doesn't manage money the way he does. "If once or twice a year she bounces a check, there's no conflict because I know who she is," Dave says. "The fact that she bounces checks is negative, but the positive is that she's not tight about money . . . she's generous, and she's taught me generosity. In watching her be so giving, I see that the benefits come rushing back at her much more so than I would have imagined." With that in mind, Dave solved the infrequent bounced-check problem by building a credit base into their checking account. No problem.

When Dave feels that he's doing more work around the house than Cris, there is still no nagging or anger. "At most, I'll tell Cris to just amp it up a little bit . . . I'll tell her I feel like I'm doing more than my share," he says. "I've probably raised my voice once or twice over the fifteen years we've known each other."

"Our attachment is more to our bodies, our friends, family, our quality of life. None of the 'stuff' adds that much to our life. It adds some. I do get pleasure at looking at these paintings, yes, but if any of them disappeared, they could be replaced."

Cris and Dave have an agreement that if either of them brings something home for the house that the other one doesn't like, such as a painting or curio, there is no discussion, no questions are asked. They find it a new home, even if it is a gift from a friend.

Cris says: "We could lose everything and we could re-create our style of living in a weekend by going to garage sales. It may sound funny, but, having so little furniture plays a big part in the success of our relationship. Without a lot of furniture or things on the wall, our house is easy to maintain. Our peaceful decorating style reinforces the peacefulness of our relationship. It makes it more possible than if we lived in an overdecorated house. We're minimalists."

She adds: "I'm so attached to making a difference in the world that my other stuff seems petty in relation to my mission."

There are other ways that Cris and Dave's organized surroundings impact their marriage positively. Cris says: "Home organization is one of my hobbies. I have hundreds of tips, and each one has made living with Dave easier. For example, our bedroom is always organized because there are only three things in it—a bed, a potted palm, and a lidded basket from Tonga. That's it! There are no wall hangings or dressers. The walls and bedspread are off-white. Nothing is stored under the bed. Our clothes are kept in a built-in closet full of white tubular hangers."

Dave adds: "I made our bedroom more serene by removing my bookcase full of books. Also, I asked Cris to delete those little decorative pillows that were on the bed. They took time to remove at night and replace in the morning. Why do women insist on having so many pillows?"

Cris and Dave create efficient systems as well. A system is a habit—the way you do a task. The routines you use to grocery-shop, do the laundry, and pay bills are all systems. Cris says there are two kinds of systems: Random Complex Systems and Planned Simple Systems. A simple system requires forethought and planning. Once it is set up, it saves you hours of time. A complex system is the result of doing something randomly, like piling your shoes on the closet floor or watering the lawn when it's brown. It wastes time. "I name my systems because it upgrades them," she says. "I like to think, 'I'm going to use the Laundry System,' not 'I'm going to do the laundry.' "

Knickknacks were once a problem in this house, but no more. Cris says, "Years ago, I lugged knickknacks home from my travels. Now I bring home practical souvenirs like a duvet from France and a reading lamp from Scandinavia. Dave is pleased that I gave up knickknacks because they increase the visual stimuli in a home. Too many create a cluttered look. I prefer a few large objets d'art and lots of blank space."

Over the years, Cris and Dave found that by not being attached to material things, more comes to them in even better ways. Dave says: "By having a spare, simple home, we're living in an ongoing vacuum, and creating space for wonderful things to come into our life. If we gave away our table and chairs, within a month somebody would come along and say, 'Do you need a table?' "

When they decided to move to a tropical island, all their worldly belongings, including a truck, fit into an eight-by-twenty-four-foot shipping container. Cris and Dave both believe in having only what's necessary or really appreciated in the house and not much more. No clutter, all white walls, clean, peaceful, organized, and spare.

"Most homes in America are visually overstimulating," Cris says. "To keep busy patterns and intense color from overwhelming us, I subtracted color and added white/off-white to our home. We have white mugs, white dishes, white sheets, white towels, white bathroom tile, and a white cat. Dave bought a white truck and painted the interior of his shop and garage white. There's still plenty of color. We love fresh flowers."

Cris believes that simple, serene surroundings have an enormous impact on a marriage. "A sparely furnished house contributes to a peaceful relationship," she says. "For example, wallpaper with busy prints pulls some of the peace out of your home, as does loud fabric on sofas. A home should be 90 percent calm and 10 percent busy.

"Your home holds your relationship. That's where you experience it . . . where you spend the majority of your time. Make it soothing."

ख़ ख़ ख़

Resources

WORKSHOPS

For information on Karen Kingston's workshops or books, see her Web site at www.spaceclearing.com.

For information on Denise Linn's seminars and feng shui certification course, write to Denise Linn Seminars, P.O. Box 75657, Seattle, WA 98125.

BOOKS

Altars: Bringing Sacred Shrines into Your Everyday Life, by Denise Linn (New York: Ballantine Books, 1999).

Clear Your Clutter with Feng Shui, by Karen Kingston (New York: Broadway Books, 1999).

Creating a Beautiful Home, by Alexandra Stoddard (New York: Avon, 1993).

Creating Sacred Space with Feng Shui: Learn the Art of Space Clearing and Bring New Energy into Your Life, by Karen Kingston (New York: Broadway Books, 1997).

Daring to Be Yourself: Creating Beauty, Harmony and Individuality in Your Life by Developing Your Own Unique Personal Style, by Alexandra Stoddard (New York: Avon, 1990).

The Feng Shui Anthology: Contemporary Earth Design, by Jami Lin (Miami: Earth Design Literacy Division, 1997).

Feng Shui for the Soul, by Denise Linn (Carlsbad, Calif.: Hay House, 2000).

The Feng Shui House Book: Change Your Home, Transform Your Life, by Gina Lazenby (New York: Watson-Guptil, 1998).

Feng Shui Today: Earth Design the Added Dimension, by Jami Lin (Miami: Earth Design Literacy Division, 1998).

Healing Design: Practical Feng Shui for Healthy and Gracious Living, by Hope Karan Gerecht (Boston: Journey Editions, 1999).

Healthy Home: A Practical and Resourceful Guide to Making Your Own Home Fit for Body, Mind, and Spirit, by Jill Blake (New York: Watson-Guptill, 1998).

A Home for the Soul: A Guide for Dwelling with Spirit and Imagination, by Anthony Lawlor (New York: Clarkson Potter Publishers, 1997).

Home Sweeter Home: Creating a Haven of Simplicity and Spirit, by Jann Mitchell (Hillsboro, Ore.: Beyond Words Publishing, 1996).

In a Spiritual Style: The Home as Sanctuary, by Laura Cerwinske (New York: Thames and Hudson, 1998).

Lighten Up! Free Yourself from Clutter and Create the Space for Miracles by Freeing Yourself from Too Much Stuff, by Michelle Passoff (New York: HarperCollins, 1998).

Living In Love, by Alexandra Stoddard (New York: Avon, 1998).

Make Your House Do the Housework, by Don Aslett and Laura Aslett Simons (Cincinnati: Betterway Books, 1995).

The Natural Home Catalog: Everything You Need to Create an Environmentally Friendly Home, by David Pearson (New York: Fireside, 1996).

Nesting: Tales of Life, Love and Real Estate, by Lois Wyse (New York: Simon & Schuster, 1999).

New Natural House Book: Creating a Healthy, Harmonious and Ecologically Sound Home, by David Pearson (New York: Fireside, 1998).

Open Your Eyes: 1,000 Simple Ways to Bring Beauty into Your Home and Life Each Day, by Alexandra Stoddard (New York: William Morrow, 1998).

Rituals for Sacred Living, by Jane Alexander (New York: Sterling, 1999).

Sacred Space: Clearing and Enhancing the Energy of Your Home, by Denise Linn (New York; Ballantine Books, 1995).

The Sanctuary Garden: Creating a Place of Refuge in Your Yard or Garden, by Christopher Forrest McDowell and Tricia Clark-McDowell (New York: Fireside, 1998).

Shelter for the Spirit: Create Your Own Haven in a Hectic World, by Victoria Moran (New York: HarperPerennial, 1998).

Simple Pleasures Home: Cozy Comforts and Old Fashioned Crafts for Every Room in the House, by Susannah Seton (Berkeley, Calif.: Conari Press, 1999).

Simple Style: The Elegant, Uncluttered Home, by Lisa Skolnik and Rima A. Suqi (New York: Friedman Fairfax Books, 1998).

Simply Organized: The Practical Way to Simplify Your Complicated Life, by Connie Cox and Cris Evatt (New York: Berkeley, 1991).

30 Days to a Simpler Life, by Cris Evatt and Connie Cox (New York: Plume, 1998).

Zen Interiors, by Vinnie Lee (New York: Stewart, Tabori and Chang, 1999).

Zen Style: Balance and Simplicity for Your Home, by Jane Tidbury (New York: Rizzoli, 1999).

Chapter 5

Create Open Time

You don't fit love into your life.
You fit life into your love.
—GREGORY GODEK

In his book, *God Is a Verb*, Rabbi David A. Cooper talks about how we perceive time in today's busy world. He says: "On the fast track of modern life, our natural priorities to attain wisdom and connect with the truth of this existence have been eroded by the demands of the outer world. The nervousness and breathlessness that accompany our constant need for more time have fed an illness of epidemic proportion during the last half of the twentieth century. Not many people yet realize the severity of this affliction. I used to refer to it as the 'time demon,' but now the world has become infected with what I call TDS, pronounced 'Tedious,' which stands for Time Deficiency Syndrome.

"A major symptom of this disease is a distorted sense of priority. Whenever work encroaches upon personal relationships and the relationships take a backseat, this is TDS. Tens of millions of marriages and family relations suffer because so many people have their priorities confused."

Amen. We are confused and then wonder why our marriages are not vital, passionate, and alive in the way we'd like. Here is a simple rule to remember—you could even paste it on your bathroom mirror and use it to awaken your consciousness each morning: *How you choose to spend your time and energy determines the quality of your life, and especially, of your relationship.*

This is how our time-starved society arranges its priorities, according to columnist Linda Welter: "People today prefer showers to tubs, sex to courtship, columns like this one to books. For most of us, time is worth too much to waste it drawing water, sending love letters, or turning pages. We value nothing more than the most efficient way to get things done."

The best gift we can give our partners is the gift of our time—ourselves. Open time gives us space to daydream, ponder, think up loving things to do for each other—take bubble baths, give bubble baths, come together. Too much scheduling makes us tight, closed, exhausted from trying to keep up, edgy, and impatient. Our spirits need the space of open time. As Ilse Crawford wrote in *The Sensual Home*, "One of the biggest luxuries in modern life is unscheduled, uncommitted time. Defend it fiercely and value it. Free time is not wasted. Your brain needs it to filter through the daily assault of information and come up with new ideas."

STAY TUNED

There are many ways to make time for your partner. One of them is to think of your marriage as an entity in and of itself—a third party that needs to be nourished. When the focus is on just getting your needs met, or your partner getting his or her needs met, there will be conflict. But when you think of getting your marriage's needs met, you'll be more aware of how your actions impact that entity.

John W. Davis and Laura Sullivan learned about the marriage as an entity philosophy during their wedding when a friend read a poem by Robert Bly (see page 152), which described the idea. They've kept it in the forefront of their consciousness ever since. Because of that, they manage to stay very finely tuned to each other's needs—especially their need for time together. Every issue, every conflict is seen in relation to that entity. "We ask how it will affect not just Laura and John, but the marriage as well," John says. "It's the womb of the relationship."

John is a therapist with a practice that he spreads among Los Angeles, San Francisco, and Seattle. He lives with his wife near Seattle, and travels to Los Angeles ten days every month and to San Francisco another three and a half days a month. By keenly tuning in to their own needs as well as the needs of the marriage, John and Laura have figured out that ten days apart is good for the relationship, but more than twelve is not. Laura says: "Our ten-day separation is like a honeymoon. The energetic tension builds up from being apart, and then when we reunite all of our juices start flowing again. But if the separation goes on too long, it's upsetting."

John says: "People who are close have psychic cords to each other. You need to be aware of when that cord is unraveling, and don't let it come unraveled. When Laura and I are apart for too long, its almost like having to relearn each other. We've ripped too much of the fabric that ties us together. How much time two people need to spend with one another is very individual, but you have to stay tuned to it and not let it go any further than is good for that particular relationship."

However you awaken your consciousness, you'll need to be continually aware of how much time your particular relationship needs not only to survive, but also to thrive. There is no easy recipe. Some people need more time together than others, so it's important to stay sensitive to your partner and his or her needs. If you give your partner nothing but leftovers, you can be assured that, sooner or later, you'll be eating alone.

NURTURE YOUR PARTNER

We don't need to totally rearrange our lives or work schedules in order to make time for romance. At the very least, we can keep the five-to-one theory at the forefront of our consciousness. It is this: *Five minutes devoted to romance equals one day of harmony.* I have to admit that I was never so hot at math, but this equation is clear: it only takes something small on your part to guarantee a big effect on your partner. When was the last time somebody did something nice for you and you didn't warm up?

Nurturing shows you appreciate your partner, that you care about her, and that you want to do what you can to make her life better. Nurturing can also take very little time, starting with something as simple as saying "I love you," or "Thank you," giving a two-minute back rub, or ideas that take a little more effort like this one:

My sister was busy with schoolwork one weekend and needed to study. She had a very loving partner. There are some partners who would have said, "Okay, go study and that'll give me time to catch up with my friends, work, whatever." Not this man. He invited her to study at his house. When she got there he brought her out to his quiet backyard, hauled out a down comforter, fluffed it up, and put it in his hammock. Then he brought out a pillow, some iced tea, and pointed the way. "You can study here," he said. My sister, of course, fell in love. How could she not?

> I do not want to make reasons for you to stay. Only reasons for you to return.
>
> —JONI VAN

Remember this: *People with good, rich relationships aren't all rocket scientists— they simply keep their focus on expressing their love for each other regularly.*

In our busy, frantic world of ringing phones, whirring computers, angry traffic, noisy this, speeded up that—we need to be nurtured even more. We need our partners to wrap us in emotional warm blankets, and we need to do the same for them. We must structure our lives so we have time and space to nurture—to offer a still point in a spinning world. That's the gift we give—and that's the gift that will keep our relationships sustained.

In order to open your time, you simply need to make choices. What or whom are you going to nurture? Are you going to fill your calendar or your intimate relationship? I had a partner who was a busy professional, yet he purposely didn't take on a lot of extracurricular social and business activities—instead, he allowed plenty of time to nurture our relationship. One particular day he was aware that I had a busy day, and would probably like some nurturing. He set his work aside for a few hours so he could take care of me that evening. He invited me to his place for dinner and when I arrived, showed me to his favorite chair, brought out a blanket to cover my legs, turned the lights low, and invited me to sit and relax while he finished cooking the dinner that he had spent the afternoon preparing. While I waited, he brought out a tray holding snacks for me to nibble on. Dinner was a lovingly cooked panoply of my favorite food.

> *But we can still have romance in our lives, no matter how long we've been together. Chill the glasses. Remember the roses. Install the new dimmer, light the candles and forget about wax dripping on the table, play the song you first heard on your honeymoon. Dress the bed in red sheets. Drive up the hill to watch the sunset and kiss (and kiss) in the car. Don't let opportunities slip through the cracks.*
>
> —DAPHNE ROSE KINGMA

This man knew how to prioritize, and how to make me feel cared for, nurtured, and loved. All it took from him was the deliberate choice to reserve some open space in his life.

SLOW DOWN

It is difficult to nurture when we're racing around trying to get ahead in our careers, decorate the perfect house, get involved in every other opportunity that comes our way . . . we're left exhausted. We have no time for ourselves, and no time for intimacy. Some modern theorists call this a "time famine," as if modern life just happened to us and we had no control over its effects. Instead, it's what I call an "intimacy famine." In my *Simple Living Guide*, I noted that it's easier to stay busy and frantic than it is to

Full Attention Kissing

❧

"Anne? What's so special about the way that lad kisses?" Anne looked dreamy, then dimpled . . . "Mike gives a kiss his whole attention." "Oh, rats! I do myself. Or did." Anne shook her head. "No, I've been kissed by men who did a very good job. But they don't give kissing their whole attention. They can't. No matter how hard they try parts of their minds are on something else. Missing the last bus—or their chances for making the gal—or their own techniques in kissing—or maybe worry about jobs, or money, or will husband or papa or the neighbors catch on. Mike doesn't have technique . . . but when Mike kisses you he isn't doing anything else. You're his whole universe . . . and the moment is eternal because he doesn't have any plans and isn't going anywhere. Just kissing you." She shivered. "It's overwhelming."

—From *Stranger in a Strange Land*, by ROBERT A. HEINLEIN

love and know ourselves and others deeply. Staying busy appears to give our lives meaning: "Just look at all of the things I have accomplished and all of the things I do in my life!" Staying busy is safe. We don't really need to get in and look at our lives when we're rushing from one thing to the next.

The less outward complexity we maintain, the more time and space we have for intimacy. It takes time and space to build relationships of any depth. For example, it requires a lot of our emotional selves to have heart-to-heart talks with our partner, rather than skimming the surface of our lives, discussing little more than who took out the garbage and who paid the light bill. We can't take the time to be sensitive to our partners and truly care for them when we are in a constant hurry. A speeded-up life not only robs us of time to connect with our partner but also makes us impatient and angry. We don't have time to listen to our partner's point of view. We don't have time for our children. We don't have time for ourselves. When we're overscheduled, we become selfish and self-absorbed, because our whole day is spent trying to catch up and our night is spent trying to recuperate. A selfish life is not conducive to intimate, loving relationships.

One way to make time for intimacy is to think of time as sacred. We often spend our time the way we spend our money, as if both were boundless. Simplicity is about making conscious choices, prioritizing what is most important, and letting go of the rest. If our relationship is most important, then why are we filling our calendars with nearly everything *but* time for our partner? A conscious relationship means saying no to outside activities that will interfere with this time. It means taking a look at the big picture, and setting aside time for what really matters. There is only one way to have more time together, and that is to make it a priority.

Some couples set aside one night a week for "date night" or "talk night." That is their priority. They know that if they don't schedule in the time, something else will come along to take its place. These couples aren't willing to let that happen. Having regular talk or date nights not only shows a partner he or she is important, but it also nips potential problems in the bud before they become full-blown hurricanes. If you put off talking about important relationship issues, they'll pile up and get worse.

There are countless other ways to go about your normal daily routine, make a few slight changes, and reap huge rewards. Think about this: If you and your partner both work away from home, you're spending maybe ten to twelve hours away from each other five days a week—that means no seeing, no talking. Short of quitting your jobs and winning the lottery, what can you do to maintain intimacy? Got E-mail? Send a love note every day. Same with a phone. Make a two-minute call every day to say "I love you" or "I'm thinking of you." If possible, make a regular lunch date or arrange your schedules so you can carpool together. Send flowers every now and then for no reason other than to show you're thinking of your partner.

There are slow-growing, grave consequences that result from our lack of attention. One incident in particular had a strong impact on me with regard to TV viewing—it happened at a couples workshop that I attended. A woman came without her husband and told the class how he started withdrawing from her over the years by watching more and more TV. He'd start watching after dinner and would usually fall asleep while watching. They no longer went to bed together. She told us how lonely the marriage had

THE BEST WAY TO CALL A TRUCE

by Sharyn Wolf

Step 1. Clear the Air
1. Admit when you've contributed in negative ways to your relationship.
2. Practice forgiveness.
3. E-mail your apology.
4. Become an expert at making up.

Step 2. Pay Your Penance
1. Do a household task she/he hates to do.
2. Complete 5 positive interactions for each negative interaction.
3. Take her/his most difficult relative to lunch.

Step 3. Develop Apology Rituals
1. Play the blues.
2. Send an apology note reminding him/her of a special past moment.
3. Try using hand puppets or stuffed animals to articulate.

Step 4. Reconnect
1. Make love.
2. Climb into his arms or put your hand in her hand.

become for her. She felt she had tried everything to regain his attention, from pleading to yelling. Nothing worked. She asked the class if they had any suggestions. Ideas were thrown around—everything from dancing nude in front of the TV to watching it with him.

I had no idea which strategy could revitalize her marriage, but the impact on the class was significant. How many marriages wind up just like this one, where one or both partners become unconscious in the relationship and check out? The partner checking out is often oblivious of the im-

3. Dance.

4. Take an emotional cleansing bath together.

Step 5. Remember Mark Finn's Advice*

Everybody's anger is justified and understandable. Being mean to the other person never helps. Attacking the other person never helps. Blaming the other person never helps. Validating the other and apologizing is never a defeat. Peacemaking is never wimpish. Being close is scary—it's the spiritual crisis of our time. You always give more than you get.

Ask yourself:

How can I assert myself without being mean?

How can I assert myself so I can be heard?

How can I assert myself without injustice collecting?

Why am I impossible to live with?

How is our future creative and alive?

—From *How to Stay Lovers for Life*

*Mark Finn is a therapist in New York.

pact his behavior has on the person he once said he loved and cherished.

If this rings any bells, try taking a TV hiatus for just one week as an experiment. Before moaning and groaning about missing your favorite show, think about this statistic: During the course of an average seventy-five-year-old American's life, he or she has spent a total of fourteen uninterrupted *years* watching TV. We're talking *years.* Can you imagine how much loving, romancing, and nurturing you could have accomplished in those fourteen years instead of slouching in front of the tube? Can you imagine how much happier and closer to you your partner would have been had you spent that much time on him or her? Can you imagine how different it would have been to have lived with a partner who was that filled with your love, rather than your neglect?

If your partner isn't interested in a full-blown TV hiatus, try talking about it. Talk about what is reasonable. How many hours are okay with both of you? Can you select shows that you could enjoy together? What other things could you do rather than watching TV?

Think also about these facts:

+ Most couples spend fewer than thirty minutes a week sharing intimate feelings.
+ The average American spends more than four hours a day watching TV.
+ Most people's lovemaking sessions take less than twenty-five minutes.
+ Most couples leave lovemaking until the very end of the day, when they're tired, preoccupied, and spent.

The good news, however, according to the book *Time for Life*, by John P. Robinson and Geoffrey Godbey, is that Americans have more leisure time than ever before: an average of forty hours a week. The bad news is that this time is usually available in short bursts scattered throughout the work-week. So, we need to use this time wisely when we find it.

Here are a few ideas of things you can do together with small chunks of time (thirty minutes or less):

Meditate
Give a massage
Take a walk
Play a board game
Read to each other
Discuss your day

Work in the garden
Go for a run
Play catch
Bake cookies

Here are other things to think about, from Gregory Godek, author of *1001 Ways to Be Romantic*:

Time Questions:

There are 1,440 minutes in a day.

- ✧ How many of those minutes do you spend near your partner?
- ✧ How many minutes do you spend being loving?
- ✧ How many minutes would you *like* to spend together?

You will live for 25,567 days—if you live to be seventy years old,

- ✧ What do you *really* want to do with those days?
- ✧ When you look back on your life, *what will you regret not having made time for*? Take action today to prevent this from happening.
- ✧ If you live to be seventy, that's 36,816,480 minutes.
- ✧ We live our lives in minutes—not years.
- ✧ Pay attention to those *minutes*—they have a way of slipping past unnoticed and unappreciated.

REARRANGE YOUR WORK SCHEDULE

For those wanting to make bigger changes, you can manage your finances in such a way that one or both partners can work part-time, work at home, or retire early. For information on how you can work within your income and still save money, take a look at the money chapter in my book *The*

Simple Living Guide. In the finance chapter of this book, I also discuss how partners can merge different money styles.

Both Keith Mesecher and Marge Wurgel arranged their work schedules in order to have more time to spend together. As a result of their planning and frugality, Marge was able to retire from her job as a public health program administrator at age forty-one and Keith, an investment advisor, works at home. Keith says: "We have more time for snuggling in the morning and have the freedom and time to make love in the afternoon far more often than we used to. My flexible work schedule also allows us to do things like go to a bargain matinee or take a trip together when we want."

Marge adds: "We also reserve 'date night' because it's a way to have intentional time blocked out on the calendar. Occasionally we have to sit down and talk about ways to spend more time together because we both have a lot going on with our own interests, and sometimes have to consciously open up space for each other."

Kate and Rusty Rhoad, parents of three young children, also prioritize their time for each other. Rusty, a chemical engineer, has turned down numerous management positions at his job to avoid the stress and extra hours. Kate, a professional organizer, works only three days per week during school hours and almost never on nights or weekends. Weekends are a key time to work together doing mundane things—even housework. And, whenever either Kate or Rusty is feeling that they haven't spent enough alone time together, they call a sitter and have a date.

The Rhoads also go out of their way to give each other time off. Rusty goes out one night a week, and Kate gets three to four nights a month out with her friends. They've even extended that to an occasional week's vacation away from the family and find that the break refreshes everyone.

Lorraine and Jeff Murray are another couple who rearranged their work lives in order to have more time with each other. Lorraine, who left her full-time position as a faculty member at Georgia Tech to be a freelance writer, says: "When I was working full-time, I think my work schedule exhausted me so much that I would sometimes be grouchy in the evenings.

I didn't feel I had much left to give emotionally, after using up all my energy all day. It was all I could do to take a walk and get through dinner. And sometimes on our walks, all I wanted to do was dwell on the conflicts at work! So it was like I was still at work. Right now, I think that my new schedule has already given me more energy at night and I think we both enjoy the more upbeat evenings as a result."

Even when Lorraine worked full-time, though, they made time for each other. Every day they take a forty-to-sixty-minute walk together and talk over things in their lives. They save Friday nights for getting together with friends, and Saturday nights are spent together at home, cooking, listening to music, and talking. "All of our rituals keep us in tune with each other," Lorraine says. "We always have a good sense of each other's concerns, desires, struggles, and successes. We feel connected."

Magrit Baurecht arranges her work schedule to periodically take time off midweek so she can spend it with her partner, Jim Nilsen. In the winter, Jim likes to ski every Tuesday. He wanted Magrit to join him, but she always declined because she felt too swamped with work from her design business to be able to take that much time off. She was so swamped that she often worked weekends and evenings to catch up. Nevertheless, she regularly talked about how important Jim was to her, and finally she realized that if he really was important, she needed to make time for their relationship. So she began to take Tuesdays off to ski with Jim and, somehow, found time to complete her work. Moreover, she gained a much-needed day of rest. By taking Tuesdays off, she not only sent a message to Jim that he was important to her; she also filled her own pot in the process.

USE RITUALS

Rituals are a wonderful way to stay connected and don't require a major shift in anyone's schedule. Many are mundane, some even whimsical, a few are time-consuming.

Defining the Good Life

❧

The American investment banker was at the pier of a small coastal Mexican village when a small boat with just one fisherman docked. Inside the small boat were several large yellowfin tuna. The American complimented the Mexican on the quality of his fish and asked how long it took to catch them.

The Mexican replied, "Only a little while."

The American then asked why he didn't stay out longer and catch more fish.

The Mexican said he had enough to support his family's immediate needs.

The American then asked, "But what do you do with the rest of your time?"

The Mexican fisherman said, "I sleep late, fish a little, play with my children, take siesta with my wife, Maria, stroll into the village each evening where I sip wine and play guitar with my amigos. I have a full and busy life, señor."

The American scoffed. "I am a Harvard MBA and could help you. You should spend more time fishing and with the proceeds, buy a bigger boat and with the proceeds from the bigger boat you could buy several boats. Eventually you would have a fleet of fishing boats. Instead of selling your catch to a middleman you could sell directly to the processor, eventually opening your own cannery. You would control the product, processing, and distribution. You would need to leave this small coastal fishing village and move to Mexico City, then L.A., and eventually New York City, where you will run your expanding enterprise."

The Mexican fisherman asked, "But, señor, how long will this all take?"

To which the American replied, "Fifteen to twenty years."

"But what then, señor?"

The American laughed and said, "That's the best part. When the time is right, you would announce an IPO and sell your company stock to the public and become very rich. You would make millions."

"Millions, señor? Then what?"

The American said, "Then you would retire. Move to a small coastal fishing village where you would sleep late, fish a little, play with your kids, take siesta with your wife, stroll to the village in the evenings where you could sip wine and play your guitar with your amigos."

—AUTHOR UNKNOWN

Cathy and Steve Gardner leave little notes for each other on a potential bad day and have both, at different times, faxed each other a drawing of the American Sign Language symbol for "I love you." "As busy as we get," they say, "it's important to be reminded that you're loved."

Another couple, Thomas and Sonya Corrigan, have very difficult work schedules yet still manage to find time for each other. Tom is a firefighter who works twenty-four-hour shifts and Sonya works part-time, from 6:30 P.M. to 3:00 A.M. Their main ritual is that they allocate a lot of "snuggling time" when they lie in bed together, hold each other, and talk . . . shutting out the rest of the world.

Another woman says it is important to her when kindness is bestowed for no apparent reason, or when nice things are done in anticipation of the other person's needs, such as fixing a favorite meal when you know your partner has had a stressful day, or surprising him with something just because you know he'd enjoy it, such as a book, a favorite pastry, or a pitcher of cold margaritas on a hot evening. This woman's husband always fills her car with gas because he knows she doesn't like to do it. She is a teacher with summers off, and often her husband will call her during the morning so they can meet someplace for breakfast or coffee. "He's very busy, but he makes the time to do this because he knows how much it means to me," she says. "And I can't imagine going through a single day without saying 'I love you,' or hearing those words from my husband."

Another husband earns tremendous points with his wife by expending very little effort at the beginning of each day. He gets up first every morning and, instead of taking care of only himself as he rushes off to work, he makes a pot of coffee for himself and his wife. Then he gently wakes her up by bringing her a cup in bed. What a way to start the day on a caring note, rather than the usual self-absorbed race out the door.

If coffee isn't your thing, there are plenty of other ways you can make slight adjustments to your schedule and reap huge rewards by devoting just a few moments to your partner. Nelson and Elaine Stover put love notes under each other's pillows. They give lots of hugs, kisses, and back rubs. As for the rest of the day, they say that with just a little more effort, mealtime can be special with flowers on the table. "That makes for a place worth coming home to," Elaine says. The Stovers also make sure that they eat dinners and breakfasts together whenever they are both home.

Think about these ideas:

Set your alarm for one hour earlier every day this week. Try a few of the following ideas:

- ✦ You could make love.
- ✦ You could lie in bed and talk with your lover.
- ✦ You could give your partner a massage.
- ✦ You could go for a walk.
- ✦ You could cook an awesome breakfast.
- ✦ You could have breakfast in bed.
- ✦ You could read an inspirational passage aloud.
- ✦ You could meditate or pray together.

—From *Love, the Course They Forgot to Teach You in School*,
by Gregory Godek

✿ *Finding Their Own Life* ✿

Denise Dryden and Jim Wurm say that a story about a glass jar filled with rocks is a metaphor for their life together. It is this: A professor wanted to demonstrate a point to his classroom, so he took out a mason jar and put in four or five big rocks. He asked the class, "Is this full?" The class responded, "Yes." The professor said, "You think so?" then took a cup of gravel and poured it into the jar. The gravel filtered down and filled more spots in the jar. "Is this full now?" he asked again. The class is thinking he's up to something, so they answer, "I don't know." Next, the professor puts in a cup of sand, the sand fills in around the rocks, and once again, the professor asks, "Is this full?" The class figures they're really being set up, so they answer, "No." Finally, the professor pours water to the top of the jar. "Is it full?" he asks again. The class says, "Yes, but what's the point?"

"The point is you have to put the big rocks in first," the professor says. "They're the focus, and if you had put sand or gravel in first, you'd never be

able to fit in the rocks. The rocks are your priorities in life—your spouse, children, job."

"This story gives you the impression that after you get the five rocks in the jar, you then have space for the sand and gravel," Denise says. "It's what our culture does . . . makes us think it's okay to cram gravel into all available space . . . that you're not complete until all available space in your mason jar is taken up. But we need room to rearrange, shake things up, give ourselves space. Simplicity is taking out that space and letting the rocks grow. For us, the bigger picture is getting the filler out and allowing room for those rocks. And the bottom line is, Don't take a story at its face value."

Jim and Denise used to fill every space of their mason jar, thinking that was the path to a happy and fulfilling existence. Life was about bigger and bigger houses, more and more stuff to fill the houses with, more money, bigger jobs, more prestige, golf club memberships, manicured nails, the right outfit for dinner. Denise says for her, the "more is better" attitude was tied to a desire for approval. "I used to think that if I have more things someone will love me more," she says. "Money was seen as a reward for doing the right things."

Jim and Denise married and immediately started a family, ultimately

"It's hard to be a team when the team never gets together," says Jim Wurm of his family in their former fast-paced lifestyle. "At that pace you're just skimming over the surface of life." Here Jim and wife, Denise Dryden, enjoy a camping trip with daughter Jesse, 12. Not pictured are their other children, Alex, 10, and Madison, 7. "We're a team now," they say.

having three children in five years. Over the years, Jim alternately worked for corporations or owned his own business, earning a higher and higher income. The family started with an attractive little house in New Jersey but wanted something more, so they custom-built a house, bought designer furniture, leased two cars at $600 a month, and had house payments of between $1100 and $1800 on different homes over the years.

"We were keeping up with the Joneses," Denise says, "paying one thousand eight hundred dollars in office rent on top of our mortgage payments, for a total of three thousand six hundred dollars a month. We were building this life, living in a new subdivision with people the same age with children the same age. Everyone was in the same spot in their career, so we felt it must be okay because everyone else was doing it."

Jim says, "Everyone in the neighborhood had the same set of constants. It was very collegial. We looked to each other for confirmation—one guy would get a promotion or a raise, and you'd talk about how you're getting new furniture for the home, or a new car, and everyone would come over and look at the new car and say, 'Wow!' There was this whole system.

"While there was a lot of excitement playing the accumulation game, I also sensed a fear that people felt they couldn't keep up, or a fear that their job would disappear, or they'd have unexpected expenses. We all tended to gloss over those issues."

Denise adds, "There were people buying food on credit cards because they were waiting for a bonus, or neighbors' phones would be turned off because they hadn't paid the bill. They'd always say it was something else. No one had savings accounts, but they had lots of credit cards."

That lifestyle finally reached its pinnacle for Denise and Jim when they moved to Texas, where they built yet another custom house in another new cul-de-sac development filled with young families the same age. This home was four thousand square feet and had five bedrooms, four baths, three TVs, three VCRs, and a sound system in every room including the garage because "You'd need to hear music everywhere." They had two leased cars, no collateral, a new mortgage, and a Spanish-speaking housekeeper. They also belonged to the local golf club. Denise volunteered for various organizations while paying for child care for their children. Two of the kids were in private preschools. Every weekend, the cul-de-sac neighbors' lives revolved around where they were going out to dinner because there was always a new promotion or raise to celebrate. Every dinner date required new clothes and having Denise's nails and hair done.

The dawning that their life in Texas was not right for them began when Jim and Denise started dreaming and then seriously planning that Denise would open a school because they didn't like the options that were available to their own kids. Denise remembers: "One day we were home, and I sat down and said, 'Oh my god, Jim, if I start a school that means we have to stay in Texas!' So we thought, do we really want to stay here, stay in this life? Then we wondered where we would go if we could do anything. At that moment, we really began to look at our lives."

"We came up with a plan and found a little town in Oregon to move to," says Jim. "We got so excited about this new passion that our world in Texas just fell away. Our neighbors said, 'You can't sell this house, you just built it.' There was a lot of fear deep down. I picked up that if they could open to it, every one of them would have wanted to leave, too, to go after their passion."

Within months, they put their house up for sale, quit the golf club, stopped going out to dinner, and gave up hiring babysitters. They had a huge garage sale and sold all their showpieces, putting what was left into two rental trailers. The things that wouldn't fit into the trailers they left on the curb for the neighbors. "We found the letting-go process was phenomenal," Denise says. "It forced us to prioritize."

The family left their Texas life—Jim in the truck with one child and Denise in the other car with the other two children. "We took off like a Conestoga wagon train and said good-bye," Jim remembers.

"It's so much easier for us here," Jim says. "We see the get-aheaders with their big houses up on the hill, filled with the same stuff we used to have. We look up and remind ourselves how nice it is that we don't have the financial and social pressure anymore."

Today, Jim operates his business from home. He says, "There is no stress of financial pressure for me now. Before, we weren't always in sync with financial decisions. I was the maker and saver and Denise always had her eye on what to buy. We don't have that stress anymore. We communicate because we're together so much more. We make plans and prioritize together. In the past, we'd just throw something on a credit card and pay it later because things would happen at such a fast clip."

Denise adds, "The problems I had with money were driven by emotions. I'd entertain myself shopping. If I felt lonely or cut off, I'd buy something for the house or for me. If Jim was traveling and I was alone with the kids and feeling isolated, I would spend money, which then caused more pressure on us. Now we have a system whereby Jim pays the bills, and we set aside an amount for the monthly food, haircuts, allowances, piano lessons . . . all of that stuff. I make choices on how to spend that. This way I get to take care of my shopping-addict side, yet it is within the confines of a certain amount."

Jim responds, "It's hard to be a team when the team never gets together. Now it's as if the board of directors of our household gets together and chats much more than before. This feels right to me. I can only live at that faster pace for so long, and I realize that at that pace you're just skimming over the surface of life, never finding depth."

The road to simplicity has been a long, challenging, and sometimes arduous one for this family. But the rewards have been great. Jim says: "Before, we were living unconsciously, like so many people do. You check in in the morning at your job, do your job, and after a period of time they pay you. That money goes to paying bills for all the things you need to have in order to be in that 'club.'

"There are requirements of that club. You don't have to think about it. It's all stated for you within the culture—you have the house, the job. None of those requirements are self-invented. They're invented by the club you join.

"Simple living is about waking up each morning and not being a member of that club. You make conscious decisions about what you want to create that day—the choices aren't spelled out—the economics aren't spelled out—none of it is predetermined. It's your own life."

❧ ❧ ❧

Resources

Beat Stress Together: What Every Couple Should Know about Recognizing Stress Reactions, Alleviating Tension, Finding Time to Relax, by Wayne M. Sotile, Ph.D., and Mary O. Sotile, M.A. (New York: Wiley, 1998).

The Big Book of Relaxation, edited by Larry Blumenfeld (Roslyn, N.Y.: The Relaxation Co., 1994).

Dancing Wu Li Masters: An Overview of the New Physics, by G. Zukav (New York: Bantam, 1984).

How to Say No Without Feeling Guilty, by Patti Breitman and Connie Hatch (New York: Broadway Books, 2000).

Intimacy and Solitude: Balancing Closeness and Independence, by Stephanie Dowrick (New York: Norton, 1991).

Living in Balance: A Dynamic Approach for Creating Harmony and Wholeness in a Chaotic World, by Joel Levey and Michelle Levey (Berkeley, Calif.: Conari Press, 1998).

Precious Solitude: Finding Peace and Serenity in a Hectic World, by Ruth Fishel (Holbrook, Mass.: Adams Media Corp., 1999).

The Simple Living Guide, by Janet Luhrs (New York: Broadway Books, 1997).

Slowing Down to the Speed of Life: How to Create a More Peaceful, Simpler Life from the Inside Out, by Richard Carlson and Joseph Bailey (San Francisco: HarperSanFrancisco, 1997).

The Speed Trap: How to Avoid the Frenzy of the Fast Lane, by Joseph Bailey (San Francisco: HarperSanFrancisco, 1999).

Timeshifting: Creating More Time to Enjoy Your Life, by Stephen Rechtschafter, M.D. (New York: Doubleday, 1996).

A Year To Live: How to Live This Year As If It Were Your Last, by Stephen Levine (New York: Bell Tower, 1997).

You Can Find More Time for Yourself Every Day: A Seven-Step Plan That Will Change Your Life, by Stephanie Culp (Cincinnati: Betterway Books, 1994).

Chapter 6

Sensual Simplicity

O for a life of sensations rather than thoughts!
—JOHN KEATS

One of the most deliciously sensuous images I've ever seen was on a poster—a black-and-white photograph, very simple, that shows a long-distance, blurred shot of a lone couple standing at the edge of a dilapidated pier. There is an old lamp hanging from a pole, and the couple is surrounded by pigeons flying and strutting all around. There are no other people in the photograph, except for a boatman steering his gondola toward land. He is a good distance away. The woman is standing on her toes, one leg thrust backward. She is stretching up to meet the man's lips in a passionate embrace. They are holding an umbrella over their heads. It must be raining, but the picture is so blurry, you can't tell. For this couple, nothing else exists at this moment but their passion. The words printed at the top say only:

"Decide now. Is your life going to be poetry or prose?"

I see this photo as a metaphor for sensuality in our lives. While we may not spend our days lost in passion on misty piers, we can do a lot to keep ardor alive in our relationships. After all, we only go around once. Are we going to sail through on autopilot, living what Thoreau calls "lives of quiet desperation," or are we going to aspire to the heights of our own sensuality and create the kind of moments that inspire photographs like these?

People often think of simplicity as deprivation: Can't buy this, can't do that. Need to live in a house with dirt floors. Have no money. In fact, simplicity is just the opposite. Simplicity is having more. Not more cars, toasters, and committee meetings, but more poetry, depth, life, and vivacity.

We're amazed when we hear tales about cats who travel across the country to return to their original homes. How did they find them? We can't believe it when we hear stories about horses and dogs whose behavior changes just prior to an earthquake. How did they know? We toss off as nutty or coincidental those people who seem to have a "sixth sense" about some event or person. We're disconnected. Our luxuries and technology have rendered our senses useless or, at the very least, downright dull. What keen sense of smell or touch does it take to flip that switch, turn that dial, push that button? None.

It's not that we ought to give up the luxury of the flipped switch, the turned dial. But we do need to awaken our senses, somehow. Simplicity is about living sensually. The world is full of robust, lusty, and evocative sensual delights . . . if only we'd notice. Our partners are sensual creatures, if only we'd notice. We are sensual creatures, if only we'd notice.

> *One eye sees, the other feels.*
> —PAUL KLEE

We can start by thinking a little less about how to have a smoothly functioning calendar and a little more about nurturing. How? First, go through your day, and your place, and think of all the ways in which you are removed from your senses. Beyond flipping switches for light and turning dials for heat, there are many sense-deadening actions with which we assault ourselves every minute of every day. Want to mask the smell? Spray chemicals. Want to clean? Spray more chemicals. Want to eat? Three taps of your index finger on the microwave pad and your frozen entree is cooked. Want to drown out your thoughts? Turn the radio dial. Want to observe, rather than be in, life? Turn on the TV. Want to avoid the weather entirely? Get out your automatic garage door opener, drive in, and never feel a thing. Is it any wonder we have a difficult time thinking sensually?

Ilse Crawford says in *The Sensual Home*: "Too often, smart-looking homes smell of next to nothing, or else of air-freshener, dry-cleaning, disinfectant, and divorce, rather than fresh air, clean washing, good food, flowers, and pets. Tests carried out in the United States over many years have shown that the very products we insist on using to make our homes seem squeaky-clean are dangerous, and can make us ill (even without our swallowing them). Dutch homes of the seventeenth century were strewn and swept through with sweet-smelling herbs. When we add artificial lemon scent to modern floor cleaners, whom are we trying to fool?"

> *What is erotic? The acrobatic play of the imagination. The sea of memories in which we bathe. The way we caress and worship things with our eyes. Our willingness to be stirred by the sight of the voluptuous. What is erotic is our passion for the liveliness of life.*
> —DIANE ACKERMAN

We're not fooling anybody, least of all ourselves. Here are some ideas to get you started living sensually:

Sight

The poetry and fiction of D. H. Lawrence is well known for good reason—he reminds us of that robust, lusty, and earthy part of us that lies dormant under our blurred lives. While so many of us spend our mornings in a chaotic cloud of movement as we zoom through life on the way to work, Mr. Lawrence suggests another way to greet the morning in his poem "Gloire de Dijon:"

> *When she rises in the morning*
> *I linger to watch her;*
> *She spreads the bath-cloth underneath the window*
> *And the sunbeams catch her*
> *Glistening white on the shoulders,*
> *While down her sides the mellow*
> *golden shadow glows as*

She stoops to the sponge, and her swung breasts
Sway like full-blown yellow
Gloire de Dijon roses . . .

We can stop and see—really see, too. When was the last time you watched your partner with this kind of awe and reverence for every detail? When was the last time that any movie or show you paid to see compared with this, the real thing? The way to feast your eyes sensually is simply to stop and start looking . . . noticing. Noticing the details. Sight is the most dominant of the senses, with ninety to ninety-five percent of all of our sensory perceptions coming through the eyes, and over 80 percent of what we learn coming to us visually.

The first connection most of us have with our partners is visual, yet we pay little attention to the sight of each other as time goes on. Instead, start watching life as it passes before you. Notice every detail about your partner as she enters the room, and then take note of how you feel. What was your partner wearing this morning as he left the house? How does she look when she's reading? How does his body move as he reaches for something on a high shelf? Have you looked lately?

Besides feasting your eyes on your partner, you can also bring visual sensuality in your life by what you choose to have around you. Think about your visual day. If you work in a typical office, you see gray metal, fluorescent lights, banks of computers, elevators, and parking garages. At home, what do you see? Chaos, clutter, and a confusing juxtaposition of patterns and colors, or clear, calm spaces that create a feeling of peace and harmony? There is an actual malady called visual stress, caused by too much going on at once for the eyes, which want to be able to rest quietly here and there. Visual stress, as you might imagine, translates into internal stress, which is not conducive to romance.

Though we can't always control our work environment, we can concentrate on providing a respite in those areas over which we have control— our homes, for one. How is the lighting in your home? Harsh or soft? The lighting is more calm with lamps and candles rather than overhead lighting. Be sure to use as much natural light as possible, one way or another. Without natural light we do, indeed, become depressed. Think about it. The worst punishment of all is to be placed in solitary confinement in a jail. There are no windows and no light. Our homes are certainly not this extreme, but many don't allow in enough natural light. Take note of what kind of clutter you have blocking or diffusing natural light. If you have heavy, overbearing drapes and curtains on your windows, remove them and use a curtain that lets full light into the room during the day. Notice how much more alive the room is with the natural play of shadow and light.

How do you eat dinner? Under harsh lights? Switch tonight and eat by candlelight. I love the ambience and mood of candlelight so much that it has actually become difficult for me to eat dinner unless there are candles on the table. In the past, I reserved candlelight dinners for special occasions. No more. Every night is a special occasion to calm down and eat dinner in the serenity created by this light. Candlelight is magical. And when it's summertime, you can extend the romantic ambience of firelight by placing several pillar candles in your fireplace—it gives the same effect as a warm fire without the heat.

Beyond your house, you can feast your eyes in nature without having to move to the country. Most of us take the great outdoors for granted. Nathaniel Hawthorne once said, "Moonlight is sculpture, sunlight is painting." So true, but most of us don't really notice, because we live under artificial light most of the day and night. It's all the same. Once again, we're cut off. I know one woman who has no TV and sometimes spends two hours in the evening watching the sun go down.

Touch

Countless studies have proven that touched infants thrive much more than those who are untouched, and that blood pressure lowers when someone is touched in a friendly manner. So why don't we touch each other more? Some researchers have found that during an average social interaction, people in cultures outside the United States might touch one hundred times, while Americans touch only once or twice. Let's at least remedy that in our own homes! And remember this bit of wisdom from the Japanese culture: Some things, once touched, take on the soul of the person who touched them.

How often do you and your partner touch each other during the day? Touch can be as simple as resting your hand on her shoulder when talking, or remembering to greet each other with a kiss. There are many intensely rewarding ways to incorporate touch into your relationship. Both of you, for example, can learn to give each other a massage—and even if one doesn't want to learn just yet, you can make the effort and start giving your partner regular massages. People often don't realize that giving a massage can be just as beneficial as receiving one. Many hospitals, community college evening courses, and massage schools teach weekend massage workshops for couples. Even without a class, you can read books on the subject, or simply experiment with each other. Think of giving and receiving massage as a dance—allow yourself the freedom to experiment with different strokes and techniques.

There is a monetary side benefit to learning massage—you'll be on your way to relying on each other for some of your health needs rather than having to go out to the "experts" to pay for them. Who among us wouldn't relish the thought of having a weekly massage, but we just can't afford the $50- to $80-an-hour price tag charged by professionals? There is no reason why we can't be each other's private masseurs, unless there are serious health problems that need to be addressed in the hands of an expert.

Learning the Language of Touch and Time

ལ

One day Daniel showed me an old [illustrated] Chinese Taoist pillow book he had found in Hawaii. . . .

[A] favorite was a bathing picture that Daniel and I decided to re-create every weekend. During the week I bought lavender soap, loofah sponges, and an East Indian bubble elixir that turned the bath an enchanting blue. He brought volcanic pumice stone for my feet, his mother's homemade tropical shampoo for my hair, and coconut massage oil for my sunburned skin. He made a life-size topographical map of my body, naming his favorite places after mountains and valleys he'd studied on maps of the ancient world. I wrote him primitive poetry, then recited it in our bath as we faced one another, encircled by candles. In our glowing water cave, we were two initiates, learning the luxurious language of touch and time.

—BRENDA PETERSON (from On the Wings of Eros)

Steve Pearce, a reporter for the *Seattle Times*, wrote this piece about his experience with couples massage:

> My wife and I now have a portable massage table in a spare bedroom, where we soothe each other as many times a week as we want. A dim light, a portable heater, and easy-listening music create a mood just like that at a professional massage therapist's office.
>
> "Stressed out today?" I'll ask my wife at the end of a tough day. "Then lie down and I'll give you a massage."
>
> Studies have shown that too much stress can be bad for your health—causing headaches and stomachaches, even raising your blood pressure. In my case, at age forty-nine, it doesn't help that high blood pressure and heart disease run in the family.
>
> In my wife's case, it doesn't help that she's a substitute teacher—a high-stress job.
>
> It can also improve your mental health as you simply feel pampered and special, and have some uninterrupted touch and attention showered on you by a loved one.
>
> There is pretty amazing therapy in touch itself, because we are touch-deprived in our society.
>
> We have found newly discovered time, intimacy and relaxation—and that certainly can't hurt a marriage.

Don't forget simple foot, hand, face, and neck massages. The next time you're sitting together on the couch watching TV or reading, do something nice for your partner and ask if he would like a foot massage. Who wouldn't like one at the end of a long day? Ahead of time, make some peppermint foot lotion by adding one tablespoon of peppermint oil to six ounces of unscented lotion. Take your partner's shoes off, and rub the lotion all over every single part of the foot. Gently pull on each toe as you massage the oil into it. You can give a hand massage the same way. So many of us work on computers all day that it's not only romantic and nurturing to give a hand massage, but therapeutic as well. For the fingers, start at the base and gently pull up on each one, one at a time. This helps to stretch tight ligaments and feels wonderful. You can add the arms if you like, too, by massaging in a downward motion from the shoulder to the fingertips.

As for face and neck massage, it's best if you sit behind your partner, with her head resting on a pillow. Rub some massage oil onto the palms of your hands, and begin stroking gently from the middle of the forehead out to the temples. You can rub the eyelids, around the nose, the hairline, chin . . . everywhere that feels good to your partner. Follow that by rubbing the back of the neck and shoulders, focusing your concentration on the tips of your fingers so you can feel knots and tight places in this area.

How else can you bring touch into your life? Imagine covering your eyes and wandering throughout your house. What would delight your senses and what would repel them? If all you had were your sense of touch to rely on, would you change anything? How many times during your day do you have the opportunity to enliven your sense of touch? How thrilling is it for the delicate nerves lining the bottoms of your feet to move over a synthetic carpet? How many times a week do you actually feel the food you are cooking and eating, or is most of it poured from a can or box, or chopped not by your hand, but by an automatic food processor? How lifegiving is it to sleep on permanently ironed polyester sheets? How comfortable is it to sit properly in straight-backed chairs and couches? What kind of fabric do you wear on your body? In what kind of style? Do you feel constricted and tight most of the day or do you feel like a sensual being?

If you don't feel sensual yourself, it will be impossible to bring much sensuality into your relationship.

Smell

I had a boyfriend one time whose scent stirred my heart in a lovely way. Mind you, he wasn't wearing some overwhelming synthetic cologne; it was very subtle—and very effective. He would come to visit me and sit on my

Herbal Household Products

❦

Rosemary Disinfectant

Simmer some leaves and small stems for 30 minutes in water; the less water, the more concentrated the disinfectant will be. Strain and use to clean sinks and bathrooms or to give a fresh scent to rooms. Add dishwashing detergent to get rid of grease on surfaces. Store any excess in the refrigerator for up to a week. Disinfectants can also be made with the leaves and flowering stems of eucalyptus, juniper, lavender, sage and thyme.

—From *The Complete Book of Herbs*

Ants

Place sprigs of pennyroyal, rue, or tansy on shelves or in cupboards to deter ants. Disturb the leaves occasionally to release more scent. This doesn't kill ants, but encourages them to go away.

—From *The Complete Book of Herbs*

Strewing

In the Middle Ages, herbs were often strewn on the floor to repel fleas, lice, moths and insect pests. They also masked unsavory smells and provided insulation against the cold in winter and the heat in summer. This practice is unsuitable today, but sprigs of herbs can be placed under doormats or carpets, or perhaps on the porch.

—From *The Complete Book of Herbs*

couch where we would talk and talk. After he left, that distinctive earthy smell would remain on the fabric of the couch and I would always go sit there and lay my head close to the scent to keep him lingering in my senses for a while. It was such a delightful way to remember him!

I remember when my friend Jane decided to bring her rosemary plant inside to grow. The scent from that plant permeated her whole room, and I just loved being there taking in the essence of that herb. Jane also named her house Lilac Lane because its long narrow driveway is bordered by lilac bushes. What a nice way to come home! I have got a Star Jasmine plant on my deck, and it's pure heaven to sit in the lounge chair next to that delightful aroma.

On the other hand, I've gone into rooms where someone has just used antiseptic cleaner, and I can't wait to get out. I don't want to spend time in a dirty room, but do we have to go so far? Some men and women can be so overloaded with synthetic perfume that my senses cringe and cower in a corner.

Modern life is good in a lot of ways, but not for allowing us to be sensual, natural beings. Fueled by Madison Avenue, it has led us far from our primal, natural reliance on all our senses, and especially our sense of smell. We don't want to smell the natural odor of our bodies, so we cover it up with all manner of chemical concoctions, and we cover our homes in the same way. Do you like the smell of all of those cleaners you're using? Have you even thought about it? Probably not. Most of us simply accept the advertising message that XYZ product is the easiest, best way to get rid of dirt, and we go out and buy it. We never stop to think about what we are really doing, in the bigger scheme of things. We're cleaning, but at the expense of our natural selves, not to mention the environment. Those products are often not only unhealthy (read the labels if you don't believe me), but they're downright sense-deadening. Do you feel uplifted to poetic inclinations when you use or smell them? I doubt it. There are many natural ways to clean your house, and a few examples are included in this chapter. You can also get books such as *The Nontoxic Home*, by Debra Lynn Dowd.

Beyond cleaning with natural products, there are other romantic, sensual ways to use scent throughout your day. You can bathe

> *Cooking is like love, it should be entered into with abandon or not at all.*
>
> —PIET VAN HOME

with natural soaps and oils. Use herbs here and there for added smell: try folding your sheets with a little lavender in the linen closet, hanging sweet herb bags in your closet (e.g., for lavender, just put a few dried lavender flowers in a cotton or linen bag and mix with a few drops of oil of lavender, and *violà!*), and making a small herb pillow to keep under your usual pillow.

Scent, as many of us now know, can also enhance our moods. Thanks to the popularity of aromatherapy, we can all tap into this wonderful world. Aromatherapy has been around since the Egyptians, who recognized the therapeutic powers of essential oils. There is also a long tradition of aromatherapy in the Far East. One of the simplest ways to relax with herbs is to add them to a bath—the essential oils in the herbs are released by the heat and absorbed directly through the skin into the bloodstream. You can also use them as massage oil, or place a few drops on commercial diffusers, or on specially made aromatherapy rings that you put on your lightbulbs. The heat from the bulb releases the scent into the air, and your whole room will take on the ambience. Scented candles (make sure they are scented with natural herbs rather than more chemicals!) can have the same effect. You can also keep handy little spray bottles filled with a few drops of an essential oil mixed with water. You can periodically mist the room as you walk through.

I also know many people who hang their sheets outside to dry. They do it not so much for the frugality of saving electricity, but because they love sleeping in the fresh-air scent of sun-dried linen.

You can put a bowl of dried lavender in your bathroom. The steam from the shower will activate the scent. Lavender, by the way, like most herbs, is very easy to grow . . . it thrives on drought and neglect (almost!). And while you're growing scented plants, consider growing herbs for your own tea. A few ideas are lemon verbena, lemongrass, spearmint, and peppermint. A good herbal tea blend is three tablespoons dried lemon verbena, four tablespoons dried lemongrass, one tablespoon dried spearmint, and one tablespoon dried peppermint. Crumble the dried herbs together, steep in boiling water for five minutes, and drain.

Taste

To begin, post the following on your refrigerator: *"If you ever wish to add to the happiness of another individual, simply ask, 'What is your favorite food, drink, or dessert?'—then serve it forth."* I didn't make this up; a sensual cook named Margie Lapanja wrote it in her book, *Goddess in the Kitchen*. I love it. And I must admit, I never thought of it myself. I always thought the highest form of cooking was preparing the best, most exotic dishes I knew how to fix. Yet Margie's advice is so incredibly sensible and *simple!* Of course people will like best what they like best, and they'll be thrilled you took the time and energy to give it to them! This little quote served to wake me up in yet one more area of romance.

How many of us ever take the time to think about this sort of thing? We're too busy cooking something fast so we can gobble it up in a blur and get on to the next thing. What a shame. What a waste of one of the highest forms of sensuality—cooking and eating. Remember when we were trying to impress our future spouses? Male and female, we'd cook romantic dinners and make a big deal out of it. We'd toss colorful greens in our salads, make pasta sauce from fresh herbs, and set the table in the dining room with linen napkins and our best serving bowls. We'd buy a bouquet of fresh flowers, bring out our candles, turn the lights down low, play classical music on the radio, and wear something special. Our eyes would be locked as we'd sit across the table from each other, hanging on every word.

Marilyn's Eggplant Dip

☙

Either broil or, if you have a gas stove, burn the eggplant on the burner for five minutes on each side while you're cooking everything else; then scoop out the pulp, add lemon, olive oil, garlic, and sesame tahini to taste and mash with potato masher.

THE KITCHEN GODDESS MANIFESTO

by Margie Lapanja

1. Do not cook if you are in a bad mood, lack the desire, or feel pressure from nagging obligation to another. And remember—you can always go out, take out, or entice someone else to "put out."

2. Keep your life full of the freshest ingredients and at least once a week explore something completely new: a new recipe . . . a new book . . . an unfamiliar song . . . a new quote for your journal . . . dance outdoors . . . take a walk somewhere you have never been before . . . kiss a baby . . . write to someone you admire and include a favorite recipe . . . talk to someone who doesn't speak your language . . .

3. Delighten up and play with your cooking! Read the recipe—close the book—then have fun! The more you play, the more you do what you love to do, the more you reconnect with your talents and power.

4. Always sit down when you eat; share most of your meals if you can.

5. Customize your creations and spice them with your own unique hallmark

What happens a few years later? Eating in a hurry, eating unconsciously, eating unromantically.

I'm here to say that we don't really need to spend any more time in the kitchen to cook and eat sensually, so let's do it when we can. My friend Marilyn works at least forty hours a week as a teacher and writer, and yet she figured out how to cook romantic dinners in very little time. There are two keys: One is to keep a cache of thirty-minute-or-less romantic recipes and menus on hand, and two is to shop at small, local markets for the ingredients of one meal only. Don't try to turn this into a major shopping trip at some supermall type of grocery store. At the huge stores, you'll spend of delicious mystery. As the saying goes, "Don't be the best at what you do; be the only one who does what you do."

6. Take a deep breath and bless your kitchen before you cook; clean up all rampant clutter, light a candle, open a window, turn on music. When in the mood, pour your favorite drink, be it wine, water, whiskey, or an ice-cold root beer in a frosted mug.

7. When recipes are given to you, save the original in the handwriting of the person who shared the recipe; their energy and intent will be immortalized every time you see their writing. Create a beautiful binder of recipes in sheet protectors. If you want to frolic and improvise, rewrite your new recipe on a page next to the original.

8. Never, ever think that food will make you fat! Delete the words "fat-free" and "sugar-free" from your culinary vocabulary and replace them with "fear-free," "guilt-free," and "feel free!"

9. Always carry a nicely printed, personal best trademark trading recipe with you wherever you go. Whenever you taste something that sparks your spirit and your taste buds, ask for the recipe. Trade, beg, or borrow—but get it.

10. Trust yourself. Add your own ingredients to this list.

—From *Goddess in the Kitchen*

more time getting lost in the aisles and waiting in line buying frozen entrees than you'd spend picking up a few items at the corner store and cooking fresh.

Marilyn's favorites are Asian stir-fry dishes, fresh fish and potatoes, fresh pesto, Middle Eastern falafels, rice pilaf and steamed vegetables, grilled polenta, various pastas, Greek salad, bread, and soup. A typical meal would start off with freshly made eggplant dip with pita (see page 131), wild-greens salad, fresh ravioli with pesto sauce, crusty olive bread, white wine, and sorbet for dessert. Here's a meal that, although it takes longer to cook, you can still complete with very little effort: Try sprinkling a whole chicken with fresh rosemary, and roast it in a clay baking pan with red peppers and small potatoes. While it's cooking, take a romantic hour-long walk, and return to a fragrant kitchen and completed dinner.

Food—the right kind, prepared the right way, served the right way—is love. Food in a hurry is not. Taking the time to share food . . . the eating, preparation, cooking . . . is a way to embellish the simple pleasures of daily life.

Romance guru Gregory Godek describes "Love Food" this way: 1, any food that comforts your lover; 2, a special meal that brings a smile to your partner's face; 3, any food that you prepare especially for your partner; and 4, a meal or treat that you serve to your partner that says "I love you."

Here is a vignette from the book *Goddess in the Kitchen*. It can give you some idea of what you've been missing by not cooking sensually. While this particular tale is written for women, it most definitely applies to men as well. Indeed, one of the nicest, most endearing things a man can do for me is to cook. With that in mind, intersperse the word *him* with *her* and *man* with *woman* and you get the picture:

> Then, it's time to beguile your passionate palates for the long haul. Consider this vision: You are charming an extraordinary paramour by gazing into his hungry eyes. Your very best, freshly baked chocolate chip cookies glow between you. As an added enticement, you have dabbed a hint of vanilla behind your ears (knowing Chanel No. 5 would have worked in a pinch). The atmosphere is aromatic and bewitching. Smiling, you nibble the edge of a scrumptious morsel and present the rest of the cookie to your eager male. After he has finished your coy offering and is completely mesmerized, invite him for a sweet, sweet kiss. The moment is mystical: You may not have expensive lipstick on your smile, but you will have a satisfied man in your arms.
>
> Make your ongoing domestic life deliciously playful. Make Pasta with Ginger Shrimp Soul Sauce and Moonlight Buttermilk Biscuits with Hot Tropics Pepper Chutney. Make the most enticing

Never-Fail Uptown Chocolate Cake to ever brush the lips. Make breakfast-in-bed Finnish Dutch Babies. Make a wish. Make love.

Got the picture? Turn your kitchen into a private bordello rather than one more place to be miserable. Cook together. Move away from the idea that cooking is only one person's job and enjoy just one more sensual pleasure together.

Hearing

When you ask most city people why they love freshly fallen snow, the common answer is this: "because everything is so quiet." It's beautiful to look at, yes, but what really sticks with their senses is the incredible quiet. Snow has a way of insulating noise like a radio booth. Other natural phenomena have the same effect. I love the book *The Spell of the Sensuous*, by David Abram. In it, he describes Long Island after a storm:

> In the autumn of 1985 a strong hurricane ripped across suburban Long Island, where I was then living as a student. For several days afterward much of the populace was without electricity; power lines were down, telephone lines broken, and the roads were strewn with toppled trees. People had to walk to their jobs, and to whatever shops were still open. We began encountering each other on the streets, "in person" instead of by telephone. In the absence of automobiles and their loud engines, the rhythms of crickets and birdsong became clearly audible. Flocks were migrating south for the winter, and many of us found ourselves simply listening, with new and childlike curiosity, to the ripples of song in the still-standing trees and the fields. And at night the sky was studded with stars! Many children, their eyes no longer blocked by the glare of the house lights and streetlamps, saw the Milky Way for the first time, and were astonished. For those few days and nights our town became a community aware of its place in an encompassing cos-

mos. Even our noses seemed to come awake, the fresh smells from the ocean somehow more vibrant and salty. The breakdown of our technologies had forced a return to our senses, and hence to the natural landscape in which those senses are so profoundly embedded. We suddenly found ourselves inhabiting a sensuous world that had been waiting for years, at the very fringe of our awareness, an intimate terrain infused with birdsong, salt spray, and the light of stars.

Most of us take for granted that the world, and our homes, are noisy places. We live with the din of modern life and don't realize how much is assaulting our senses every minute of every day. Once again, we have little control over what goes on outside, but we do have total control over what we allow inside our homes.

The sensual home is not necessarily absolutely quiet. Rather, it's a place with *selective* sounds. To select, go through your day with awareness and notice the noises you hear—the food processor, lawn mower, weed whacker, blender, vacuum cleaner, car engine, TV, radio, piano, violin,

Open Your Senses to Every Moment

୧୨

You can learn to enjoy your sensuality in each and every moment. Right now, listening to music, let the music vibrate the pores of your skin. Washing dishes, let the suds bathe your hands. Walking the dog, learn to enjoy being pulled. Every day there are hundreds of things you can enjoy. You can enjoy the leisureness of a stroll, or the sweat of jogging, or the tang of a breeze. Every moment can be an experience that lets you grow in sensuality. Right now you can feel this paper, this book, this space, the sounds around you, even your own breathing. Being open to all that and with all that will gradually turn you on to life more and more.

—WILLIAM ASHOKA ROSS (from *On the Wings of Eros*)

THREE STEPS TO A GOOD MARRIAGE

1. Be generous. A spirit of generosity is the opposite of the scarcity theory, which says, "If you get yours, I won't get mine." An example of generosity in the midst of conflict is this story: A husband is angry at his wife. They fought and he had to go to a meeting. He slammed out the door. Then he drove to a pay phone and called his wife. He said, "I love you. I'm still angry, but we'll work it out."

The myth about goodwill is that it's designed to help the other person, but it actually helps you. And remember, there is a big difference between goodwill and resignation. They may look the same, but the difference is what's inside you.

2. Take care of yourself. If you find you're frequently complaining because your partner isn't affectionate enough, for example, taking care of yourself means you can initiate the affection. If you slaved all day to give a big dinner party and after the guests have all left, your partner doesn't give you the compliment you want, you can say, "Boy, that dinner party went really well!" This is better than fuming and stewing that your partner didn't compliment you.

3. Draw a line. If your partner does something intolerable, draw a line and set boundaries as to what you will and will not accept. Do not use any ideas in this book to stay in an abusive relationship.

people talking, cat purring, mothers singing to babies, people yelling, kids screaming, water running, fire crackling, computers humming, airplanes flying overhead, phones ringing, and so on and so on. Whew! All these sounds, good and bad, can be exhausting. In fact, noise can be so detrimental that there are laws enacted in some places that say you can't make certain noises past certain times in certain places. A group of island dwellers near my house got a law passed outlawing Jet Skis. The Jet Skiers said they had a right to ski in public water, and the island dwellers said they had a right to peace and quiet. Peace and quiet won.

Diane Ackerman, in her book *A Natural History of the Senses*, relates the following study: "Arlene Bronzaft, a psychologist, discovered that exposing children to chronic noise 'amplifies aggression and tends to dampen healthful behavior.' In a study of pupils in grades 2–6, at PS 98, a grade school in Manhattan, she showed that children assigned classrooms in the half of the building facing the elevated train tracks were eleven months behind in reading by their sixth year, compared to those on the quieter side of the building. After the New York City Transit Authority installed noise-abatement equipment on the tracks, a follow-up study showed no difference in the two groups.

"And we wonder why kids can't read, we wonder why the drop-out rate is so high in New York. Jackhammers, riveting, and other construction noises are part of what we associate with life in big cities, but by hanging steel-mesh blankets over the construction site to absorb sound it is possible to erect a building quietly. As civilization swells, even sanctuaries in the country could become too clattery to endure, and we may go to extremes to find peace and quiet: a silent park in the Antarctic, and underground dacha."

Short of moving to Antarctica, what can you select out of your home? First, count the number of automated machines you have around. One of the first to go for me was my weed whacker. The last few times I used that thing, I remember being in a very bad mood, thinking, 'This is the meaning of my life? To stand outside every week assailing myself (and the neighbors) with the high-pitched whine of this contraption? Isn't there some other way?' There was. I gave it away, dug out the weed patch once and for all, and quickly planted it so the weeds couldn't grow back at the same ferocious speed as before.

The second thing to go was the gas-powered lawn mower. I am always offended by the neighbors' mowers, and was even more offended by mine because it was directly under my ears. Now I use a push mower and again have the benefit of peace and quiet plus a little exercise.

Next went a few electric (not all!) kitchen machines. I hung on to those I use regularly but pray for the day when I can figure out a way to do all my chopping and grinding by hand. I still need the vacuum cleaner, but with area rugs on hardwood floors, I can use a broom equally as much.

I'm also very conscious of media noise. When I'm alone, I do not need the company of the latest sitcom, talk show, or endless news analysis. When I really want to relax, I make some tea and curl up on the couch with a book. I turn off the radio and light a candle. I'm there!

So, how about your house? Once you get rid of the invasive kinds of noises, you'll be amazed to find that pleasant sounds fill the space you thought was empty. Consider these: birdsong, crickets, the sound of the tea kettle (why use a microwave to brew hot water when you have the singing of a kettle on the stove?), a clock ticking, someone humming, your lover saying something sweet in your ear, beautiful music, conversations, singing, windows rattling in the wind . . .

The next time you're about to reach for the TV dial, how about asking your partner to read with you? It's very romantic to snuggle up and take turns reading to each other. I'd much rather hear the sound of a loved one's voice than the endless blaring of split-second chatter on the tube any day.

You can also consider listening to music together. Lie in each other's arms and put on something rapturous. Or turn out all the lights, put on one of my favorites, "Moonlight Sonata," and dance in the dark. Who says life is too busy for romance?

Our gift of hearing is like health—it's one of those things we take for granted until we lose it. Take good care of your hearing by consciously choosing to have in your life the most pleasant sounds you can find. When your hearing is gone, you won't have a choice, as Helen Keller points out. She once said:

> I am just as deaf as I am blind. The problems of deafness are deeper and more complex, if not more important, than those of blindness. Deafness is a much worse misfortune. For it means the loss of the most vital stimulus—the sound of the voice that brings language, sets thoughts astir and keeps us in the intellectual company of man.
>   . . . If I could live again I should do much more than I have for the deaf. I have found deafness to be a much greater handicap than blindness.

❧ Loving Sensually ❧

At night, in that drifting state between wake and sleep, sometimes John will reach over and caress Jennifer's head and hair. He also loves to wash dishes by hand—the smoothness of the plates against the warm sudsy water—and he loves the smell of the almond dish soap. He says of the dishwashing, "So long as you have to do all of these things, you might as well enjoy them."

Jennifer loves to rub John's feet—not always because they are tired, but because she savors the touch of his skin.

When they met, John Kenning and Jennifer Waldron had both been divorced for over twenty years, and say that one of the elements that bonded them to each other was their shared appreciation for the sensual world and for beauty. Jennifer says: "I remember the first time John came to my

house, he noticed the little details. He appreciated what I did, and he'd say things like 'That's amazing' when he looked at an arrangement of flowers or a picture on the wall. And when I went to his house, I liked the way he had arranged his furniture. All of this told me that this was a person who sees beauty.

"Together, we absolutely love beauty. Our garden is ex-

Jennifer Waldron and John Kenning say that their shared appreciation for the sensual world is a great strength of their relationship: "We eat well, and love cooking together. Every night is a ritual," says John.

quisite. We have wind chimes and a little portable fireplace. We do simple things such as placing a single rose on a washbasin or putting new candles out or taking a mountain hike. I love that about John. He loves to put his hands in the dirt, sit on a warm rock, or compose a picture to take."

The earth literally moved when this couple got together. On their first date as they sat in a restaurant, an earthquake began to shake the tables and vibrate the dishes. John started singing Carole King's "I feel the earth move under my feet . . ."

"That was it," he says. "We were off and running!"

Meeting each other felt like "coming home," they say. Within six months, they had moved in together and within another eight months they were married. "We wanted to be married in a place that would allow us to experience all of the natural senses of the outdoors," Jennifer says. "I remember feeling the light wind, and hearing the rustle of the leaves mingled with John's brother playing guitar."

Even Jennifer's dream had a hand in the marriage. "I'd been doing a lot of dream analysis and journaling about my dreams," she says. "I didn't know what to do about my wedding ring. It was from a dream that I got the design . . . it was very powerful. I dreamt about a sort of Buddhalike figure and on his chin was a big piece of turquoise that went up into a diamond on his ear. I took that image to a jeweler and that became my ring."

The personal work that each one had done during their years as single people prepared both Jennifer and John to be more open and receptive to the sensual realm of daily life.

Jennifer says she has taken classes in massage and acupressure, and also creates pottery. But what has had the most impact on her is the massage she has treated herself to three times a month for the past ten years.

"I found it to be absolutely essential," she says. "As a single person you never get touched, or the touching is either in an intimate, sexual way or as a ritual, such as a hug, a pat on the back, or a handshake. It's rarely therapeutic touch. Before, my body was an iceberg . . . very rigid. My muscles were tight. I used to work in high heels and suits. I had also never done the interior work on myself. My massage therapist introduced me to the mind-body connection to feelings. During our sessions, we do a lot of visual imaging and I talk about what I am experiencing.

"Once you connect with your inner life, you can connect more easily to other people's inner lives, too. And now I feel more free to touch and be touched. I could go to my father who was dying and hold his hand and not be afraid to keep holding on."

John had also spent many years healing with body work. He went to a Reichian body worker who uses a combination of yoga, acupressure, and yogic breathing to help clients release buried energy that Reichians believe represents buried feelings being stored in the muscles and cells. "I did this for three years, and everything got released," John says. "Old thoughts, issues, hurts, and wounds. I learned to relax into my body. I could be very open with my body and not as stiff and immobile as I once was. I could express my feelings for the first time rather than stuffing everything down the way I used to do.

"Most men in our culture have not been raised to be comfortable with our bodies. We don't have the opportunity to speak about our experiences or feelings that we have around our bodies. There is an old saying: 'What doesn't get expressed, gets suppressed.' So most of my life I didn't get to express my feelings or what I was thinking. It all got repressed.

"When all of those old wounds and thoughts are emptied out of your body you can then fill it with good stuff. Now I'm able to receive more."

Jennifer agrees that all the body work both of them got over the years has helped them to be able to receive from each other. "For me, there was always the feeling that if I'm going to receive something, I have to pay it back, so if John is going to rub my back, for example, I'm going to have to get up and rub his feet."

"Receiving can feel like you owe. My years of getting a massage changed all of that. I was finally able to understand that my payback was being a good client. The lesson was that *letting* her do the work was my way of paying her back.

"Another reason why we can receive and not feel like we have to immediately pay the other one back is that one of our agreements is we'll both be fully up to the plate for each other in this relationship. That means we're always giving to each other in one way or another. It may not be an immediate exchange, but in some way we're there for one another."

John says: "I can receive a back rub from Jennifer and at the same time realize that I don't have to earn the back rub by doing her feet, because she's gifting me with this back rub that she's offered. It's a gift of intimacy. That becomes a mutual act."

Deep trust in each other has also allowed John and Jennifer to receive without feeling there are strings attached. John says: "When I first met Jennifer, I instantly trusted her. I knew I had nothing to fear. I felt safe."

"The trust has also built up over the time we've known each other," Jennifer says. "He's let me know that it's okay to disclose anything. No matter what I tell him, I get a reaction that's loving and cherishing. His form of support for me is that he never discounts me, tells me I'm wrong, or argues with me. He seems incredibly open to who I am. I trust that in him."

John adds: "The litmus test is 'Can I be me and still be loved?' There's nothing that opens a guy up faster than knowing he won't be judged and will be accepted . . . that it's safe to be with this person."

Open communication has added to the trust level as well. "It's how you listen and how you talk to each other," Jennifer says. "Nothing is left on the back burner to simmer. That's what breeds resentment, competition, and distrust. It's also essential that we've both agreed not to use sarcasm. We see that in so many couples, and it's very destructive."

Communication also includes being clear about the kind of touching they need at any particular time. John says: "We are very clear about the difference between sexual massage and touch. If my hip is bothering me and I ask her to work on it, at that moment I don't want sex. I just want her to work on my thigh."

Either of them may want simply to give touch as well. "Sometimes I'll have a need to touch John in a therapeutic way," Jennifer says. "I'll ask him if I can rub his shoulder or his feet."

Jennifer had another kind of sense-awakening experience after a conversation with a single co-worker many years ago. He told her that he had gone out and bought the most beautiful piece of china, one place setting of the most exquisite silver, and the most gorgeous wineglass that he could afford. Every night he would set this out for himself, light a candle, and treat himself to a sensual dinner. He felt that he deserved the beauty of this setting.

"I took that to heart and decided that as a single person, I deserved it too," she says. "I got out my own good dishes and shut off the TV. I decided to be really present with my eating."

"I learned from Jennifer to enjoy my meals," John says. "Before that, I think I stood up for three-quarters of them. I was always rushing. Now I've slowed down and I honor the place and space that we've created by sitting down to eat a meal together. We eat well, and we love cooking together. Every night is a ritual. We create a nice place for ourselves at the table, put flowers in a vase, and choose fine music. Then we light candles all over the house."

There is a seamless flow to the dinner routine. Both John and Jennifer love to cook, so one or the other will always want to try a new recipe and they discuss what it will look like, smell like, taste like. Whoever doesn't cook, does the dishes. John says: "It's usually serendipitous. We don't have a plan, but the weather, the time of the year, will present itself. If it's raining and cold, I may want to do my chicken garlic soup. The day presents itself in a culinary way."

"We also love to sing together," Jennifer says. "On the first road trip we took, we started singing in the car and discovered that we both have beautiful voices. And we appreciate music. We even have a whole drawer devoted just to dinner music."

It is fitting that their most cherished Christmas gift to friends and family is a booklet they made that is filled with relics of their sensual world. Each page includes one recipe, a piece of music to go with it, and a wine selection. They also included a quote for every meal. Their favorite quotation is a metaphor for their lives. It is from James Beard: "A gourmet who thinks of calories is like a tart who looks at her watch."

തയ തയ തയ

Resources

The Art of Kissing, by William Cane (New York: St. Martin's, 1994).

The Best Things in Life are Free, by Todd Outcalt (Deerfield Park, Fla.: Health Communications, 1998).

The Complete Book of Herbs, by Lesley Bremness (New York: Viking, 1988).

The Complete Book of Massage, by Clare Maxwell-Hudson (New York: Random House, 1988).

The Complete Guide to Massage: A Step-by-Step Approach to Total Body Relaxation, by Susan Mumford (New York: Plume, 1996).

The Complete Illustrated Guide to Shiatsu: The Japanese Healing Art of Touch for Health and Fitness, by Elaine Liechti (Boston: Element, 1998).

Eros, Consciousness and Kundalini: Deepening Sensuality Through Tantric Celibacy and Spiritual Intimacy, by Stuart Sovatsky, Ph.D. (Rochester, Vt.: Park Street Press, 1994).

Goddess in the Kitchen, by Margie Lapanja (Berkeley, Calif.: Conari Press, 1998).

The Goddess's Guide to Love, by Margie Lapanja (Berkeley, Calif.: Conari Press, 1999).

Gracious Living in a New World: Finding Joy in Changing Times, by Alexandra Stoddard (New York: William Morrow, 1996).

Herbal Rituals, by Judity Berger (New York: St. Martin's, 1998).

The Joy of Sensual Massage: A Guide to the Complete Massage Experience, by Jack Hofer (New York: Perigee, 1989).

Massage, Aromatherapy and Yoga, by Carole McGilvery, Jimi Reed, and Mira Mehta (New York: Lorenz, 1999).

A Natural History of the Senses, by Diane Ackerman (New York: Vintage, 1990).

The New Guide to Massage: A Guide to Massage Techniques for Health, Relaxation and Vitality, by Carole McGilvery and Jimi Reed (New York: Lorenz, 1996).

On the Wings of Eros: Nightly Readings for Passion and Romance, compiled by Alicia Alvrez (Berkeley, Calif: Conari Press, 1995).

Pleasure: A Creative Approach to Life, by Alexandra Lowen, M.D. (New York: Penguin, 1994).

The Re-Enchantment of Everyday Life, by Thomas Moore (New York: HarperPerennial, 1996).

Simple Pleasures: Soothing Suggestions and Small Comforts for Living Well Year Round, by Robert Taylor, Susannah Seton, and David Greer (Berkeley, Calif.: Conari Press, 1999).

Touching: The Human Significance of the Skin, by Ashley Montague (New York: Perennial Library, Harper & Row, 1986).

Chapter 7

Heart-Based Commitments

She kisses back. I tell her now, for real, that I'll swim with her
through anything the years throw at us, through weather bad and
good, through indifferent days and months when the whole sky
is gray and overcast with doubt. I tell her that I love her,
that I wouldn't let her swim alone through the lake's dark
and tangled coves.

—BOB ZORDANI, "A FISH STORY,"
FROM *ON THE WINGS OF EROS*

A sense of commitment is surely one of the essential elements of
any enduring relationship. But just what is commitment, exactly? If nothing else, it is what breeds deep, enriching passion—and who doesn't want more of that in his or her life? Commitment
breeds passion because people are far more likely to be open, vulnerable,
trusting, and real when they know their partner will be there for them over
the long haul. When we've got the feeling that our partner may bolt at any
time, we can't open to our full essence—and everyone loses.

The reward for this kind of passion is the depth, caring, and real intimacy that is the hallmark of living simply and loving simply. Living simply means living deeply and intimately, rather than skimming over the surface. Living with depth is immeasurably satisfying . . . living with one foot out the door is a life of always yearning, always wanting what isn't quite there, always dissatisfied, always thinking the answer is "out there."

Commitment Simple Loving–style is a broad-based, conscious decision we make in our hearts that we are going to love this person in every way we can. We need to continually tend that decision, and we need to take it very seriously before ever making a commitment.

There are several ways to look at committing from the heart that include commitment in the big picture and in the smaller, daily portrait of our lives together.

THE BIG PICTURE

The Third Body

A man and a woman sit near each other,
and they do not long
at the moment to be older, or younger,
nor born in any other nation, or time, or place.
They are content to be where they are,
talking or not talking.
Their breaths together feed someone whom
we do not know.
The man sees the way his fingers move;
he sees her hands close around a book she hands to him.
They obey a third body that they share in common.
They have made a promise to love that body.
Age may come, parting may come,
death will come.
A man and a woman sit near each other;

as they breathe they feed someone we do not know,
someone we know of, whom we have never seen.

—ROBERT BLY

Some couples look on their marriage—their union—as the third body, a term coined by Robert Bly in this poem. The third body is literally a third element in the marriage; it is the marriage itself. There are the wife, the husband, and the marriage—all to be reckoned with. How will a particular decision affect each of you? Will whatever you want to do be something that will nourish or subtract from the third body—the marriage? Looking at it this way helps to take the destructive self-centeredness out of relationships. Rather than thinking of what's best for *me*, it encourages us to think in terms of What's best for the *marriage?*

This third body is the soul of the relationship. Connie Zweig and Neil Schuitevoerder write in their article "Nurturing the Third Body: The Soul of Your Relationship," "When the needs of the third body are met, it nurtures you by providing a loving air that hums quietly between you. When it is neglected, it leaves you feeling neglected, dry and alone. And when the third body is wounded, you sense a wrenching tear in the fabric of your love.

"Once you form a partnership it acts like an invisible glue that holds you in unison. You may experience it as a big, fluffy cushion on which to relax or a pliable container in which the relationship can grow. But with your recognition of it, your sense of safety and comfort can deepen. You can risk more vulnerability and authenticity with each other because you feel bound together as if in a joint soul."

When taken seriously, the third body is your regulator—guiding your actions and shaping your thoughts and feelings as individuals and as a whole that is greater than the sum of two. It has its own values or rules of conduct, such as keeping agreements with each other rather than acting singly, on individual whims.

A Sense of Purpose

Another element that helps to keep relationships thriving is a shared sense of purpose. Why is it that successful businesses have mission statements, but most marriages do not? Many of us get married because we enjoy each other's company, we have a lot in common, we love each other, or we want to have children, and we stop there. If a business operated with such a narrow, limited focus, it would surely fail! If there is no valid, defined, and acknowledged purpose for being together—if the couple doesn't even know why they've created it—chances are they'll have trouble keeping the marriage alive.

If we can see that our relationship has a purpose greater than serving the needs of either partner—if it is more important than either one of us—then it will take precedence over individual needs.

This doesn't mean ignoring our own needs and becoming martyrs to the relationship; it simply means that we stop and evaluate the impact of our actions in terms of the greater relationship. Is there something about ourselves that we can change that will enhance the relationship? If we choose to make that change, we do so for the relationship, not just for our partner. Remember: If the relationship is strong and flourishing, our own life will be augmented as well.

Susan Dixon wrote in her article "Marriage: What's the Point?": "Couples who share a common vision of life's purpose and how to achieve it meet another requirement fundamental to the success of their relationship; they are friends of each other's excitement. Supporting each other in the low moments is not enough. We should be able to celebrate the high times together as well. What excites one should excite the other.

"Our commitment is to the relationship. For if a relationship has been conceived in love and dedicated to a higher purpose, it will take on a form greater than its creators. The focus will be on what is best for both partners, not on who wins or loses.

"As we commit to nurturing the relationship we discover there is no room for competition or resentment, fear or blame. Instead, we see that there is a place of love, a space of mutual creation where we can remember who we are and why we have come together."

Nelson and Elaine Stover are firm believers that a marriage must have a mission—a larger picture in order to hold it together well. Elaine says: "You both need to decide what your marriage is about, and you need to re-define it over the years.

"For us, our mission has evolved to be service oriented—helping people live more simply and sustainably—helping them get more meaning out of life. This is our work—it's not just going to a job—it's our mission in life."

For the past thirty years, the Stovers have worked all over the world volunteering for an organization called Institute for Cultural Affairs (ICA). Sometimes they were paid a small stipend when they lived in third-world countries, but much of the time, one of the Stovers held down a paying job while the other volunteered full-time for the organization. They've lived in Australia, India, the United States, Egypt, and Europe.

Nelson says: "The difficulty most families have is that they don't create a big picture. We rebuild that picture every two or so years. It's not an exact science, but when the vision gets out of focus, we know it's time to revise it. Sometimes a natural phenomenon happens, sometimes you realize you're getting older, sometimes you've accomplished all of the things you set out to do and it's time to look at it again."

Elaine and Nelson also sit down every four to six weeks and write in their family journal. Elaine says: "First we read the last entry, then say what's happened since, such as significant events, people . . . then we chart it and Nelson writes it up. Doing this makes your daily life significant—otherwise everything becomes a blur . . . it oozes together and you don't have a chance to reflect on anything. Most people don't take time to reflect on their lives, or they do it personally, not together."

Focus on the Importance of the Relationship

Author Harry Browne says he commits to *himself* never to do anything that would have a negative impact on his marriage, because it is so important to him, and because he loves his wife so much. Given the long, long road he traveled to get together with her, it is no surprise that he wants to maintain this marriage at all possible costs.

Harry met his wife, Pamela, in an airport in 1970. Their plane was delayed, and they found themselves seated next to each other in the waiting room. A conversation ensued. Although they lived in different states, there was enough interest for Harry to make the trip to see her once. They kept in touch for the next few years and finally lost contact with each other. Over the next ten years, Harry went on to other relationships. Three times he tried to locate Pamela, to no avail. Finally, in 1985, thoughts of her became so strong that he made the decision to turn over every stone in the country to find her. He had no idea whether she was married, still alive, or even interested in talking to him. But he had to follow his heart. "I made phone calls around the country and badgered people until I got a lead on where she was," Harry says. "Finally I reached her by phone. She lived in North Carolina, and I lived in California. We talked. During those years she had been married and divorced. It was obvious that we still liked each other very much. She agreed to visit me in California for ten days, and that was it. At the end of ten days we decided to marry."

Harry is so thankful he found Pamela that he does everything in his power to keep the marriage thriving. He says: "I don't like the word *commitment*, simply because it implies it's a contract that would require you to do something against your best interests at sometime in the future. If you're making a commitment, it should be to yourself, to make sure you don't make a major mistake, and thereby lose something that is best for you.

"My commitment is to continually remind myself of what I have and not throw it away or jeopardize it over something insignificant. For instance, if you're going to get angry with your spouse, save it for something really important."

This kind of internal commitment requires a regular assessment of the larger picture. He says: "Don't make a crisis out of something that is trivial compared to what you have to lose. That doesn't mean suppressing your feelings and telling yourself, 'Whatever she wants I'll just go along with rather than rock the boat.' With Pamela and me, she knows how I feel, I know how I feel, I know how she feels. I want her to be happy and can't stand it when she's not, so we'll do whatever we need to do to accommodate each other's needs without bending ourselves out of shape. She is free to be herself and I am free to be me. Neither of us tries to change that.

"To us, commitment is simply the realization that this is something so special and precious that we want to do everything to preserve it."

Recommit Regularly

Recommitting is like a tune-up for our cars. We can't simply buy a car and assume it will run forever. We need to continually bring it in for service. Same with commitment. A Catholic nun inspired my friend Danielle to recommit regularly to her marriage. Danielle was seriously considering leaving her husband of twenty years because, she complained, they were growing apart, some of the things he did really bothered her, and they no longer shared many of the same interests. She looked wistfully at her single friends who could live the way they wanted to. Then an unexpected lesson came. By chance, a friend invited her to visit the nun who had taught the two women in high school many years before. Danielle agreed to make the trip to the retirement home.

"I remember sitting out on the veranda with Sister," Danielle said. "It was a really nice day, we were in a relaxed mood, and she was reminiscing about her life. She told me the story of how she entered the convent right out of high school, so that would mean she had been a nun for around sixty years. She said that this life she had chosen had been very good to her. What really struck me was the next thing she said: Even though she loved her vocation, throughout all of those years, she regularly had to recommit to it! I was astounded! I had always assumed that nuns, especially, had this special calling and that once they accepted it, that was it— no more decisions or quandaries—they knew it was the right path for them.

"It hit me that no matter what you choose in life, you need to recommit to it all the time. I can't tell you how much that helped me in my marriage. I realized that I needed to continually recommit to my husband."

THE DAILY PICTURE

Keeping a commitment alive and flourishing means making choices every day that will affect the marriage in a positive way. Cris and Dave Williams, profiled on page 89, say they have a continual desire to ensure that, above all else, they both feel secure in the relationship. That desire affects their decisions about how they will behave every day. Dave, for example, has always had women friends in his life. During the course of their twelve-year marriage, there have been a couple of occasions when Cris felt jealous of one of these friendships. No problem. No question. "A couple of times she's come to me and said, 'I'd rather you didn't have that relationship,'" Dave says. "So I'll drop it. My relationship with Cris is far more important."

Cris says: "It's important that we both feel very secure in the relationship, and security is a fragile thing, so I have to bend over backwards not to do anything that will make Dave feel insecure. I never press him to do something he doesn't want to do. That helps him feel secure. If he says he doesn't feel like going to a party and I was excited about going to it, I won't press it. I'll drop it. I'll honor his feelings. I either might go to the party myself or not go. More often than not, I'll just stay home.

"In a day, security is shown in a lot of ways, like he'll come up and give me a hug, or he'll anticipate a need I have, such as if he walks in and I'm fixing dinner, he'll help. I don't need to ask him."

Ann and Jim Street focus on what they love about each other rather than on their differences. On the outside, they are very different: Ann is more emotionally driven, creative, free-flowing and unscheduled, and Jim more analytical and precise. He likes the mountains; she likes the ocean.

She wanted many children; he wanted just a couple. He likes things organized; she's too busy creating to be organized. Despite the differences, they never considered leaving each other.

"When the kids were little, we had agreed that Ann would be home and she'd do most of the cooking," Jim says. "Very often I would come home from work hungry, and wanting to have a nice dinner, only to find the house a wreck, with Ann and the kids' creative projects all over the place and no dinner anywhere. This would go on for three weeks in a row sometimes. I'd feel bad about it, but then I'd say, 'Well, what we all love about Ann is her creativity, and I wouldn't trade that in for an organized person any day.' Then we'd all help get dinner.

"People are a package, and you can't really choose one quality over another. I always ask myself, Would I be willing to give up something I love in exchange for getting rid of something I don't like, such as lack of organization? The answer is always no. I love her. We've never reached any different conclusion."

Jim says: "We make decisions based on love. If something matters a lot to one or the other, we'll give in simply because we love each other so much—we don't want the other one to be unhappy."

That theory was tested to the limit the year the couple took a vacation to the Amazon rain forest. Ann, who always wanted more children, fell in love with a six-year-old Ecuadorean orphan living in the rain forest, named Remi. She wanted to bring him home. The most unresolved, ongoing, intense conflict in their marriage had been over the issue of having more children. Jim wanted no more than the three they already had. After much talking, soul-searching, and intense discussion, Jim gave in and they adopted Remi. Ann says: "He agreed because he loves me and wants me to be happy, and I love him and want him to be happy. We're constantly weighing this balance. It's not about who is right or who is wrong, or who gave in more. It's about wanting to make each other happy.

"If something matters a lot to one of us, we'll let the other person know because we love each other so much we don't want the other one to be unhappy."

KNOW YOURSELVES VERY WELL BEFORE EVER MAKING A COMMITMENT

All of the focus on third bodies or the larger picture will be an exercise in futility if you have chosen the wrong partner. In order to avoid the pain of divorce, and I've been there, we need to be utterly conscious and aware before ever making a commitment to anyone. If we don't do the homework necessary to know ourselves and what we need, how can we possibly know what partner is best for us? And if we don't get to know our partners at a very deep level, we'll be in for surprises later.

His Holiness the Dalai Lama has this to say: "On the subject of love and marriage, my simple opinion is that making love is all right, but for marriage, don't hurry, be cautious. Make sure you will remain together forever, at least for this whole life. That is important, for if you marry hurriedly without understanding well what you are doing, then after a month or after a year, trouble starts and you will be seeking divorce. From a legal viewpoint divorce is possible, and without children maybe it is acceptable, but with children, it is not."

Mary Baker Eddy concurs, with the same caution. She wrote: "After marriage, it is too late to grumble over incompatibility of disposition. A mutual understanding should exist before this union and continue ever after, for deception is fatal to happiness."

Bev and Tom Feldman decided to spend their engagement period getting to know each other on a deep level, rather than planning for their wedding. They wanted to do everything they could to ensure that their marriage would last, and intended to start their married life consciously. Bev says: "For most of us, the engagement period has been commercialized into a time of romanticized high-pressure consuming: picking out china, silverware, linens, appliances; buying wedding outfits; and planning the wedding and honeymoon. But marriages last on average just seven years. We decided to use the engagement time as it was originally intended: to focus on getting to know each other at a deeper level, and to create the foundation for an enduring relationship."

The Feldmans created a plan for their engagement period. They agreed to spend a weekend day together, once a month, doing what they called "engagement work." They would spend all day, from 9 A.M. to 7 P.M., either Saturday or Sunday, with no breaks except lunch. During these weekend "workshops" together, they agreed not to answer the phone or pagers, there would be no TV or other distractions and no opting out by complaining that they were too tired. Each workshop had a theme and a specific agenda to cover, and there might be homework in between. They also set it up so one friend would be available by phone to facilitate them in case they got stuck. More than once they called for help. This went on for six months.

"Part of structuring it like this was that we were willing to be with ourselves and each other when the going got rough," Tom says, "and there were times when it got rough. We had to be responsible for the experiences of our lives. It was very hard at times.

"The requirement was that each of us would be willing to go through whatever was presented and be fully present and fully honest with ourselves and with each other. When we spoke, it would be authentic and at a very deep level. It wasn't always easy or pretty. There were periods of silence.

"We wanted to look at areas of our lives that we had never spoken about—such as our romantic pasts. We wanted to explore what hadn't been said, to ask what hadn't been asked, and really examine who we were. We wanted to press ourselves and each other to make our past patterns in relationships conscious so that they would not unconsciously dictate our present reality."

At the end of the six months, they would decide if they were ready for this marriage. They wanted to do what they could so they would not wake up five years later with a mortgage, three kids, and a divorce on their hands.

"By the end of this work, our relationship was an empty space," Bev

EVERYDAY LOVING

Show Up!

"Showing up" in a relationship means being fully present and putting your all into being the best partner you can be. Some spouses think they're "showing up" simply by being in the house, but that's not enough. A few of the ways we don't "show up" in relationships are the following:

1. *Keeping one foot out the door.* Would your attitude be different if God came down and told you this was it—you could not leave this relationship, ever? Assuming it is not an abusive one, how would you handle your conflicts? With one foot out the door, we never have to give this relationship our best effort because we're silently thinking to ourselves, "I'll just leave." Whether we actually leave or not, that mindset keeps us from "showing up" fully, and that's hardly fair to our partners.

2. *Fantasizing.* Rather than staying in the present with whatever is going on in the relationship, many people spend their time fantasizing about everything else but the issue at hand. They are not giving the relationship the focus it needs.

3. *Working long hours.* Career demands provide people with a handy excuse to check out of the marriage. Remember when your relationship was new and exciting? Did you manage to find more time for it then? Take a hard look at your deeper motivations for being away from home this much.

4. *Working on relationships other than your marriage.* Are you spending more time being a wonderful person with your golf partners, co-workers, the people in your book club, or—heaven

forbid—with an affair, than you spend with your partner? No wonder you get along so much better with all those people—they're getting your attention! Reorganize your priorities and put your energy into your marriage.

5. *Getting sick a lot.* Everyone gets sick now and then, but if you find that you're chronically ill, there's probably something else going on. When you're sick, you can't give 100 percent to your relationship and you're in a lopsided relationship at that—you the needy one, and your partner the caretaker. A healthy relationship involves two equal partners, both giving and taking in fairly equal proportion.

6. *Watching a lot of TV.* Television is a very common tool to use to check out of a relationship. The excuse is often that "I'm so tired after a long day at work, all I can do is sit in front of the tube at night." If your job or your life is so miserable that this is all you have left, then figure out how to get your life back and do it now. You're doing a grave disservice not only to your partner but to yourself as well.

7. *Drinking or using drugs to excess.* This is obvious, and more serious than the other styles of checking out. If you are the one with the problem, get help. If you are in an intimate relationship with someone who has a drug or alcohol problem, tell her if she doesn't get immediate help, you'll need to leave until she does. There simply is no way for someone with any kind of addiction to be a fully functioning, fully present, fully available partner.

8. *Staying in the past or the future.* We don't show up in present time because we still haven't gotten over or forgiven our partner for something he did in the past, or when things seem so dismal that we can't allow ourselves to be fully present

or happy until she changes. If what your partner did in the past is so bad that you have tried, but are unable to let go or forgive, then what is the point of staying in this relationship just to be miserable? If, for whatever reason, you plan to stay in the relationship, then you need to let go and forgive in order that everyone, including you, is not living in daily purgatory.

9. *Assuming your real soul mate is out there somewhere.* Your real, down-to-earth, tangible, and flawed human partner can never match up to a mythical soul mate. If you do manage to find your soul mate, you'll find that, in time, he or she is flawed, too, and you'll be no further along the path to perfection than you were with the first partner. So don't leave a relationship until you have done literally everything in your power to make the current one work—and that means showing up fully, 100 percent, with all exit doors closed. If you don't do everything you can, including taking a look at your own behavior, you will, without a doubt, take your same baggage and issues into the next relationship.

says. "We completed the old and we were able to say, 'Well, now here we are. What is it that we want to have in our marriage, and what are we not willing to have? We saw that life as a married couple, versus two single people being together, would be very different, even though we had lived together for seven years."

Tom says: "I wanted us to create something different that would have us grow together, where each person is fully empowered to live their life, full out, one hundred percent. Each of us is also one hundred percent responsible for the entire relationship, and that's very different from being fifty/fifty. In day-to-day life, the way that plays out is if one of us needs to do something, including work, the other does what needs to be done to help make that happen. Because we are both freelancers, there are certain days I work and certain days Bev works. There's no funniness about it—there's no 'Oh, that's not what guys do. They don't cook dinner and keep house.' We both do it all for each other."

When the period of their engagement work ended, Bev and Tom decided they were ready to marry. To honor their work and commitment, the couple invited twenty friends to an engagement ceremony.

The most important part of the ceremony was when they spoke to the group about what they intended to create as a married couple. They spoke of wanting to have a family, and to have their own house. The ceremony finished with a party. A few days later, they went on an *engagement moon*—their version of a honeymoon.

Within eight months, all the Feldmans' intentions came true. They married and bought a house, and Bev became pregnant. Daughter Silver Greene Feldman was born in November the following year. They've been together for eighteen years and married for twelve. Silver is now eleven.

But the Feldmans' work is not finished. They continue to identify and process their issues, and they continue to set aside regular time to reassess their lives and relationship. Tom says: "The underlying commitment to the relationship work has remained. No one should think that because we did that work we're now cured. With some regularity, we've done relationship work similar to our engagement work more or less every year. It means sitting down and giving time to this as a separate and important entity—not just in passing over dinner. We schedule it.

"We are not perfect. We are not ideal. We are human. We have plenty of problems, but we really have each other, our daughter included. We're all in this together and we're all here for each other."

A Commitment to Their Marriage and
Common Values Keep Them Together

A *shared sense of idealism* was the initial spark that brought Ann Medlock and John Graham together, and it has also sustained them throughout eighteen years of marriage.

They say that sustaining their commitment to each other hasn't been difficult, in part because of their unified vision. John explains: "It's about going back to the vision of our relationship, and how close we are, how much we love each other, how much work we're doing together that is so magnificent. The fact that I've been grumbling about something she's done assumes a new perspective when I remember that. Being annoyed doesn't mean much in the larger picture of what we have together.

"Commitment means much more than sexual fidelity. It means soul mate stuff. The universe put us together to do some deeply important work. Our marriage is romantic, but it's also an enterprise and I'm committed to that enterprise, not just to Ann Medlock, sexy lady, this woman I love."

Ann and John are leaders of the enterprise they call the Giraffe Project, which finds and tells stories of unrecognized heroes in our midst who "stick their necks out for the common good." To get more people to become Giraffes themselves, the project has developed school programs and teaching guides to bring stories of these heroes to young people, inspiring them with real-life role models. The project also gives heroes' stories to the media, presents speeches and workshops, and is creating a handbook for parents called *Raising Giraffes*. "Our mission is to get people of all ages to lead meaningful lives," Ann says.

Ann started the project when she lived in New York and worked as a freelance writer. "I was disgusted with some of the writing jobs I was doing and with what I saw happening in the media," she says. "My feeling was that the news as a whole was so full of people doing ghastly stuff, that true balance would only come in finding people who were doing great things and getting them in the news. I decided to be a free flak for heroes."

John's wakeup call to live by his ideals came about in a more dramatic fashion. He tells the story: "In the summer of 1981 my first marriage was collapsing, and I had left my job in the Foreign Service. I thought I'd try working as a lecturer. My first lecture was on a cruise ship. Off Alaska, in the North Pacific, the ship caught fire. I was one of the last people rescued from a lifeboat in the midst of a heavy storm. We were rescued against impossible odds, and it was clear to me that the only reason I lived was to do something meaningful with this life I'd been allowed to keep.

"When I came back, my dad died. I left my marriage, moved into a tiny apartment by myself, and tried to start a career doing lectures, which wasn't going well at all. Clearly, whatever I was supposed to be doing I hadn't figured out yet and my life wasn't looking too good."

Ann Medlock and John Graham say their "unified vision" keeps them together. "We're totally in sync in that we're on the same mission."

Ann and John had been in the same writers' group for two years when she asked him to write the bylaws for the Giraffe Project. He did the job as a volunteer, and as they got to know each other on a deeper level, they both realized that they were "wildly idealistic." John says, "Ann wanted to start the Giraffe Project and change the whole nature of media in America and I wanted to save the world from the atom bomb."

That sense of idealism has never left, and Ann and John continue to create and re-create their vision, and use it to sustain their life together. John says, "It's a given that we both devote our lives to this cause of being teachers, and helping people stick their necks out to serve. We're totally in sync in that we're on the same mission. Ann does some parts really well, much better than I do, and I do other parts better than she does. The two parts fit together perfectly. It makes us more confident that this is the vision—our coming together makes it whole.

"We continue to hold the mirror up for each other—egging each other toward doing our very best, not faltering, not giving up. Sometimes we don't want to hear it, but there it is on the wall—our marriage vow to help each other live up to our gifts.

"We're both very strong personalities. Sometimes I suspect her of trying to shove me around because she's such a strong person. Nothing stands in her way, and I don't want to get shoved around. There are definitely times when she accuses me of the same thing—of using my six-foot-four body and loud voice to overrule her. But we always circle back around and work it out equitably. And it gets better and better."

Ann says, "Power and control is such an issue with couples. I think there's an assumption that if one person in a couple is strong, the other has to be weak, as if there were a finite amount of power within the couple. But why not see that there's all the power in the world available and that one partner's power doesn't have to be a subtraction from the other's?"

❧ Meaningful Lives

Rather than getting locked into power struggles between themselves, Ann and John focus their unified power and talents on encouraging other people to lead meaningful lives. Ann and John so firmly believe in their mission that it is very easy for them to do without material wealth. Ann says: "We choose to live in a way that makes extravagance impossible, but we think we live luxuriously. We laughed when a television show interviewed us and talked about sacrifice. We thought, 'What did we give up? What are we sacrificing?' Then we realized they were talking to an audience full of people plugging away at jobs they hate, just for the money. They needed to hear that there's another way to live. Well, there is. Doing service, sharing that fulfilling work with the person you love—what could be more luxurious?"

To contact the Giraffe Project, call (360) 221-7989 or visit their Web site at www.giraffe.org.

℘ ℘ ℘

Resources

FACILITATORS

Bev and Tom Feldman are available to facilitate engagement work. They can be reached at (818) 790-7418 or at tom@agoodlife.com or bev@agood life.com.

BOOKS

Before You Say "I Do": Important Questions for Couples to Ask Before Marriage, by Todd Outcalt (New York: Perigee, 1998).

Chicken Soup for the Couple's Soul: Inspirational Stories About Love and Relationships (Deerfield Park, Fla.: Health Communications, 1999).

The Conscious Heart: Seven Soul Choices That Inspire Creative Partnership, by Kathlyn Hendricks, Ph.D., and Gay Hendricks, Ph.D. (New York: Bantam, 1997).

Conscious Loving: The Journey to Co-Commitment, by Gay Hendricks, Ph.D., and Kathlyn Hendricks, Ph.D. (New York: Bantam, 1990).

Create Your Own Love Story: The Art of Lasting Relationships, by David W. McMillan, Ph.D. (Hillsboro, Ore.: Beyond Words Publishing, 1997).

Don't Sweat the Small Stuff in Love: Simple Ways to Nurture and Strengthen Your Relationship While Avoiding the Habits That Break Down Your Loving Connection, by Richard Carlson, Ph.D., and Kristine Carlson, Ph.D. (New York: Hyperion, 1999).

The Eight Essential Traits of Couples Who Thrive, by Susan Page (New York: Dell, 1994).

For Fidelity: How Intimacy and Commitment Enrich Our Lives, by Catherine M. Wallace (New York: Vintage/Random House, 1998).

Getting the Love You Want: A Guide for Couples, by Harville Hendrix, Ph.D. (New York: HarperPerennial, 1988).

Heart-Centered Marriage: Fulfilling Our Natural Desire for Sacred Partnership, by Sue Patton Thoele (Berkeley, Calif.: Conari Press, 1996).

Hidden Keys of a Loving, Lasting Marriage, by Gary Smalley (Grand Rapids, Mich.: Zondervan, 1988).

How to Stay Lovers for Life, by Sharyn Wolf (New York: Dutton/Plume, 1998).

Journey of the Heart: A Path of Conscious Love, by John Welwood (New York: HarperPerennial, 1990).

Light in the Mirror: A New Way to Understand Relationships, by Barry and Joyce Vissell (Aptos, Calif.: Ramira Publishing, 1995).

Love Is a Decision: 13 Proven Principles to Energize Your Marriage and Family, by Gary Smalley (New York: Pocket, 1989).

Lessons in Love: the Course They Forgot to Teach You, by Gregory J. P. Godek (Naperville, Ill.: Sourcebooks, 1997).

Love Sweeter Love: Creating Relationships of Simplicity and Spirit, by Jann Mitchell (Hillsboro, Ore.: Beyond Words Publishing, 1998).

The Love Test: Romance and Relationship Self Quizzes Developed by Psychologists and Sociologists, by Virginia Rutter and Pepper Schwartz, Ph.D. (New York: Perigee, 1998).

The Maiden King—The Reunion of Masculine and Feminine, by Robert Bly (New York: Henry Holt, 1998).

The Marriage Spirit: Finding the Passion and Joy of Soul-Centered Love, by Dr. Evelyn Moschetta and Dr. Paul Moschetta (New York: Simon & Schuster, 1998).

The Mastery of Love, by Don Miguel Ruiz (San Rafael, Calif.: Amber Allen Publishing, 1999).

Neale Donald Walsch on Relationships: Application for Living, by Neale Donald Walsch (Charlottesville, Va.: Hampton Roads Publishing, 1999).

Odyssey of the Heart: The Search for Closeness, Intimacy and Love, by John H. Harvey (New York: W. H. Freeman, 1995).

Passionate Marriage: Sex, Love and Intimacy in Emotionally Committed Relationships, by David Schnarch, Ph.D. (New York: Norton, 1997).

The Seven Principles for Making Marriage Work, by John Gottman, Ph.D. (New York: Crown, 1990).

Shortcuts to Bliss: The 50 Best Ways to Improve Relationships, Connect with Spirit and Make Your Dreams Come True, by Jonathan Robinson (Berkeley, Calif.: Conari Press, 1998).

Staying Together: Embracing Love, Intimacy and Spirit in Relationships, edited by Mark Robert Waldman (New York: Tarcher/Putnam, 1998).

The Triumphant Marriage: 100 Extremely Successful Couples Reveal Their Secrets, by Neil Clark Warren, Ph.D. (Colorado Springs: Focus on the Families Publishing, 1995).

Why Marriages Succeed or Fail and How You Can Make Yours Last, by John Gottman (New York: Fireside, 1994).

Chapter 8

Talking from the Heart

One always loves the person who understands you.

—ANAÏS NIN

When was the last time you felt really listened to and understood? When was the last time you put aside your own agenda and focused on everything your partner was saying, without interrupting, judging, or attempting to solve their problem? Most of us aren't so great at this skill—we unconsciously dive into a defensive mode, or listen to someone else while formulating our response or rebuttal.

After I began "waking up" in relationships, I knew that one of the most important things I could do was learn to be a better listener. I've since discovered some very effective ways to hone that skill. I also discovered something else about listening deeply. When someone is allowed to express himself freely, he not only feels the exhilaration of being understood; something even more important can also happen—he begins to clear emotional blocks and release physical energy. The more free we are of these blocks, the more clear we can be as human beings, and the more clear we can be in communicating to our partners.

I look at these blocks like an overfull, paper grocery bag. When the bag is empty, it is clear and open. Then you start adding boxes, cans, and cartons of food. Each time you load another conflict into the bag, you add more weight and bury your emotions deeper. After a while, the bag is so full that the items in it are totally immobile. Sometimes the bag will burst when you least expect it.

That's us. Every conflict we don't address gets buried and, pretty soon, we are unable to think clearly. We start mixing old issues in with the new, hurling accusations such as "You never!" or "You always!" Similarly, clearing old family "stuff" can help keep your old baggage out of your marriage—that way you're not mixing hurts and disappointments from your family of origin in with what is going on in the present.

On the other hand, keeping your bag empty doesn't mean making a mountain out of every molehill, and sharing every thought that comes into your mind. It means openly dealing with the big issues in a constructive way.

This kind of deeper communication is at the heart of a committed relationship because it builds trust and intimacy. When you let your partner know she is safe to let her hair down with you and not be shamed, belittled, or argued with, she naturally feels free to share more and more.

As Henry James Borys says in *The Sacred Fire:*

> In an intimate relationship, when we communicate only information and ideas, then our communication actually violates our intention in being together. It violates our feelings (or our potential feelings) for each other. If we keep it up, our relationship will begin to lose its life, for its life is feeling—love. In an intimate love relationship, the purpose of communication is not just to exchange information, but ultimately to create a communion of feeling, to enliven and deepen the experience of loving companionship and intimacy.

Sharing freely from the heart encourages intimacy in a way that talking to prove a point or win an argument does not, because it shows your partner that you care about her thoughts and feelings, and also that you're willing to be vulnerable and open about your feelings.

BE HONEST

Before anybody can share anything, though, you must set an absolutely firm foundation of honesty in your relationship. You simply must be able to trust each other, or any communication style you could possibly ever use is nothing but a sham. Honesty means many things in a relationship, from not doing things behind your partner's back such as having affairs or participating in questionable business practices, to being honest about how you are feeling or what you need. And being honest—really honest—inspires passion.

Laura Sullivan reflected on the value of honesty in her relationship when an old friend recently asked her how her marriage was going. Laura answered, "Wonderful! Better than ever, after fifteen years together."

"What do you think it is?" the friend asked. "Is it honesty?"

"I was surprised by the question," Laura said, "but when I considered it, my first response was, "Absolutely. Honesty and trust are fundamental. Without these there is no relationship."

Laura and her husband, Reichian therapist John W. Davis, have developed absolute honesty in their relationship, in part, by following the Reichian method of full disclosure. Wilhelm Reich was a student of Freud's and is considered the father of body-centered psychology. This means that everything is brought to the surface when it arises. In this way, issues stay current and are not mixed in with eons of unfinished business.

Laura says: "We feel it is important to express and release the emotional energy around any conflict as soon as possible. We try to express ourselves fully, knowing that the other person won't leave the relationship over an emotional discharge. Sometimes one of us might upset the other so much that one chooses to walk away, but no physical violence is ever al-

LEARN YOUR PARTNER'S LOVE LANGUAGE

Everyone speaks a different love language. Your job is to learn which one your partner speaks, and their job is to learn yours. This is important because our natural tendency is to show love the way we like to receive it, but that doesn't necessarily register with our partner. Gary Chapman's book, *The Five Love Languages: How to Express Heartfelt Commitment to Your Mate*, lists the five most common languages:

1. *Verbal affirmation and hearing.* These people regularly need to hear from you that they are appreciated and loved, provided you mean it. So, use generously the words "I love you," or "I appreciated it when you did . . ." Don't forget words of encouragement, kind words, forgiving words, gentle requests, and empathic mirroring.

2. *Quality time.* These people need you to spend time with them. Don't give them teeny increments of your leftover time—they want to know that they are important in your life and that you make quality time for them. Do things to-

lowed. This 'let's deal with it right now' method allows us to clear the air and reconnect in our love very quickly. We don't let things fester because we didn't want to go into it. We go right to it and clear it, even if we still disagree. That clearing allows us to stay connected to our love."

Both John and Laura say that this level of absolute honesty has kept their marriage vital, passionate, alive, and full of energy. "We tried other communication systems where we kept everything calm, and found that the energy for our relationship was dampened," John says. "When we switched to this method, everything was alive and fresh, and the energy was more intense. Even our nonverbal skin chemistry gets renewed, and our sex is better now after fifteen years because it seems fresh. We're full of passion for each other. There is no fear."

gether with a positive attitude, work side by side, take time for heart-to-heart conversation, do things they enjoy.

3. Receiving gifts. These people feel loved when you give them things. The gifts do not need to be expensive—just a simple gesture, every now and then, that you thought about them during the day and that you are not taking them for granted. That gift can be of yourself, such as being with them during a crisis. To these people, little things mean a lot.

4. Acts of service. These people love it when you help them in some way. It could be listening while they prepare to give a speech, fixing a broken pipe or computer, cooking a good meal, and so forth. They also appreciate it when you share household chores, and especially when you think of it first, before they have to ask. Remember how you helped when you were first falling in love? Go back to that point again!

5. Physical touch. These people feel loved with lots of physical contact—sexual and nonsexual—especially when initiated by you. When talking, gently touch their leg or arm. Remember to greet and say good-bye with a hug and kiss. Hold them when they cry. When sitting on the couch, sit near each other. Rub each other's feet or give a two-minute shoulder massage.

Laura says, "When our skin touches, there is a delicious electrical exchange that happens. Sometimes just a pleasurable little charge, but other times it is a long deep energy recharge or balancing. A chakra tune-up. Some people might call this chemistry. Whatever it is, it feeds us. I think of it as life force, or chi—a basic building block of human energy function."

John describes how unresolved arguments can dampen the chemistry between a couple. He says: "Take, for example, if you and I had an argument and didn't resolve it. Then I come to you wanting to make love. You'll probably tell me to get lost. Then imagine if we still didn't resolve that argument. And that goes on into other disagreements. Pretty soon our bodies are afraid of each other's, there's so much resentment built up. Because Laura and I work through our issues and arguments as they come up, we're always fresh. You want a clear mind so you can have a flowing, alive body."

The reason why this style works for John and Laura is because they both know that their partner is totally honest with them, and thus, they know they can trust and rely on what the other says to them at all times. They don't need to wonder if there are hidden agendas, or whether their partner is dissatisfied with them but just not talking about it. They also place in very high regard their marriage vow, which said: "NO MATTER WHAT." That vow was and is so important to them that in the early years of their marriage they kept it tacked to the wall. That was their agreement—that they would stay together no matter what.

Laura says: "Right from the start we created a safety net to allow for this freedom of fuller expression for what we were feeling. Your partner needs to know he can go through his stuff and you'll be there for him, and vice versa. You have to be the one person he can feel safe with no matter what's going on.

"This gives us a foundation of trust and security that allows love and passion to grow."

John says: "People often think that they should leave the relationship because their partner pushes too many of their buttons, and that they can go out and find a person who doesn't push them. But there's no one who won't push your buttons. Instead, I say, find someone who will push you because that's how you'll grow. Laura and I push a lot of buttons, and our relationship is dynamic, passionate, alive, and powerful. It's not a set of compromises.

"The buttons we've pushed have made us stronger. We've learned that in the process of pushing each other we've lifted, opened, and strengthened ourselves. It has allowed for a fertile field so new things can continue to grow. The opposite would be true if we tried to control the other person so they never pushed us. We'd wind up fifteen years later having a lot of areas where no one is allowed to go, and there would be no fertile field. Just a lot of barren rock."

John says he sees many people who have electricity in the beginning of their relationship and then lose it because they haven't paid attention, or didn't deal with issues as they came up. He says: "Relationships are fragile and take attention and effort. A relationship is not like you're Michelangelo and have just created a beautiful work of art that you can leave there for years and years to look at. You have to continually tend it.

"In the midst of all of this you have to keep your eyes on the prize—your relationship. In the very end, what is more important, being right or being alone? You need to know when to let go. For some people, being right is the most important thing in a relationship. For us, the relationship is most important."

THREE WAYS TO COMMUNICATE FROM THE HEART

The following are three methods you can use to communicate on a deeper level with your partner:

1. Counseling Each Other

Pick a time each week when you both can devote one hour (or more) to "talk time." Make it a regular time, and mark it on your calendar so you don't fill it with something else. This act alone signals that your relationship is important, and by setting aside regular time to clear the air, you'll find that problems and issues don't lie unresolved, causing more problems later. Once you get used to regularly sharing, it becomes easier and easier and your relationship will maintain more clarity.

Before you start, take some deep breaths to focus your awareness, and open your heart to your partner. It doesn't do much good to schedule "talk time" if you go into this with a closed heart, an inflexible attitude, or the sense that this is taking too much of your time.

Allow each person equal time to talk about anything she or he wants, with the other agreeing to listen. No arguing, no belittling, no interrupting. When the first person is through, the second gets his or her time. It's good to devote at least thirty minutes to each person; but if all you have is thirty minutes total, then each person uses fifteen. It's important that each person receive equal time because that keeps the relationship equal—one is not the caretaker of the other. This not only keeps partners on an even keel with one another; it also encourages both people to be responsible for their own "stuff."

Sit somewhere comfortable, close to each other, and look directly into your partner's eyes. It often helps to hold hands or touch knees—some small gesture of physical connection—but do this only if your partner is comfortable with it. When you are in listener mode, your job is to focus 100 percent on your partner. You are not there to solve her problem or give advice—you are simply there to listen. It is not easy to pay total attention to one person for even twenty or thirty minutes. One of the hardest challenges is to ignore your own thoughts and opinions as they come up during the other person's time. Our minds are constantly going off in other directions, and it takes a high degree of awareness to catch yourself when your mind is wandering off of or reacting to what your partner is saying.

Sometimes these sessions start out with your partner feeling lost about what to talk about, or talking about mundane things. Listen very, very carefully, and you will start to notice a deeper issue buried in the chatter. After you feel comfortable just listening for a few sessions, you can take the next step and help your partner go more deeply into his emotions. You can do that by staying with him on whatever subject he is talking about, and perhaps asking questions or making comments that will help him go further. What you really want from these sessions is a deeper understanding of yourselves.

If your partner cries, know that is a good thing because he is clearing a bit of blocked energy. At first it can be uncomfortable "letting" someone cry, because our tendency is to help people "feel better"—but the last thing you want to do is block the flow of tears. Tears are very healing. Let him cry until he is done.

Inexpensive Ideas for Keeping the Romance Alive

ରେ

by Michael Webb

Bored with the predictable and costly flowers, chocolates, and dinner routine for Valentine's Day, birthdays, and anniversaries? Michael Webb, syndicated columnist and editor of The Ro-MANtic newsletter, shares some very creative (and inexpensive) ways to say "I Love You" on these special days—and throughout the rest of the year.

- ◇ Sleep under the stars—Buy some glow-in-the-dark stars from the toy department and arrange a special message above your bed.
- ◇ Computer romance—Change the screen saver on the computer to a scrolling message. For added effect, use a wingding or character font that can't be read without decoding.
- ◇ Got milk?—Hide a bunch of silly prizes and a card in your love's favorite cereal.
- ◇ Jump-start the romance—attach your card or gift to a three-foot string and tie it to the bottom of an automatic garage door. When your honey comes home, the gift will magically arise to greet him.
- ◇ Warm the heart—While your love is in the shower, put her towel in the dryer for a few minutes so it will be toasty warm when she steps out.
- ◇ Music to their ears—In your own voice, record a book, fairy tale, or poetry on tape for your dearest to listen to on the way to work or while he or she is out of town.
- ◇ A winter picnic—Move the living room furniture and have a picnic in the middle of the floor complete with blanket, picnic basket, and all the fixings (a roaring fire in the fireplace would add to the effect).
- ◇ Welcome home!—Use chalk to write a welcome-home greeting on the sidewalk.

    —From *The RoMANtic Newsletter: Hundreds of Creative Tips to Enrich Your Relationship.* Call 1-888-4ROMANTIC or order via the Web site, www.TheRomantic.com.

Sessions can also start off with your partner angry at you. Let her be angry. As long as there is no physical violence, let her rant and rave until she is done. You want to help her get her emotions out of her system, and anger is simply one more emotion that blocks energy. Once the anger has dissipated, she can think more clearly about a solution. If you are not ready to listen to her anger, then wait until you are ready and try again.

Whatever is going on, let your partner talk for the full time allotted. If you've never communicated at this level before, you'll both need to build trust in each other so that you feel safe talking openly. At first, it's difficult to talk about our vulnerabilities. We're afraid people (including our partners) will judge us or, worse yet, reject us because we don't have it all together. Once you can trust each other, you'll discover a real human being underneath who has similar fears, vulnerabilities, and baggage. We're all human beings, and none of us has it all together. Sharing like this helps us bond. Once the bonding starts, compassion naturally flows. This is what you want in your intimate relationship.

If you stay on the surface of disagreements or issues, all you can see is the disagreement—you feel one way and your partner feels another. Maybe you can battle it out or find some surface compromise or, worse yet, one can bully the other into agreement. When you take the time to understand where each person is coming from at her or his deepest, most vulnerable level, then you can work together to solve the problem from a compassionate, heart-centered place.

2. Spiritual Companioning

Spiritual companioning is a less formal, more spiritually based way to counsel each other. It is less formal in that you don't need to make sure each person has equal time, and you may or may not need to set aside regular time to do it. You can be a spiritual companion whenever your partner needs to share, and vice versa. The spiritual element is that it is grounded in "virtues language."* The goal is the same—you actively listen and help your partner "empty her cup." Like the first method, it is a way to help your partner find resolution, rather than attempting to do it for her.

Linda Kavelin Popov, who teaches spiritual companioning as part of

*For more information on the Virtues Project, see pages 48 and 67.

her Virtues Project, says: "There is a big difference between sympathy, empathy, and companioning. Sympathy is when you feel sorry for someone, empathy is when you can feel their feelings, and companioning is when you bring compassion and detachment together so that you can walk intimately with others without taking on their feelings as your responsibility. The ability to witness another's feelings without needing to fix them is a powerful gift to give anyone."

It doesn't matter how your partner is feeling—your job is to stay detached. When your partner is angry, especially with you, Linda uses the motto "Be curious, not furious." This means instead of getting defensive or angry back, you get curious: Why is he angry? If your partner's anger pushes too many of your buttons, you can still refrain from becoming furious by taking a break. When you are ready to detach, you can come back and get curious.

Curious means being emotionally and mentally "present" when your partner is expressing his or her feelings. Then ask "cup emptying" questions starting with "what" and "how." For example, if your partner is really upset, ask, "What's upsetting you?" or "What are you angry about?" Remember, though, to never ask "why." Asking why often feels like an interrogation or a request for instant analysis.

You want to ask open-ended questions and show the utmost nonjudgmental curiosity. Being curious means you really, truly want to know—be genuine. This allows you to bypass defensiveness, which gets nowhere, and get to the heart of the matter. Let her fully express herself before asking another question. Once your partner has named a feeling, you can then help her "empty" further by asking a more focused question such as "What is the most difficult part of this?" or "What worries you the most?" or "What is most confusing?"

Linda says: "When a person's cup seems empty, give a few more moments of silence. There is a coffee slogan, 'Good to the last drop.' Sometimes the last drop contains the pearl of truth. When a person gets to the bottom of her cup, the truth is always found there. You have given her the opportunity to hear herself think and feel."

Finally, when your partner is really through, you can ask closure questions such as "What is clearer to you now?" or "What has been helpful about talking?" or "What have you appreciated most about talking?" Linda warns it is essential that the listener not have an agenda for what "the" right answer is. Serving as a spiritual companion takes a great deal of trust in your partner's process.

As a way to restore the dignity and self-esteem for someone who has opened his heart and soul to you, you can offer a virtues acknowledgment such as "I see your courage."

Betsy and Pete Smith, who have been married for twenty-nine years, say that one of the best things about their marriage is that their communication has opened up after learning the art of spiritual companioning. "We didn't have the skills before," Betsy says, "and now our marriage is much richer. Things don't build up like they did before . . . I would be so frustrated but not be able to say what I was feeling. Then Pete would clam up and go behind a book or newspaper, and I'd get more frustrated and didn't feel heard. The cycle went around and around."

Pete says: "I'm not unlike most males in that there's a tendency to want to fix whatever is bothering Betsy—especially if emotions are involved. Before, I'd want to just get it over with and let me go on with my life. Since we started practicing spiritual companioning, I've learned to listen and try to probe, using active listening techniques to help her empty her cup. I don't judge—I just listen."

Betsy says: "Earlier in our marriage Pete didn't want me to cry, for example. He was very uncomfortable with it. Eventually I started feeling like I shouldn't cry, but I'd feel cut off from myself and from him. I'd want to be closer, but I felt like he'd try to fix whatever it was, or ignore it and hope it went away. Now, he really hears me. I've been able to share things at a really deep level . . . my deepest fears, terrible things that I wasn't willing or able to share before. Now I know he's going to be there. I feel much more loving toward him. At one point I had a lot of grief over a particular issue, so Pete and I went away for the weekend together. He just held me and provided the safety I needed to cry and cry. Sometimes he'd ask me questions, like 'What's the hardest thing about this for you?' or 'What does that mean to you?' Pete's support really helped me to understand what my grief was about."

3. Compassionate Communication

Another method that encourages communication from the heart is one developed by a man named Dr. Marshall Rosenberg. He calls it Nonviolent Communication (NVC). It is founded on language and communication skills that strengthen our ability to remain human, even under trying conditions.

Dr. Rosenberg's quest for learning a new way to communicate started at a young age, when his Jewish family moved to a Detroit neighborhood. "I was exposed to a considerable amount of violence," he says. His observations about human nature—wondering why some people were led to violence against others, and some were filled with compassion—led him to get a doctorate in clinical psychology. But still, he didn't have the answers he sought. "I realized that clinical psychology was based on pathology—diagnosing people as mentally ill was just another form of judgment. I wanted to focus on what people needed to live well."

In college, he worked with Carl Rogers, who was studying the characteristics of helping relationships (e.g., a person helping someone in pain to feel better). Three characteristics of those helpers arose: acute empathy, authenticity, and liking one another.

"We identified these and wondered how to teach the skill to others," Dr. Rosenberg says. "I noticed that the characteristics Rogers identified were apparent in those people no matter what else was going on around them. We all know people like that, where no matter how bad things are, they are still an inspiration to us.

"From my studies and observations I learned that people who functioned well didn't judge others, knew how to present clear requests that others saw as a request and not a demand, and no matter how other people communicated to them, saw their humanness behind the needs."

Balancing Rituals for Couples

c~3

by Joel and Michelle Levey

If you want to keep your relationship alive, it's essential to give some time on a regular basis to connect deeply, even if it's only for a few wholehearted minutes each day! Here are some balancing rituals that can be easily integrated into your schedule. You can use these on a daily or weekly basis, and the time you give to them can be adapted to fit in with the changing rhythms of your lifestyle: if there is not time for it one day, that's okay. Just find what works for you and keep trying.

Hair Brushing

One of our favorite quick ways to connect is to brush each other's hair. Michelle particularly loves this. It seems to nourish the "roots" of balance in our joint psyche, linking us back to tribal days when people regularly shared moments of tender loving care through grooming each other. Bioenergetically, it also helps clear our energy field of accumulated static electricity, which is especially important after long days in front of a computer monitor.

Foot Rubs

In this same category of physical rituals that move us toward balance is the special gift of giving each other a foot rub. This is a great one for quiet moments after a hard day's work or play—or anytime! The soles of the feet have receptors connecting to all the organs and structures of the body. Foot rubs are one of the best ways to give and receive a balancing and revitalizing mini-massage, especially if you use some aromatic essential oil like lavender or juniper. You don't have to be an expert on reflexology to give your partner a deluxe treatment (though there are many guidebooks available on the subject), and even little cards that map out the terrain of each foot in detail). Just trust the inner guidance of your heart and let your hands "go for the sole."

Get Wet

Anything to do with water is a helpful strategy for balance—bathing or showering together, swimming, washing one another's feet, listening to the soothing sounds of a waterfall or ocean waves on recorded environmental music tapes, or even going for a walk in the rain (especially if you live in Seattle, as we do) are all wonderful ways to reconnect in a balancing way.

Read to One Another

Two friends of ours experimented with unplugging their TV and reading poetry to each other in the evenings instead. Another couple we know are working their way through The Hobbit and can't wait to jump into bed to get to the next chapter.

Take a Walk

Friends of ours decided to go for a walk after work around the reservoir in their town as part of their daily routine. This strategy proved immediately beneficial, both for their own individual sense of health and vitality, and for their health, vitality and balance as a couple. People with children can bring the kids along too!

Morning Tea and Meditation

Another couple we know found that reestablishing an old family custom of "morning tea and meditation" in bed made a major difference in the quality of their relationship and the energy with which their day got off to a start. For other couples, praying together in the morning or evening has become an integral element of staying balanced together.

The Four Rivers of Life

One couple whom we worked with started to incorporate a time of deep reflection and truth-speaking each evening. Using a simple process we'd introduced them to, which involves four questions as a tool to give structure to their contemplations, they each take turns listening and speaking deeply as they share what is true for them. Here are the four questions:

✦ Where today was I inspired by something or someone?
✦ Where today was I surprised?
✦ Where today did I find myself being challenged or stretched to grow or think in new ways?
✦ Where today was I touched or deeply moved by something that came into my life?

We first learned this series of contemplations from Angeles Arrien, who received them from her Basque ancestors. In the Basque tradition, these four questions honor the Four Rivers of Life: the river of Inspiration, the river of Surprise, the river of Challenge, and the river of Love. According to the wise elders of this tradition, it's impossible for us to truly stay in balance without jumping in and bathing in these four rivers on a daily basis.

—From *Living in Balance*

Since then, Dr. Rosenberg has become an internationally known peacemaker and founder of the Center for Nonviolent Communication. He is also author of *Nonviolent Communication: A Language of Compassion.*

He says: "As NVC replaces our old patterns of defending, withdrawing, or attacking in the face of judgment and criticism, we come to perceive ourselves and others, as well as our intentions and relationships, in a new light. Resistance, defensiveness, and violent reactions are minimized. When we focus on clarifying what is being observed, felt, and needed rather than on diagnosing and judging, we discover the depth of our own compassion. Through its emphasis on deep listening—to ourselves, as well as others—NVC fosters respect, attentiveness, and empathy, and engenders a mutural desire to give from the heart."

An element of NVC is that if focuses on separating *needs* from *wants.* Dr. Rosenberg points out that all people everywhere have the same hierarchy of needs: air, food, water, protection from the elements (clothes, house), understanding, empathy, connection, spirituality, and contributing to life. The difference is not in the needs, but in how we seek to fulfill them.

He says: "We simplify our needs by getting clear about them and not getting them confused with the way our culture encourages us to get them met. A need contains no reference to a specific action.

"For example, someone may think they need a gun, but the need is for *protection,* not the *gun.* The gun is only a service to get the need of protection met. In that case, I show people that members of their family are three times more likely to get killed if they have a gun in the house. In the case of the gun, I help them find other ways to get protection.

"Many people try to meet their needs through *strategy* (gun, for example) and it results in a lot of conflict.

"Another way is this: say someone is tense and nervous, so they think they need to watch TV or grab a beer. They immediately think *strategy*—beer or TV—but if they get in touch with the need, they can find ways to get those needs met in a less toxic, less costly way."

Dr. Rosenberg has taught his methods to as many couples in conflict as warring tribes and nations. "I worked with one couple on the brink of divorce," he said. "The husband told me he needed to get out of the relationship, but I pointed out that wasn't a *need*—it was a *strategy*. He had several judgments about his wife—one was 'You never understand me.' She answered, 'Yes I do.' He replied, 'No you don't.'

"I said, 'Wait a minute, what is your need behind that?' I helped him to see it was a need for understanding that was not getting met. Then we worked to put that need in the form of a statement to his wife: 'I have a need for understanding that's not being met.'

"Then I asked him what he would like her to do to meet that need of understanding. I suggested that when he was talking, she would repeat back to him what he said before reacting. He was thrilled. 'That's exactly what I mean,' he said. Finally he was able to make a request to his wife. 'I have a need for understanding that's not getting met sometimes. Would you be willing to repeat back what I say so I know I've been understood?'

"The wife's complaint was that he wasn't sensitive to her needs. I translated that she had a need for more closeness and tenderness. Her request was, 'Would you be willing to sit with me and check in about how you're feeling, and ask how I'm feeling for even five minutes when you come home, instead of going directly to the computer?'

"At the moment I helped them get connected with their needs, I can't tell you the gratitude they both had. They were eager to learn more, and years later, this couple is still together."

Dr. Rosenberg pointed out that using compassionate communication does not depend on both people using it. In a couple situation, even if one partner lapses or doesn't want to learn it, the other partner can still use it by listening attentively and focusing on needs, not strategy.

❧ *Communicating in the Silence* ❧

It was an exquisite paradox: the year that Joel and Michelle Levey spent in a silent retreat was the year they learned the most about deep, soul-to-soul communication.

With words and chatter swept away, the path was cleared for their hearts to meet. "It was the most intimate year of our lives," they say.

Joel and Michelle, both meditation teachers, signed on for a group meditation retreat that was premised on everyone being absolutely silent for the entire year—no talking to anyone. Throughout that time, there was also no physical contact—Joel slept in one room and Michelle in another. The only way they could communicate was by focusing their thoughts on each other. In order to do that, they planned ahead of time that at the same time every day, they would sit in their adjoining rooms and meditate on each other. "We'd stop what we were doing and I'd sit and hold him in my heart and he in mine," Michelle says.

"We were like two soap bubbles merging," Joel explains. "We'd sit for fifteen to twenty minutes a day like this, just focusing our thoughts on each other. Oftentimes it was such a sweet infusion of tender loving energy. That was how we kept our relationship really nurtured. We couldn't spend time talking or being physical, so this was a way to connect with wholehearted awareness of our love for each other.

"In our ordinary lives, we tend to connect on a more superficial, scattered, turbulent level. When we were silent for a year, we were quiet at the level where the connection really exists.

"It was so clear to me how important it is to nourish and commune with the heart and core of our relationship, having learned from what was missing previously. We see so many relationships where people are starving for deep bonds and connection, but they may be really busy with a lot going on outside. When the busyness falls away, they're left with so little, because they haven't tended their inner connection."

Since that year, Joel and Michelle have continued with their ritual of focusing on each other when they cannot be physically together. When they are separated on business trips, they set their wristwatch alarms to beep in unison—even if they are in different time zones. When the alarm goes off, no matter what they are doing, they focus for just a minute on each other and send their love. "Just because we're separated

Joel and Michelle Levey have learned to honor their different styles of communicating: "We've learned not to push and pull when we're in the middle of a conflict," says Michelle.

physically, it doesn't mean we can't still hold each other in our hearts and connect," says Michelle.

While their silent communication has enabled them to connect deeply with their hearts, Joel and Michelle have also nourished their verbal communication. Both place great emphasis on being transparent. Joel says: "I don't value masks in others, and I don't pretend everything is fine if it's not. We're both pretty good about telling it like it is—that is, to the degree we are mindful of what is really true for us. Say what you mean, mean what you say, and be who you are."

Michelle adds: "We're each fiercely determined to be authentic about being who we are. Growing up, I saw the games people played with each other, and I remember thinking that was unacceptable to me. For me, it comes back to that intense drive to discover and reveal the reality and truth about ourselves, each other, and the world. We honor being straightforward. It's intense sometimes, but our commitment is to risk."

When there is conflict in the relationship, the Leveys have learned to honor their different styles. "Often what I need to remember is honoring space," Michelle says. "Joel will want to stick with the issue and keep working it, and I'll need to clear a space and cool down. We've learned to be aware of each other's styles and to respect that. We both need the opposite at those times, so we've learned not to push and pull when we're in the middle of a conflict.

"We're both fiery people, and we're both intense. We're not 'oatmeal.' People tend to think of meditation teachers as very calm and placid, but that's not always true of us. There's a lot of high-spiritedness and vitality. We're very energetic—not indifferent or apathetic. We feel things strongly . . . it doesn't take long to get the match going!"

Since the Leveys are both intense people and spend so much time together, working, traveling, and writing, they've found a way to create needed solitude. "We don't need to physically go apart to find that feeling of solitude because we can be quiet together. We know how to be alone together," Michelle says. "We can walk in silence and it's fine. We can drive for a long time in silence, or enjoy the silence in the house. A lot of people in relationships have issues about 'alone time,' but I don't need to leave Joel to find my own space."

✣ A Marriage of Service

Over the years, Joel and Michelle's marriage has been one of deep, shared inner work integrated with active lives of service in the world. One of their wedding vows was to help others on their journey of awakening to their true nature and potentials. They have co-authored several books, including *Living in Balance—a Dynamic Approach for Creating Harmony & Wholeness in a Chaotic World; Simple Meditation & Relaxation;* and *Wisdom at Work.* The Leveys also serve as consultants for major corporations, health care professionals, and even the U.S. military. They spent six months designing the "Ultimate Warrior Training Program" for the U.S. Army Green Berets at the request of the Pentagon.

Joel says: "Outwardly, our life is anything but simple. We run our business by ourselves, travel sixty to eighty percent of the time, and have two houses—one in the city, and the other an organic farm in Hawaii. We've found that there is inner simplicity and outer simplicity. The inner simplicity is presence, spaciousness, being clear in the midst of confusion, stillness in the midst of turbulence. It's a frame of reference for the larger perspective—a commitment to what our life is about. We're not doing this work just for the money—it's to see clearly and help others reduce their own suffering and realize their full potential.

"We're dedicated to this higher purpose. We get stretched thin at times, but because of this commitment to the larger picture and the life we share, we're growing ever more resilient."

Michelle adds: "At our corporate trainings, people are inspired that we can work professionally with our spouse. One of the most crucial things we pay attention to in our marriage is catching the whispers before they become screams. It's not a particular ritual—it's the practice of inner listening and mindful dialogue with each other."

Joel says: "Part of our practice is that one of the first things we do each morning is contemplate the preciousness of our lives—the gift of another moment together. Death is certain, but the time of death is not. We never know for sure that when we leave the house in the morning, we will see each other again. If I'm awake in this relationship, I walk out the door with the awareness that I may not see Michelle again."

Michelle adds: "So what really matters is living with the realization that our time together is brief and precious. When there's conflict, we ask ourselves, 'How important is it in this transient and impermanent life?' We realize that love is more important than being right. We think about this every day, before we get out of bed in the morning, and the last thing at night."

☙ ☙ ☙

Resources

For information on the Virtues Project, see its Web site at: www.virtues project.com.

For information on Dr. Marshall Rosenberg's Center for Nonviolent Communication, write P.O. Box 2662, Sherman, TX 75091, or call (903) 893-3886, E-mail cnvc@compuserve.com, or visit the Web site at www.cnvc.org.

BOOKS

Communication Miracles for Couples: Easy and Effective Tools to Create More Love and Less Conflict, by Jonathan Robinson (Berkeley, Calif.: Conari Press, 1997).

The Dream Sharing Sourcebook: A Practical Guide to Enhancing Your Personal Relationships, by Phyllis R. Koch-Sheras, Ph.D., and Peter L. Sheras, Ph.D. (Los Angeles: Lowell House, 1999).

The Healing Journey for Couples: Your Journey of Mutual Discovery, by Phil Rich, Ed.D, M.S.W., and Stuart A. Copans, M.D. (New York: Wiley, 1998).

How One of You Can Bring the Two of You Together: Breakthrough Strategies to Resolve Your Conflicts and Reignite Your Love, by Susan Page (New York: Broadway Books, 1997).

The Language of Love: A Powerful Way to Maximize Insight, Intimacy and Understanding, by Gary Smalley (New York: Pocket, 1991).

The Lost Art of Listening: How Learning to Listen Can Improve Relationships, by Michael P. Nichols, Ph.D. (New York: Guilford Press, 1995).

Nonviolent Communication: A Language of Compassion, by Marshall Rosenberg, Ph.D. (Del Mar, Calif.: PuddleDancer Press, 1999).

10,000 Ways to Say I Love You, by Gregory Godek (Naperville, Ill.: Sourcebooks, 1999).

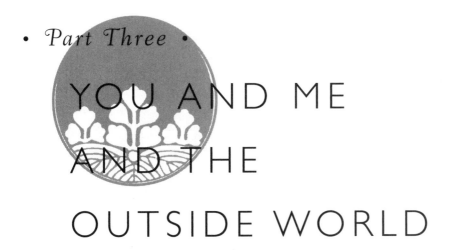

Part Three

YOU AND ME

AND THE

OUTSIDE WORLD

Chapter 9

Making Financial Peace with Your Partner

If you want to take the true measure of someone,
observe how he handles sex, time, and money.

I don't know where this quote originated, but think about it. How you handle your money impacts your time, and both time and money impact your intimate relationship in a big way.

Here's a brief overview: Every dollar you spend means you need to work more hours at your job in order to earn another dollar to replace the spent one. Every hour you spend working is another hour you are not devoting to your relationship or to other parts of your life. Every hour you are not spending on your relationship impacts the quality of that relationship. This is hardly to say that we should all go out and live in chicken coops and eat seeds from the ground so we don't have to work. Nor that we shouldn't find jobs and careers that we love and that give us mental and spiritual fulfilment. And I don't believe we should spend all our waking hours devoting ourselves to relationships. Not at all. But most of us are so far off in the opposite direction—never stopping to consider how money *really* impacts our intimate relationships—that we need to wake up our consciousness and look at the link. With this new awareness, we can then make *conscious,* not unconscious, choices about how we manage our money.

For example, if you are in debt, it really doesn't matter how many love notes you tuck under your partner's pillow—you can't possibly be the kind of focused partner needed in order to do your part to have a good marriage. That's because debt keeps people awake at night, distracted, anxious, and working extra hours just to pay it off. In that state of emotional affairs, how can you have the peace and feeling of abundance necessary to be a loving partner?

Even if there is no debt, but you're living from paycheck to paycheck with nothing saved, you're living on the edge, which is hardly conducive to romance, either.

There's also the more hidden impact that money has on relationships. That's the one borne by our consumer culture that continually encourages us to find fulfillment by consuming more and more. We will be happier with a bigger house. We will be more satisfied with a newer car. Our lives will be better with that new vase for the entryway table. My spouse will like me more with this new outfit. You get the picture—it never, ever stops. There is no end. How does that mindset affect relationships? Our focus is out there—on consumption—rather than inside, either on developing ourselves to be better human beings, or on connecting intimately with our partners. This is a difficult treadmill to step off because we are bombarded constantly to purchase more and more. We can't get through a day, even an hour, without hearing or seeing an advertisement for something, and the nature of advertising is to make us feel that whatever we have is inadequate compared with what they are offering. The seduction can be overwhelming.

What happens when the seduction takes over? We buy, buy, buy, thinking we're somehow buying happiness or fulfillment. And for couples, the buying is rarely done in unison—one wants to buy more than the other. What's next? Fights and arguments over money. Indeed, we've probably all heard that money arguments are one of the chief causes of marital discord, including divorce, in America.

KEEP TRACK OF CONFLICT IN ORDER TO AVOID IT

by Donna Miller

1. Keep a "hard times" journal so you can learn from your conflicts. After a conflict in which the problem didn't get resolved in a way that you would have liked, ask yourself the following and write it in your journal:

- ❖ What could I have done differently that would have worked better? This keeps you focused on yourself, rather than on what a rat your partner is. If you want things to go differently next time, you need to focus on the only person you have the power to change—and that's you, not them.
- ❖ What did I learn from this conflict? Again, keep the focus on you because it's only your personal growth that you can control. You can acknowledge that you're still angry at your partner, but try to look further to see what that anger stirs up in you.

2. Have a regular relationship night. It can be as often as the two of you want or need—weekly, monthly, quarterly. During relationship night you can haul out your hard-times journal and talk about what you've learned. For those who feel it's not fair to focus just on yourself and not on your partner's shortcomings, remember that intimate relationships are like teeter-totters—when one person shifts, the other has to shift! We may not know how he or she will shift, but in general we know that when one partner begins responding in a more loving, compassionate way, it's pretty difficult for the other to remain negative.

Remember the movie *The Gods Must Be Crazy*? For those who haven't seen it, it's about a tribe of people in Africa who lived peacefully and co-operatively for years and years. They lived a totally self-reliant life, using no manufactured items whatsoever. All was well until one day, a small airplane flew over and the pilot, having finished his bottle of Coke, threw the empty bottle out the window. The bottle landed in the middle of the tribe's village and all of a sudden, the villagers got greedy and started fighting over this mysterious bottle. They had never seen such a thing, and they all wanted it. The fighting and power struggles continued until finally, one of the villagers took the bottle and threw it into what they thought was the end of the earth. Then they returned to living peacefully and cooperatively.

That's us with the Coke bottle—always wanting more and more and never satisfied. We even go into debt—spending money that isn't ours—in order to get more than more. Can you imagine if you were a visiting alien observing earthly behavior? People running around like ants, frantically working overtime and lying awake at night fretting in order to pay for all their stuff that they *know* will make them happy? And doing it over and over and over again. Then mysteriously, they wonder why their marriages are heading south and there's no time left for intimacy.

Another by-product of our consumer culture is the power struggle that results. In most relationships, one partner earns more money than the other. If spending money is one of the chief avenues of pleasure for that couple, the partner who earns more money has more power. Don't think for one moment that power over money doesn't invade the rest of the relationship, all the way to the bedroom. On the other hand, if a high-consumption lifestyle is not the couple's main focus, then money takes on less importance, except as a means to live on and have for retirement.

What to do? Unless we want to move to that mythical village in Africa or to a desert island, we will continue to be bombarded by advertising and comparisons with the Joneses next door. We need to take a hard look at our lives and marriages and decide what is really important. If an intimate marriage is more important than having a houseful of exotic accoutrements, then we need to shift our priorities. That takes developing consciousness.

Here is how I manage my spending: I'm not the type to sit down with graphs and charts every month, so instead, I simply take my consciousness along with me as I go through my day, and especially when I go through stores. I can be in a store looking for a certain item and I'll pass by a display of cute sweaters. I'll immediately think to myself how nice it would be to have that sweater and how it will make me look good. I'll reach for the sweater and, as I do, my voice of awareness calls out and asks, "Now, Janet, would you really rather have this sweater or would you rather have freedom? You know that if you spend fifty dollars on this sweater, that's fifty dollars more that you have to work to earn, and fifty dollars less in your freedom account. So which is it?"

Usually, my freedom voice wins, but every now and then I'll buy the sweater, or whatever it is, and spend the money. Just as long as *most* of the time I'm choosing to hang on to money rather than give in to these impulse purchases, I feel I'm doing just fine. There's nothing wrong with indulging once in awhile. But I never indulge to the point of going into debt. If I don't have an extra $50 in the bank for that sweater, then I don't buy it, period.

You need the same kind of consciousness in order to begin your budgeting. Do you want to devote more energy to your personal relationships and interests, or to spending in the pursuit of happiness? You can ask yourself this question every time you are about to part with your money—especially for impulse purchases. At first, you'll feel like an addict trying to say no to drugs that you're dying to have, but after a while, it'll be very easy because you'll start to see how you really don't need all that stuff, and how your life is no less happy because you didn't buy it. In fact, your life will become better because you won't have a house full of junk, plus you'll have less debt. You'll also have time that was previously spent shopping to spend on being a better partner. That time will pay off handsomely because your partner will be happier, and you know what a happy partner means to you.

Are There Wedding Bells in Your Future? Before You Tie the Knot, Talk with Your Fiancé About Finances

❧

by Juliette Fairley

Is someone you know planning to marry soon? Do him or her a favor and advise focusing on the bottom line.

Many financial experts agree that money is the main cause of friction between married couples. In fact, about 54 percent of divorces have to do with money issues, according to Brooke Stephens, investment advisor and author of *Talking Dollars and Making Sense* (McGraw-Hill).

"The first thing you should do with your wedding money is pay off the debt incurred from funding the wedding," Stephens said. "But keep in mind what you are investing for. That's why you have to talk about goals and expectations in advance."

Marriage is stressful enough, but when you figure in the added burden of money, you have a double whammy. Newlyweds can get a smoother start in life by following these six tips to investing your wedding money.

* Talk about money ahead of time. Find a quiet time to talk about money, says Olivia Mellan, a psychotherapist who specializes in money conflict and author of *Overcoming Overspending* (Walker). "Pick a quiet time when you are not under stress," she said. "The time to talk about money is not during tax time or when you are buying the house." Mellan also advises talking about money once a month.

  Marilyn Steinmetz, a certified financial planner based in Hartford, Conn., notes that arguments arise when one spouse is a spender and the other a saver. "The couple has to come to a compromise by talking about money ahead of time," she said. "The spender has to work out the reasons he or she is spending."
* Settle on mutual goals. Mellan says each spouse in the marriage should write out short- and long-term goals. "You see which goals come up in common and then put the two lists together for a mutual list," she said.
* Pay off debt before marriage. "I work out a budget with the individual so that he or she can pay off the debt," Steinmetz said.

Mellan says if one person is in debt, the other shouldn't be responsible for helping to pay it.

"That debt should be kept separate and should be the responsibility of the person who incurred it, unless the other person is willing to help them pay it off," she said. "But it shouldn't be expected of them."

❖ Ask wedding guests to give cash gifts. Whatever money you get from the wedding, put it in a money market account. That way it can start accruing interest right away, says Sheldon Cohen, senior partner at Cohen & Goldstein, a law firm that specializes in matrimonial law in Manhattan.

Later, you can shift into a stock fund money set aside for long-term goals, such as purchasing a house, a future child's education or your own retirement.

Cohen also advises keeping a written record of what money was received in case the IRS inquires.

"Keep the guest list so that if there's an audit you can show where the money came from," he said. "Also, set up an appointment with your attorney and accountant so that you can find out what tax bracket you are in."

❖ Determine the vehicles you will invest in. Start by figuring out what each person's risk tolerance is, Mellan says. "A lot of men tend to be risk takers and women tend to be risk adverse, so they need to find a middle ground," she said.

Steinmetz says the first thing a couple should do is set up a money market account so that they can save money for their short-term goals.

"In most couples, one person takes the initiative with investing," she said. "It's 50–50 between men and women. Some men are too busy so the woman takes over with investments. In other cases, the woman wants no part of it and the man is interested. I see both scenarios equally. Ideally, you want to do it together."

❖ Don't merge all of your money too soon. Mellan says merging money all at once is a big mistake. Most newlyweds face broad-based intimacy fears and merging assets right away could add to stress in this area.

"It's crazy to put things together right away. You want to merge slowly over time," she said. "Set up a joint account and based on your income and assets each person contributes a certain amount. But have your own personal accounts on the side."

—From *Investor's Business Daily*

Beyond shopping consciously, what can you do if you are in debt? Never fear, there is hope. Rush thee either to your kitchen table with pad and pencil to come up with a plan, or to the phone to make an appointment with a free credit-counseling service. The bottom line is, get out of debt and do it quickly! If you don't think that's possible, read the story at the end of this section about a couple who started their marriage with the wife-to-be $11,000 in debt. Together, they created a plan to rid themselves of that debt in one year, earning minimal salaries.

There are three basic concepts that you and your partner need to follow if you want to get your finances under control, rather than having them control you:

1. **Spend less than you earn.** If you're not disciplined, you'll need to get rid of your credit card(s) in order to do this. If you don't want to get rid of them permanently, then put them in a Ziploc bag full of water and put the bag in the freezer. By the time the bag thaws, the urge to splurge should have passed. If you don't have a credit card handy, you'll have to live within your means. Whatever it is that you earn, just make sure you spend less. Did you know there is a book titled *The Millionaire Next Door*? One of the ways regular people with regular jobs become millionaires is by spending less than they earn. If you've created a lifestyle that requires you to spend more than you earn, then sit down together and come up with a serious plan to get yourselves under control.

Living a life that is purchased by debt is simply living a borrowed life, and a very shaky borrowed life at that. Whom are you trying to impress? How does this impact your marriage? What does this say about how authentic you are? What kind of a skating-over-the-surface life is this, anyway? You're living for show, not for intimacy. So cut back wherever you need to in order to live not *within,* but *under,* your means. Then you can save the rest. Believe me, you'll sleep much better knowing you have something to fall back on. Can you imagine what a good, peaceful night's sleep will do for your marriage?

2. Save your raise. Here's another trick the millionaires and other good money managers use. If you managed to live on your lower income before, why is it you all of a sudden feel the need to live on the higher amount now? The "I deserve to reward myself" rationale is the best way I know of to stay permanently on the treadmill. You earn more, so you spend more, so you have to earn more, and so on. Bank the extra money, and use every cent of it to pay off your debt quickly, or at the very least, bank half the raise and spend the rest. Whatever you do, stay conscious and watch that voice that thinks you need to reward yourself with better clothes, better cars, better paraphernalia, just because you got a raise. All you're doing is digging your own debt-ridden hole, and that does nothing positive for a marriage.

3. Pay yourself first. Trick number three is that immediately upon getting your paycheck, take a specified amount out and put it into a savings account or investment for yourself. If you don't, you'll surely spend it all because you're a human being living in a seductive consumer society that wants your money. Decide now to save at least ten percent of your earnings and do it religiously every time you get paid. Period. No questions asked. Don't miss your payment for any reason. There are thousands of ways to hang on to your money, ranging from holding off on going out to lunch every day, to shopping at consignment stores when you really need something, to fixing things instead of buying new ones, and so on. Many frugality books spell out in detail how to save money on everything imaginable. There is no excuse not to be able to pay yourself first, unless you are in debt. In that case, pay off your debt as quickly as possible, and then begin your program. With no debt, you'll be free to create a meaningful life for yourself, rather than one dictated by monthly payments to creditors.

WHEN ONE SAVES AND THE OTHER DOESN'T

What if you are a saver and your partner never heard of the concept? There's still hope. Since simplicity is not about being divisive, there are ways to work together in an open, loving way.

The best way to begin merging ideas is to sit down together and clarify your values as a couple. What do you want from life? Get out of the typical day-to-day mindset that focuses on the immediate, such as whether to buy a new car or house, or whether to paint the bathroom yellow or green, and so on. Move your imagination into the big picture and develop a couple vision. Once you have that vision, it will be much, much easier to proceed with a financial plan together because you're both going in the same direction. It only takes one person to start the vision rolling.

It Only Takes One to Change

✧ Andrew and Sally MacGregor were busy leading their traditional lives with two different money styles, until Sally was inspired to live more consciously. Andrew says: "Sally was the one who first became interested in the concept of voluntary simplicity. She read the book *Your Money or Your Life* (about managing money according to your values) while I attended a weekend conference. When I returned, she was excited about becoming Financially Independent (FI). I had no idea what she was talking about. She was frustrated that I couldn't share her enthusiasm. My hesitation about this concept grew from my fear that this type of lifestyle would not allow me to have the material things that I wanted. Once I read the book, we could talk about the principles behind FI. This led us to further reading about how to simplify our lives. We now are united in the pursuit of a simpler, more sustainable life."

A Common Vision

"Sally still tends to be a saver and I tend to be a spender. However, we are now closer in the way in which we approach money. This is due to our practice of voluntary simplicity. Our shared vision provides a way in which to evaluate purchases, savings, and long-term financial goals."

Sally and Andrew also took a big step and moved out of a big city to a small town, in order to further their goal of living a more simple life. They didn't want the stress of both having to earn a high income and realized it would be difficult to reach their goals if they stayed in the city. They knew that buying a house would be next to impossible and if they did, they would both have to work to support the mortgage. When they had children, they'd need day care rather than having one parent staying home.

Once the MacGregors settled on a community, it took a year for both to find jobs. Then they bought a house. Andrew says: "This move was in great part due to our shared vision. We are convinced that this will lead us confidently in the direction of our dreams."

✧ Lorraine and Jeff Murray were able to change their lifestyles because of creating a common goal. Lorraine says: "When we were first married, we were fairly 'laissez faire' about money and explored life in the fast lane. It wasn't until we read simplicity books that we began to have a financial direction. We looked at our 'big picture' goals related to our values and life purpose, and got the sense that we might not have to work nine to five until we were sixty-five, *if* we were willing to make significant changes. Just six years later we met one big goal: I quit my high-stress, fifty-hour-a-week job (thirty miles from home!) and am able to work part-time at home as a freelancer.

"In six years, we were totally out of debt and don't even have mortgage payments, plus we have saved considerable money. We get a lot of joy from life's many 'freebies,' like a beautiful moon rising or the sun setting, a home-cooked meal, our hobbies, getting together with friends, singing in the choir. I'd say that our common goal of living simply and getting out of debt has contributed tremendously to our relationship because we've de-

Unimagined Wealth

ꙮ

by Lorraine Murray

There are two ways to get enough: one is to accumulate more and more. The other is to desire less.
— G. K. CHESTERTON

He who knows he has enough is rich.
— TAO TE CHING

Too often, the word frugal suggests "selfish," as images of Scrooge pop to mind. But as my husband and I have mastered the fine art of penny pinching, we've found the opposite to be true: A frugal lifestyle can set the stage for community service.

When we first married, Jef and I relished dining out, trendy clothes and seaside jaunts. Having abandoned our childhood faiths years before, we gave little thought to community service. Instead, we were consumers par excellence, earning money to spend it.

Then we had two wake-up calls. First, a friend handed us a copy of *Your Money or Your Life*, a provocative book by Vicki Robin and Joe Dominguez. Gradually, as we recognized the emotions that prompted our splurges, we began freeing ourselves from the "earn to spend" cycle.

veloped goals as a couple, rather than as individuals. For example, we share the goal of not having to work full-time until the accepted retirement age. We want to spend more time helping those in need in our community."

❖ Once there is a common vision, it is easier for couples to be more accepting of spending differences. Keith Mesecher and Marge Wurgel say that in their daily lives, they are both on the same financial path. Because of that common value, if one has a passionate desire to purchase something or put money toward an endeavor that would help bring great satisfaction, they support the other in spending the money. Marge says: "As an example, Keith loves to sing and make music, so he is spending money on converting the garage into a music studio. In our daily lives we spend rather similarly, and both are working to increase our nest egg for financial

But the book also prompted us to discover what things in life really mattered to us. What would we do if we had only a year left to live?

The second call came quickly on the heels of the first. Returning from a business trip to New York, Jef mentioned he'd visited St. Patrick's Cathedral and lit candles in memory of his dad and my parents, who'd died years ago. I felt stricken. A keynote of the Catholic faith in which I'd been raised is to pray for the living and the dead. I'd failed on both scores.

Once the spark of our faith was reignited, we began attending Mass at a nearby church. Sunday after Sunday we were surprised at the many warnings in the scriptures about centering our lives on the pursuit of riches.

One Sunday we met four nuns sent by Mother Teresa to open an Atlanta home for poor women with AIDS. When we began helping them renovate a house, we saw firsthand how a frugal lifestyle can nurture one's desire to serve others. The sisters, who live very simply, don't waste precious time and energy desiring and acquiring the trappings of middle-class life. Instead, their time is spent joyfully helping the poorest of the poor.

Today we continue to shift our focus away from materialism. We've started a voluntary simplicity study group at our church to help others create lives more in tune with their values. The extra time we've gleaned from breaking our addictions to shopping and keeping up with the Joneses has helped us get involved in other ministries as well.

We've learned you can't serve two masters. Ceasing to worship at the altar of consumerism, we've discovered a world of riches more precious than ever imagined.

independence. We believe that our similarities about money have made our lives together easier, and we feel equally committed to seeing that the other gets what he/she needs."

✧ Another couple came up with a compromise and enlisted the help of an investment advisor. The wife says: "My husband likes to buy expensive cars every year. While we can afford it, it seems like a total waste of money to me. He still gets his car, but I get money to invest every month. It's our way of evening things out. It's just one of those things where we will never agree. I figure that we are still two different individuals, and even though we are married, we are not joined at the hip. I spend what a lot of people might think is a crazy amount of money on books. But my husband just shakes his head. So I guess that we just try to accept each other as we are."

They have a financial advisor who helps them with investments, and say that's where most of their disposable income goes. The wife says: "I realize how fortunate we are to be financially secure, but we could spend everything we earn if we weren't disciplined . . . lots of people do. We never carry credit card balances. I know a lot of people think that if you make a lot of money it is easier to be debt free, and it probably is. But people who earn a lot of money just tend to buy more expensive stuff. Everything is relative. I see a lot of people who don't know how to live within their means."

SEX, MONEY, AND POWER

We can also work out money differences by taking a look at our money personalities. Some of us need the security of more money in the bank, while others spend to meet unmet needs. Once we both understand what motivates our money personalities, we can work together from a place of compassion and understanding, rather than anger and accusation.

Linda Barbanel is a psychotherapist who specializes in the psychology of money. She outlines the different money styles in her book, *Sex, Money & Power*. Linda says that fights appear to be over the actual money, at least on the surface, but in fact, they are about people's different money personalities.

The money styles Linda identified are *The Keepers*, who see money as something to hold on to, and to use to enhance feelings of safety and security; *The Love Buyers* who use money as a replacement for what is lacking in other aspects of their emotional lives—using money to provide a boost to self-esteem and personal reinforcement; *The Power Seekers*, who use money to control people because they feel that financial control is the same thing as control of human emotions and events; and *The Freedom Searchers*, who use money as an escape from the everyday demands of life. With enough money, Freedom Searchers believe that they can avoid being pushed around and be left entirely to their own devices.

Once a couple understands their different money styles, they can then learn to communicate about money differences in a constructive way. Here are a few guidelines you can use to settle money disputes:

Together, a couple can try to:

1. Identify and discuss their differences.
2. Identify the things they both agree on.
3. Strategize ways to attain common goals.

To establish a calm and productive atmosphere for a discussion, agree ahead of time that it's in both partners' interests to resolve the differences. Here are some ground rules to follow:

1. Only one person may talk at a time.
2. No interrupting or ridiculing.
3. No attacking.
4. No yelling.
5. Each partner should make an effort not to criticize or maintain a negative, close-minded attitude.

❧ *Debt-Free in One Year* ❧

by Pat Lunneborg
(reprinted from the *Simple Living* journal)

How did they do it? How did Christine and Jeff Dobson in their first year of married life get rid of $11,000 credit card debt and $8,000 car payments, working as a Starbucks barista and a fund-raiser for an opera company?

Christine and Jeff Dobson got rid of an $11,000 credit card debt and $8,000 car payments in one year. "I think the key to the whole thing is talking about it, putting it out in the open," Jeff says of their financial difficulties.

Christine, thirty-one, and Jeff, thirty-three, met in 1991 when both were in college and majoring in theater. Over the years, they dated, broke up, dated some more, and married in September 1996. They had only one problem: Christine's financial situation.

Christine says: "I went to college with a credit card in my hand and proceeded to use it for four years. My parents paid it during that time but made it clear that, after graduation, that card was mine. Very quickly I had eleven thousand dollars on it with nineteen percent interest. Sometimes I didn't even make the minimum monthly payment, which was less than one hundred dollars. The credit card company would call me at work, and it got ridiculous. I did consumer credit counseling for a while, and they spoke on my behalf and said I could make the minimum payments. When we got engaged, Jeff knew what I was going through."

Jeff responds: "Right before we got married I took a two-week cross-country driving trip to Moab, Utah, and brought along the book *Your Money or Your Life*. Christine's mom had given it to her for Christmas years ago and it was still sitting on the shelf, unread. I read that and also *You Can Be Financially Free* by George Fooshee. His book is about getting out of debt, and it has charts showing that if you have this much debt, say ten thousand dollars, at a certain interest rate, and you were to pay it off in four years, this is how much you'd have to pay every month. Let's say four hundred dollars a month. His idea was you figure out what you think you can do and then cut it in half. So we're looking at two years of paying around eight hundred dollars. I took it one step further and said, 'Why don't we do it in one year?' So we tore up the credit card and were prepared to pay one thousand dollars a month. I paid off my credit card balance, which was about one thousand dollars before we married."

"One of the reasons I married Jeff is because he is very creative, he's always coming up with great ideas, sometimes wacky ideas, but this one definitely wasn't wacky," Christine says. "We knew we had a big chunk of change to pay off and I agreed we should get rid of it as fast as possible. We made this huge chart and hung it on the wall like it says to do in the book."

Jeff says: "I think the key to the whole thing is talking about it, putting it out in the open. It bordered on obsession and it was all we were thinking about. She was making twenty-five thousand dollars and I was making fifteen thousand dollars. There had to be a way to make it work. I talked to everybody about what we were trying to do, even the customers where I work. As a result, one of my customers who had to leave the country suddenly because of a family illness offered us his house free for ten months. We stored some of our stuff in his garage and some at Christine's mom's. The owner paid all the bills."

They saved on food by eating sandwiches and buying in bulk. Jeff says: "It was perfect timing. Starbucks introduced sandwiches at my store but it wasn't going over very well, so we had to throw them away at the end of the night. I brought them home and we lived on five different types of sandwiches."

As for transportation savings, Jeff explains: "Christine's brother was driving a 1970 Honda Civic, so we gave him the car we were paying on and took his little Honda. After that, he was making the car payments."

They get their clothes at exchange and trading places, and Christine also trades with her friends. Both employers provide health insurance.

Christine says: "We started economizing with our wedding. Ours cost no more than six thousand dollars and no one put out more than a thousand—my mom, my dad, Jeff's parents, ourselves. I bought my gown off the rack for five hundred dollars. Instead of gifts our friends brought food to the reception that we held at my mom's. A friend brought the wedding cake, another did the pictures. Our honeymoon was a camping trip."

Their gift-giving habits also changed. Jeff says, "We try not to give gifts, and stopped doing Christmas. We just went to a wedding of some good friends and rather than give them a gift, I videotaped their wedding."

As for savings, Christine explains: "We worked so hard to get out of debt that we're rewarding ourselves a little right now and haven't started saving yet. I'm not going to beat myself up because we bought a few things that we can enjoy. I'm starting a new job in September and I'll be making thirty-five thousand dolllars, so one way to save would be to pretend I'm not making that additional ten thousand dollars."

Jeff adds: "We do have money in mutual funds and stocks. Through Starbucks I have seven thousand dollars in 401(k)s and fifteen thousand dollars in stock shares. In another year I'll be fully vested and after five years that amounts to a good amount of money through my job. Whenever we have a big ticket item, we save for it and buy it on sale. For example, we wanted a computer so we studied them until we knew what we wanted, then we waited for nine months and picked it up for cheap at an after-Christmas sale."

"We're also saving money by living in a very small apartment that's filled with furniture we're holding for our friends. All our furniture is borrowed."

෨ ෨ ෨

Resources

The Average Family's Guide to Financial Freedom, by Bill Toohey and Mary Toohey (New York: Wiley, 2000).

Getting a Life: Real Lives Transformed by Your Money or Your Life, by Jacqueline Blix and David Heitmiller (New York: Viking, 1997).

Invest in Yourself: Six Secrets to a Rich Life, by Marc Eisenson, Gerri Detweiler, and Nancy Castleman (New York: Wiley, 1998).

The Millionaire Next Door: The Surprising Secrets of America's Wealthy, by Thomas J. Stanley, Ph.D., and William D. Danko, Ph.D. (Atlanta: Longstreet Press, 1996).

The Mindful Money Guide: Creating Harmony Between Your Values and Your Finances, by Marshall Glickman (New York: Ballantine, 1999).

The Poverty of Affluence: A Psychological Portrait of the American Way of Life, by Paul Wachtel (Philadelphia: New Society Publishers, 1989).

The Secret Meaning of Money: How to Prevent Financial Problems from Destroying Our Most Intimate Relationships, by Cloé Madanes (San Francisco: Jossey-Bass Publishers, 1998).

Sex, Money and Power: Smart Ways to Resolve Money Conflicts and Keep Them from Sabotaging Your Closest Relationships, by Linda Barbanel, M.S.W., C.S.W. (IDG Books Worldwide, 1996).

Shattering the Two-Income Myth: Daily Secrets for Living Well on One Income, by Andy Dappen (Montlake Terrace, Wash.: Brier Books, 1997).

The Simple Living Guide, by Janet Luhrs (New York: Broadway Books, 1997).

Slash Your Debt, Save Money and Secure Your Future, by Gerri Detweiler, Marc Eisenson, and Nancy Castleman (Kalamazoo, Mich.: Financial Literacy Center, 1999).

Your Money or Your Life: Transforming Your Relationship with Money and Achieving Financial Independence, by Joe Dominguez and Vicki Robin (New York: Penguin, 1992).

Chapter *10*

Simple Ways to Stay Connected When There Are Children

*Life belongs to the living, and he who lives
must be prepared for changes.*
—JOHANN WOLFGANG VON GOETHE

When I first had children, I came across a most moving saying. It was written for men, but applies equally to women. It said: *"The best thing a father can do for his children is to love their mother."* For women we could say: *"The best thing a mother can do for her children is to love their father."*

Amen. Amen. Amen. So many of us don't see it this way. We think the best way to love our children is by loving and caring for them directly, which is true, but we stop there. By the time we've loved our children, gone to work, and finished our housework, we are often left with little time or energy for our partners. Yet in so doing, we are doing a disservice to ourselves and our children: we are not providing the kind of role model our children need, and we are not cherishing and nurturing our partners in the way they need.

What better role model could we possibly give our children than letting them see the two people they love most loving each other? This is love in action, and this is the imprinting that they will take with them into their own marriages. Ron White, profiled on page 227, has been devoted to his wife, Mary, for over twenty-five years. He said simply: "I learned that from my dad, who adored my mother . . . it was obvious."

Loving, cherishing, and respecting each other ought to be the foundation of any relationship, and especially relationships with children. That foundation sets the tone for your entire life together, and also provides a legacy for your children to pass on to their children. What a better world we'd be living in if all of us were raised in households with parents who adored each other, and acted on it.

When there are children, everyone is stretched thin with added chores and responsibilities, whether both work outside the home or one is the parent at home and the other works elsewhere. Respect and love, then, are shown in the minutiae of everyday living: helping with chores, chauffeuring children, and running errands. I've heard too many parents, particularly women, bemoan the fact that their partners are not taking enough responsibility for either raising the children or sharing the household chores. The frequent complaint is that they feel invisible around the house—as if they were no more than maid, nanny, or cook. This kind of neglect is hardly conducive to love, romance, or good role modeling.

For those who think that the quantity of work they perform around the house has little impact on their romantic lives, think again. I came across a very interesting questionnaire about housework. We've all read the research that says women today still do the majority of housework. Let's assume that is true. Perhaps those who are not doing the housework have little incentive for doing their share? After all, if I could get out of doing housework, I would too. But this interesting little study certainly provides a wake-up call as to the benefits of doing an equal share of housework. It was conducted by marriage counselor Sharyn Wolf, C.S.W. She calls it "For Men Only: A Sexual/Housework History." It goes like this:

When we first met, we had sex __ times a week.

The last time I scrubbed the toilet was __.

When we began living together we had sex __ times a week.

I have purchased __ cans of Pledge in the past two years.

I would like to have sex __ times a week.

Rotten food is regularly removed from the refrigerator by __.

After we lived together for a year, we had sex __ times a week.

The last time I removed and washed the microwave tray was __.

In the past three months we have had sex __ times a week.

I shake the toaster crumbs out __ times per week.

Sex is initiated by me __ times a week—by my partner __ a week.

Tile fungus generally builds up for __ weeks before I notice it.

Sharyn concludes: "The biggest turn-on might not be a lacy negligee you bought her but you changing the sheets, making the bed, fluffing the pillows, and inviting her to join you under the quilt which you recently washed. A tray which you've placed next to the bed might contain a sprig of flowers, a bottle of mineral water for dehydration, a snack just in case you're there longer than you thought—all those things can only add to her pleasure."

A friend told me that when he was in his late twenties, a marriage counselor once asked his wife if she ever loved him. He understands her answer now, although he didn't comprehend it at the time. His wife said she loved him when he cleaned out the sink. "I was furious," he says, "but I think I get it now. When there are children to care for, love is more than hugs, kisses, back rubs, and sex after the kids go to bed. In a relationship, sometimes a big part of love is in recognizing and caring about the details. It's calling before you leave from work to see if your partner needs anything else picked up from the grocery store for dinner. If it's not your night to cook, love is in clearing, dishwashing, wiping the counters, sweeping the floor. And yes, cleaning the garbage out of the sink."

Sometimes couples share the chores on paper, but not in reality. A wife described the problem: "He has his assigned tasks and I have mine. We

DOES BLAME WORK?

by Sharyn Wolf

It's easy to get caught in a contest of who failed whom because, if it's not your fault, you don't have to do anything. You can sit back, yell, "Fix it, fix it" like a child, and wait for your partner to come through. You can blurt out the sorry situation to others and obtain great sympathy. Take this test to see if blame has worked to solve any of your problems:

T   F   When I tell my partner that something is her fault, she is appreciative that I noticed.

T   F   In our relationship, the one who is blamed takes immediate action on this information, and fixes the problem. Things improve.

T   F   My partner and I generally agree on who should take the blame.

T   F   Knowing who to blame has filled our relationship with funny stories to tell.

T   F   The more we blame, the closer we get. Our relationship has deepened with blame.

Blame, rather than a way of disengaging ourselves from the problem, is a way of saying: I'm a failure. I can't conceive of any contribution I could make to working this out. I'm not capable. I am incapable because of you.

Yes, nothing frustrates us more than someone who doesn't take responsibility for his behavior, but blaming him won't get him to change that. Rest assured! Blaming will not lead to his one day slapping his forehead with his hand, accepting your point of view, and saying, "What an idiot I've been. You're right. Of course, it's my fault."

have agreed to do them on a weekly basis. However, despite all of our efforts to talk about it, he continues to perform his chores when he chooses to, and sometimes not at all. That leaves me feeling very disrespected, because I want to be able to rely on the agreements we make together, and also not get left with the bulk of the household chores. When he does that I am not inspired to be loving towards him."

Love is also shown in the way the parents support each other as human beings. One couple divides not only the household and parenting chores but also the week so each one has a night off, free of responsibilities. Another night is reserved for the two of them to be together, *sans* children.

The idea that a marriage is a third entity in need of nurturing applies equally to marriages with children. When that third entity is not part of the couple's framework, daily life can become an endless power struggle. One wife remembers: "We sometimes invited guests to our house on Friday nights, but to my embarrassment, my husband would often arrive late, just in time to sit down for the meal. Then, without discussing it beforehand with me, he would leave right after dinner and go to the movies or out for a night with his friends. Where was the love in our family picture? Where was the modeling of respect and regard?"

When that third entity is present, however, the marriage and family can become a beautiful dance of love and respect. That entity provides a framework from which to make decisions. Before accepting a social invitation that would impact your family time, first check in with your partner. Even if it is your partner's turn to cook but she has a project to finish, you jump in and cook. The third entity goes beyond divvying up the chores 50/50—rather, it makes decisions based on what is best for your family and your partner at any given time.

I liked what one dad had to say about this. He admitted he was a workaholic, yet still kept his family a priority. This man loves his work and owns his own business, and he also loves his wife and family. He said he looks at life like a pie. There is only so much to go around. So he divided his pie in half—into work and family. That was it. If he tried to throw anything else in there—like playing poker with his buddies or taking up a new

Team Safer

The Family That Works Together Thrives Together

∽

by Marilyn Meyer

I met the Safer family a couple of years ago at a friend's Friday night Sabbath dinner. There were about twelve of us gathered around an extended oak table. We lit the candles, welcomed the ministering angels who would guard our homes in peace, placed our hands on our children's heads, and blessed them in the tradition of our ancestors. My daughters and I were ready to complete the familiar ceremony and eat, when I overheard an untraditional question from the father, Alan Safer.

"Martin and Emily, what was something special that Mommy did for you this week?"

Emily, aged eight, answered first. "She drove the car pool twice and bought me a new Boxcar Children book."

Martin, who was only five, needed a bit of prodding. He finally recalled that she stayed home with him when he was sick and baked his favorite cookies.

I've since witnessed this ritual numerous times. Always it begins with the children's praises, followed by a few thank you's from Alan. These are not heroic deeds; it's in praising the ordinary that he models his love for his wife: cooking more than her share, taking the car in to be repaired, selecting just the right movie for their Saturday night video.

The Safer family views themselves as a team working together, "the Safer team." Decisions

sport or hobby—he'd throw the pie off, and the two things he loved most would suffer. He was not willing to compromise either one.

REMEMBER SIMPLE PLEASURES

Once the foundation is set for a respectful, loving marriage, there are many ways to nurture romance that require little time or money.

One couple I know, briefly mentioned in the introduction, works very do not have to be absolutely "fair" and there's no keeping score. "It's team Safer; the important thing is that as a family unit, we have to work together as a team." Decisions are made by consensus, based on not merely what's equitable and fair, but also on the unconditional regard Alan and Laurie feel for one another. As parents they have a united front when it comes to making any major and even most minor parenting decisions. "Let me talk to your mother (father)," is the usual response to requests. Both firmly believe that the most important factors are providing love and predictability for their children.

An example of this is when either of the children is sick and needs a parent in the middle of the night for comfort. It is Alan who gets up with them. He knows and understands that Laurie does not easily fall back to sleep. She'd be up for hours and exhausted the next day. "Besides," he adds, "I'm a cuddler; I like cuddling my kids when they feel sick."

For the five years prior to the birth of Emily and Martin, Alan and Laurie carpooled together to their jobs downtown where they shared offices in the same suite. After work they'd stop for dinner, and perhaps share a movie. On the way home they'd catch up on chatter.

After Emily and Martin were born, the Safers located a child-care center near their office, so they could drop their children off together, have lunch with them whenever possible, and drive home together as well.

"Having children added a level of stress to our lives but not to our relationship," Alan says.

From the beginning the bottom line was forming a "we," finding peace and showing love. The first one home cooks and the remaining parent cleans up. However, if Laurie comes home exhausted, Alan takes over, no questions asked and vice versa. Love is in both perceiving each other's needs and asking for what you want.

hard on their organic farm. Both people work from sunset to sundown, all while raising three young children. Their incredibly intense lifestyle would provide an easy excuse not to take time to nurture each other, but they take whatever time they have and use it to their advantage. One ritual is this: Every night after they put their children to bed, they sit together and he brushes her long hair while she reads to him. How romantic, and how simple! This small act of devotion does a lot to keep them connected in a loving way. The busier the couple, the more important it is to take even a few minutes out of the day to relate like this. A little ingenuity can go a long way toward keeping love vital and alive.

Whether you have limited time due to children, a busy career, or any other reason, don't let that stop you from being romantic. There is no excuse! Here are some ideas that I've gleaned from various books and conversations. Use them to jump-start your own imagination.

- One husband, stuck in yet another traffic tie-up on his way home from work, reached into his glove compartment to take out a cassette and found a tape with a bow on it. His wife had taped a selection of his favorite songs, introducing them like a DJ, but with personal comments, and a dedication "to the one I love."
- A wife returned home, exhausted after a grueling business trip. She dropped her luggage in the hall and closed the front door. She was greeted with a big, warm bear hug. Her husband sat her down, took off her shoes, and made her a cup of tea to revive her while he finished making dinner.
- Don't forget simple love notes. Use anything from Post-It notes to the backs of envelopes and handmade cards. Leave notes everywhere—in a shirt or jacket pocket to be discovered during the day, on the coffeepot, in a briefcase.
- Send flowers to your partner's place of work for no reason (and if one works at home raising children, send them there). Find a single gardenia or flower from your garden, put it in a nice bowl of water, and leave it on your partner's bedside table to be discovered in the evening or morning. Bring a surprise breakfast to your partner and don't forget to put a little flower in a cup.
- I heard of one wife who took advantage of a thunderstorm and hauled out a multitude of candles. She lit them around the room, then got out the book *Dracula* and began reading in an ominous voice. You don't have *Dracula* lying around? Find something! What a way to turn the mundane into something special.
- Don't forget bathtime. Without asking, pour your partner a nice, warm bubble bath after a long day at work. Set candles around the room. Have ready a thick towel and invite him or her in for a personal bath.

✧ If you like to lie in bed and read at night, take advantage of the situation once in a while and put aside your novel. Pick up something racy or a tender poem and read it out loud. Even if you don't want to read poetry or racy books, it's still romantic to read anything out loud together.

✧ Here's a more elaborate idea that requires making sure the children are fast asleep: One woman wanted to give her partner a special Christmas surprise, so she went to bed first, knowing her husband would be along shortly. She got a string of small Christmas lights, plugged them in next to her bed, climbed in with no clothes on and wrapped herself with the lights, then covered herself with the blankets. When he came in, everything looked like bedtime-as-usual until he pulled away the covers to hop in! What a surprise to find his very own personal Christmas tree waiting for him!

✧ I met one couple, now retired in their 70s, who has fond memories of the year they took their four children out of school and went on a round-the-world trip together. I asked them how they managed to keep their romance alive that year, what with everyone crammed into tents and hotel rooms. They still smile when they talk about it. Every time it was at all possible, after the kids were well asleep, they'd sneak out a window or door and go off together somewhere close by. It was only recently that they told their now-grown children about this, and none of them had suspected a thing!

✧ One couple keeps a blank book on a bedside table. When either one has to be gone, say on a business trip, they always leave a message of love for the other person inside the book. The collection of messages provides a heartfelt reflection on a slice of this couple's life together.

If you need more ideas on how to keep your love alive without ever leaving the house, there are plenty of books listed in the resource section

The Need to Give and Receive Affection

 ∽

by Lloyd J. Thomas, Ph.D.

As a culture, we have sexualized the expression of physical affection. We have made physical touch a taboo. We have robbed our children of the critical benefits of affectionate touch. We have declared physical touch as a sexual advance, and thereby categorized it as "harassment" or "abuse." And we wonder why people don't feel loved, don't feel safe, and may not even feel alive. It is very sad, bordering on tragic.

We need to make a clear distinction between physical contact that is nurturing and that which is sexual. That distinction is critical to the emotional health of each of us. We need affection. We need sexual contact. But they are two different needs. We can never have enough sex to satisfy our need for affection. We can never have enough affection to satisfy our need for sex. Indeed, most extramarital affairs occur not so much out of a need for sex, but out of an unmet need for nurturing affection.

The ability to give and receive physical affection is a very powerful, non-verbal means for communicating safety, caring and love. It is an extremely important skill which enhances and strengthens the bond between parent and child, between couples and between friends. Warm, gentle, and nurturing physical contact alters our biochemistry. It strengthens our immune system. It increases our sense of well being, our sense of security, and allows us to trust ourselves, and the environment in which we live. It is almost always experienced as pleasurable.

Some children are born with a high sensitivity and reactivity to touch. They may experience caresses as overwhelming or painful. They become what is called "tactually defensive." They may respond to physical affection with withdrawal, hyperactivity, crying or avoidance. However, this genetic condition is extremely rare. It can be overcome by continued, but infrequent, touch, accompanied by soft soothing sounds and pleasant sights.

of this chapter. And for those who would like to leave the house for a regular date, do not use the excuse that you don't have the money to pay for a sitter. I know many, many couples who trade sitting with friends. One cou-

The most common reason for people's difficulty in expressing affection is that they have never witnessed such affectionate exchange between their parents, or have never received such touching as a child. Children learn what they see or experience. If Mom and Dad never hug, kiss, caress, hold hands, sit close to one another, snuggle with each other or "play footsies" in front of their children, then their children grow up ignorant of such behavior and sometimes even frightened of it. The same affectionate void occurs when children themselves never receive such activity.

Another reason adults have difficulty expressing affection is that it is linked with "pain forthcoming," or associated with loss. If I greet a child with words of delight, but pinch his cheek at the same time, he will equate my touch with mild, but noxious, pain. Certainly, when the only physical contact between a parent and child is painful and abusive, children become frightened of all kinds of physical contact. The grown-up version of this association is a fear of vulnerability. Adults believe that if they open themselves up to receiving affection, they are always opening up to being hurt again. In similar fashion, if I hug and kiss my children only before I leave for work, they will learn to equate the demonstration of affection with loss of contact.

Finally, there is the issue of what affectionate expression is gender appropriate. It is not generally accepted in our culture for men to express vulnerable, soft, warm, tender emotions . . . especially to another man. It is not considered "manly" for them to cry or demonstrate a weakness. The warm, nurturing expression of physical affection has been culturally defined as feminine . . . the role of the woman. This is very unhealthy for both men and women. Under this belief, we rob ourselves of a very enriching, if not vital, aspect of psychological and relational health.

If you learn to freely and comfortably express your affection as well as be open and receptive to it from others, the quality and nature of your life will be highly enriched. You may even remain physically, mentally and emotionally healthier. As a culture, let's start giving ourselves permission to freely express our affection for one another in a non-sexual but nurturing manner.

Lloyd J. Thomas, Ph.D. is a corporate, personal, and professional life coach and licensed psychologist. For information, contact Dr. Thomas at (970) 568-0173 or DrLloyd@CreatingLeaders.com.

ple does this every Friday night, and has continued the tradition for over twelve years. One Friday night their friend's two children spend the night at their house, and the other Friday night their kids spend the night at the other house. The kids have a great time and so do the parents. Start asking the parents of your children's friends if they are interested in this kind of arrangement. You don't need to start out with overnights—even two hours would be a great beginning. Parents rarely turn down an offer for a free night out.

Another group of parents, all with limited funds, started a baby-sitting co-op more than fifteen years ago in order to give one another a break from child rearing once in a while. Then the group evolved into a weekly potluck and socializing group. Start one of these groups the same way—by asking. Never let it be said again that you don't have time for romance!

The romantic ideas, of course, are the icing you put on an already tasty cake. If the foundation of your marriage is shaky, you need to get that in order first. How can you even think of brushing your wife's hair if you're full of resentment? Why would you want to make a tape of romantic music for your partner when you're angry that he's not pulling his weight in the family department?

TALK ABOUT IT!

The Simple Loving answer is: Learn the communication skills in chapter 8 and talk to each other about whatever is going on. Remember, no attacking, no put-downs, no sarcasm while the other person is talking, no matter how much you disagree. Listen to each other with an open heart until each of you is finished. Daphne Rose Kingma said it well: "Negotiating the mundane means that you accept the dish pans and trash cans of life and decide together how chores are going to be done. Then, instead of being bones of contention, and the most significant things in life, chores can recede into the background so you can do the really important things—like discovering your destiny and making love."

Children or no children, Simple Loving means keeping your relationship in the front of your consciousness most of the time. That doesn't mean you can't or shouldn't focus on other interesting things, including your work and spiritual life, for example, but it does mean you need to remember that your relationship is an entity that needs to be fed, loved, and nurtured every single day.

❧ *Romance on a Shoestring* ❧

After Ron and Mary White had their third child, Ron went to the doctor complaining of extreme exhaustion and stress. The doctor gave him a prescription: "You and your wife need to have good quality time together. I don't care if you don't have any money or think you don't have the time. Find a way to do it."

"That's when we started having our weekly dates," Mary says. "When we first started we had zero extra money, so we'd get a family member or friend to watch the kids until the oldest one could take over. We'd do free things, like taking walks in parks, sitting on logs, sometimes buying ice cream, or taking along a picnic. We'd go to museums and places that had free days, or send the kids to my sister's house, while we made a romantic dinner. We'd put on romantic music and have candles all over the house. When we got a little more money, we'd go to matinee movies, or take a round-trip ferry ride. We still go to matinees. I don't know that we've ever gone to a full-priced movie."

The Whites have also bartered to keep their romance alive. They'd watch their friends' kids or do other favors in return for baby-sitting. In exchange for staying at a cousin's waterfront cabin, they'd offer to clean it or give them a gift. And every week Ron barters his time with a local florist to have a bouquet of flowers delivered to Mary at her work. He hasn't missed a week in seven years. "I just thought it would be nice for her to have flowers at her desk," Ron says.

Ron and Mary met when they were seventeen and sixteen, married at ages twenty-one and twenty, and recently celebrated their twenty-eighth

Ron and Mary White married young, at ages 21 and 20, and never had extra money for things like extravagant dinners. "Sometimes I'd feel sorry for myself, wishing I had things my friends had," Mary says. Then Ron would do something really special for her and "totally shatter all those superficial feelings."

anniversary. They've never had extra money, yet through ingenuity, thoughtfulness, a sense of purpose, and a fervent devotion to keeping time open for each other, they've maintained a loving, close, and respectful marriage that has survived and thrived with their three children.

"Our lifestyle has been very purposeful," Ron and Mary say. "We had family goals that we wanted to attain on a limited budget, such as the best education we could afford for our kids, and we wanted to spend as much time as possible with one another. With three children at home, we knew we had to be very creative."

Over the years, Ron's creativity has had no bounds. On the twentieth anniversary of the day they met, he arranged for a co-worker, who once earned his living as a singer, to go to Mary's office and serenade her at her lunchtime. The song was "Brown-Eyed Girl," by Van Morrison, Mary's favorite song when she was sixteen.

"I was overwhelmed," Mary says. "Sometimes I'd feel sorry for myself, wishing I had a house with a view, or things my friends had. I'd be jealous. Then something like this would happen, and it would totally shatter all of those superficial feelings. The love that extends through these kinds of things is so thoughtful and so unusual . . . especially from someone of our generation. Everybody around me kept saying what a sweet thing this was; that their husbands didn't even remember the day they got married, let alone the day they met. All day long I felt like a celebrity. It was so special."

Again, a few years later Ron wanted to do something special for an anniversary, still on a limited budget. Although he wanted to squire Mary around town in a limo, the cost was prohibitive. So he rented a Lincoln Town Car, and agreed to pay another co-worker to dress up like a chauffeur. He knew all Mary's favorite spots, wrote down the addresses, and asked the friend to drive the couple to each one of them.

Mary remembers that event, too. "Ron always picked me up from work, but usually it was from the back of the building. This time he called me at work and asked me to wait in front. I had no idea what to expect. I walked out and saw a Lincoln Town Car waiting for me, with Ron and his friend standing outside. I got in, and he handed me a teeny bottle of my favorite wine and a wineglass, and gave me a little box of chocolates and a bouquet of flowers.

"It's hard to describe my feelings . . . that someone cares about me enough to do these thoughtful things. We can't afford a lot, but these are so much more meaningful anyway because they really display true love and affection. There's so much thought behind it, like remembering the song I liked when I was sixteen, or remembering my favorite view spots in the city. It's knowing we don't have a lot of money and figuring out ways to do these things . . . that's what is so meaningful to me.

"One of the really important things that makes our relationship so good is being mindful of little things. If I'm reading the paper and casually mention a book that sounds interesting, the next day he'll go out and buy it for me. That really means a lot. Or sometimes when

"We wanted to spend as much time as possible with one another. With three children at home, we knew we had to be very creative," says Ron. Left to right: Ron, daughter Brie Ana, 20; son Sean, 26; Mary; and son Colin, 22, enjoying family "game night" together.

he works a lot of hours, I'll be really careful about keeping everything clean and organized and I'll make food ahead of time. When the kids were young I'd take them out of the house for a few hours to give him a break. I know when he's tired, and I'll do what I can to keep his stress down."

The gift of time for each other has been a big factor in keeping the Whites' relationship flourishing. It has been many years since Ron recovered from the illness that inspired their weekly dates, but Ron and Mary still go out of their way to make time for each other. Ron's workday starts and ends earlier than Mary's, so every day he comes home, prepares dinner, then leaves again to pick up Mary at her job (she takes the bus to work in the morning).

"I pick her up in order to have time alone together," Ron says. "On the way home we talk about our day . . . it keeps our connection going. When you live in a house with children, you can't always be alone, so this gives us daily 'alone' time.

"Our main focus has always been on each other, not on group activities, like golfing or joining a country club. We wanted one-on-one time. And we'd always notice when we hadn't had our date . . . during the week we'd start getting edgy. We'd even notice that edginess if we had spent the date with another couple because we didn't have that time that we needed so much."

ↄ   ↄ   ↄ

Resources

The Book of Love, Laughter & Romance: Wonderful Suggestions and Delightful Ideas for Couples Who Want to Stay Close, Have Fun and Keep the Enchantment Alive, by Barbara and Michael Jonas (San Francisco: Games Partnership, 1994).

The Couple's Comfort Book: A Creative Guide for Renewing Passion, Pleasure and Commitment, by Jennifer Louden (San Francisco: HarperSanFrancisco, 1994).

Frugal Luxuries: Simple Pleasures to Enhance Your Life and Comfort Your Soul, by Tracy McBride (New York: Bantam, 1997).

1001 Ways to Be Romantic, by Gregory J. P. Godek (Naperville, Ill.: Casablanca Press, 1995).

Sex Begins in the Kitchen—Because Love Is an All-Day Affair, by Dr. Kevin Leman (Grand Rapids, Mich.: Fleming H. Revell, 1999).

Simple Fun for Busy People—333 Free Ways to Enjoy Your Loved Ones More in the Time You Have, by Gary Krane, Ph.D. (Berkelely, Calif.: Conari Press, 1998).

10,000 Ways to Say I Love You, by Gregory Godek (Naperville, Ill.: Casablanca Press, 1998).

2002 Romantic Ideas: Special Moments You Can Share With the One You Love, by Cyndi Haynes and Dale Edwards (Holbrook, Mass.: Adams Media Corp., 1998).

Chapter *II*

Simple Loving Ceremonies

I am yours forever
And our co-equal love will make the stars laugh with joy.
—CHRISTINA WALSH

Ceremonies are a way of sharing our magic with the world. We gather with those we love to publicly acknowledge the cycles of our lives—weddings, birthdays, graduations, anniversaries, and other milestones. Ceremonies invite us to leave our mundane tasks behind and, just for that moment, revel in the joy that love has brought to us.

Ceremonies, like rituals, are a way to remind us of our roots—family members, relatives, and important people in our lives gather together and we have a panorama of who we are and where we came from. We can find comfort in these events in the midst of a quickly changing, swirling world.

We also want to make these events special and from our hearts, rather than attempting to re-create what we saw somewhere in an advertisement. These Simple Loving ceremonies, then, are not as much about the material side of an event as the deeper meaning behind it. They are an outward manifestation of our examined lives.

WEDDINGS

Simple Loving weddings are not just about creating a great party—they are the doorway to a conscious, intentional, and heart-centered life. Simple Loving weddings focus far more on the meaning of the celebration, rather than on the celebration itself. Couples who marry with this as their framework acknowledge that the wedding is important, but it is far less important than the life they are embarking on. One bride said: "Instead of a full-blown, fancy wedding, I went back to basics. This is supposed to be about me and Kevin, and it's supposed to be a celebration of our families that expresses the way Kevin and I feel about each other—and about our lifestyles."

How you conduct your wedding ceremony can be seen as a metaphor for how you conduct your life. Will your wedding be driven by outer, material values or by your own, unique, inner set of cherished beliefs? Is most of your life driven by your heart and soul, or more by an unconscious following of the dictates of other people and other institutions? If you are planning a wedding, ready to begin a new life with someone, now is the time to step back from the excitement and look deep within yourself to determine what it is you really want from your life, and your wedding. It can take courage to step out of the mainstream and create a wedding ceremony that is truly your own, but in so doing, you'll be setting the stage for your entire life and marriage.

Rev. Diana B. Dawn has performed weddings for over twenty years and says she will not marry couples who come to her focusing only on the event, or who haven't thought enough about what it really takes to make a marriage work. One of the first questions she asks couples is How many people does it take to make a marriage work? She says: "Most people say two. I say no, it's one. The only person you're accountable for and the only reactions you can be accountable for are yours.

"The reason I call my wedding ceremonies 'intentional' is because I want each person to be fully awake and conscious of that moment. I also

RELATIONSHIP AS A SPIRITUAL PATH

If love is to be a spiritual path, the question to ask is "How can I love better?" Each day, ask yourself:

1. How can I love the people in my life?
2. Am I more concerned with loving my partner, rather than seeing what I can get?
3. Is my potential partner someone who lets me love him or her?
4. Am I encouraging my partner to grow and discover her best?
5. The quality of my love is who I am throughout the day. How do I treat other people, including the clerk at the store, the bank teller, my parents, co-workers, and neighbors? That's a sign of who I am.
6. Am I too busy thinking of what I can get to focus on what I can give?
7. Do I love myself enough to take the focus off me and put it on other people?
8. Have I involved myself in so much therapy that it's time to quit the self-focus and realize I'll never be perfect and it's time to get out and love others?
9. Conversely, have I done enough inner work, which could include therapy, to enable myself to be a good partner? Do I recognize that there are cycles in life when I'll need to turn inward and when it's time to reach out?
10. Am I conscious of how I relate to others? If I'm in a bad mood, am I conscious enough to come home and say, "I just don't feel like I can be loving right now—I need to be alone for an hour" or do I come home in the same mood but unconscious, slamming the door and yelling at my partner or children?

want to know that they are marrying with the intent to spend the rest of their lives together as awake and conscious of themselves as they can possibly be."

Rev. Dawn says that a truly meaningful, intentional wedding does not

GREEN WEDDINGS

by Carol Reed-Jones

The basic principles of a green wedding are:

✧ Avoid disposable and one-time-use items, including women's hosiery with wedding bell appliqués; disposable cameras; plastic cake decorations, fans and gloves for female attendants; cheap wedding favors that guests will only throw away; specific table decorations.

✧ Check to see if you can use borrowed, rented, or secondhand items.

✧ Ask yourself: Do we really need this item?

✧ Select wedding garb that can be worn again.

✧ Use organically grown food.

✧ Reduce electricity—consider candles and "unplugged" music.

✧ Cut down on excess transportation by having the wedding near the reception.

Simplify whatever you can, wherever you can, without compromising the meaning that this day will have for you. Fewer small details to attend to will translate into more fun, more time for your guests, less stress, and less overconsumption.

need to cost a fortune. In fact, she feels that the more money a couple spends on the wedding itself, the less energy they are spending on what matters—their life together. She says: "I would love to do a study sometime on weddings that cost one hundred dollars versus those that cost twenty thousand dollars, and see how long those couples stay together. What I see in my practice is that those weddings that cost a lot involve people who have put all of their energy into the party and not on their intent.

"The value of the wedding is in your intent. If your intent is to have a glamourous photo album, then it isn't about communication, honesty, trusting each other, and growing together, because that's what the minister and the couple are affirming. You ought to be affirming your life together, yet you just put all of your money into the band, the photographer and the hors d'oeuvres."

Rev. Dawn says the value of a publicly made intent is embodied in the story of a couple who finally got married after having lived together for eighteen years. During those years, the couple had even purchased a house and raised children together. One week after they got married, they were coming home from the grocery store. The husband pulled the car over and said, "I've got to tell you this. I have to apologize for the last eighteen years. I didn't know how deeply I could be committed and love someone until now. I feel I've ripped you off of that deep sense of commitment that comes from making those vows that we just made." He had tears in his eyes when he realized that there was an incredible golden thread that had not been there for eighteen years. What was missing all those years was the intent, the commitment, the affirmation of sharing a life together. This couple hadn't made public their commitment to each other.

"When people are focusing mainly on the wedding festivities, I remind them of something," Rev. Dawn says. "The party is for a day. The relationship is your life.

"Couples must have that sense of foundation in order for me to marry them," she says. "I look for common denominators, such as whether they both feel the same about children, where they want to live, do they have similar spiritual beliefs, which can be embodied in nature, church, or philosophy. It doesn't matter whether both are of the same religion—it matters if they have the same foundation. We look at what they see in their future, and why they chose this day to get married. We look at what things are important in their lives—what thrills them—is it music, the outdoors, dancing, meditation, sports? Then we incorporate those things into the celebration."

One couple, who both loved canoeing and the outdoors, were married near the beach. They involved both their families and friends in the ceremony, even asking friends to read verses as part of the vows. They broke homemade bread with their families. At the end, they got into a canoe and paddled away. Rev. Dawn says: "These are the things that brought this couple together—canoeing, the outdoors, a sense of family. And even though they didn't practice a formal religion, the value and nurturing they had received from that as children was really crucial."

Another couple, who wanted to devote their life to working for peace, turned and faced the congregation during their ceremony, and read together the Prayer of Saint Francis. They said: "[It was] our own prayer and aspiration for a life lived together in humility, peace and sacrificial love."

A couple who valued elegant, natural simplicity were married outdoors in a public rose garden. The bride arrived with her parents, wearing a beautiful, simple dress borrowed from a friend. The groom was escorted by their two female witnesses, one of whom carried their rings in a seashell. The setting reflected their common connection with nature, and the quiet beauty of the ceremony spoke clearly of their shared value of simplicity.

These stories speak to the heart of a Simple Loving ceremony: *intentional and values based.* Whatever your values or intentions, they ought to be reflected in your ceremony. If you're not clear about your values either alone or as a couple, you can begin to crystallize them during the planning process.

Heart-Centered Weddings

An intentional wedding is created from the heart—springing from the depth of your souls, rather than just another exercise in following the dictates of a consumer-driven world. As Daphne Rose Kingma says in her book *Weddings from the Heart*, "A wedding from the heart is more about what you say, do, and feel, than what you wear or how many courses you serve at the reception dinner. It's about love and not about impressing people; it's about your love—what it means to you, where you want it to take you, and what hopes you have for it.

"This is not to say that your beautiful dress or the exquisite flowers aren't important, nor that you shouldn't have a traditional photograph of you feeding your new spouse a piece of wedding cake. What it does mean is that you will do these things only because they have meaning for you two, because they genuinely reflect what you feel, because they speak to your heart."

Robbie Fahnestock has been a minister for twelve years and says his perception about weddings has changed during that time. He says: "For years, I thought a wedding ceremony was to witness two people entering the halls of matrimony. Now I think it's about re-marrying our own self-love that we've forgotten about having in our life. For most of us, we've learned to be something other than loving human beings—we're taught that we're supposed to go to college, get a job that you may not like, look good, work out, be in competition with each other, get married. We come to a wedding and we remember. If we allow ourselves to be open we can get in touch with that loving part of ourselves at a wedding. A marriage is about 'I accept you unconditionally. I love you just the way you are and I am tickled to share my life with you.' That's about all of us, not just the two people getting married.

"One wedding in particular that I performed was really the embodiment of that. I officiated along with a Native American priest. The part that touched me was when the priest began with a Native American ceremony to help people forgive others. He said in his culture, prior to a wedding, people are asked to forgive each other so as not to bring those ill feelings into the ceremony. The wedding was a time to let go of our resentments. That set the tone, and I witnessed several people forgiving each other that day—people who hadn't talked to each other for years were talking. The intention this couple had was that this would be a heart-centered wedding, and it was. I was blessed to be a part of it."

Diane Rabin and Harv Jaffe also focused on the heart at their wedding. "I was the bride on a budget," Diane says. "My source of love and energy is people. The ambience and intimacy, and the genuine type of atmosphere is created by the people at the ceremony. They become the hall, the flowers, the music, the decorations—like a human tapestry.

"Harv and I are blessed with a lot of friends from different areas of our lives, and the common thread with all of them is the heart. When you have that heart you don't need all the pomp and ceremony."

Diane and Harv's friends came forward and offered to help with the wedding in every way possible. One friend offered the use of her house for the event. Another one volunteered to bring pastries and hors d'oeuvres. One woman offered to bake the wedding cake. Another found a dancing bride and groom for the cake topper, because Diane and Harv love to dance. Yet another friend, a teacher, asked one of her students if he'd like to play the violin at the wedding. He agreed, and brought along other musician members of his family to play the piano, cello, and harp as well. Another friend sang, and another took photos. More friends cooked for the pre- and postdinner parties. Still more friends offered to buy plants so the host's garden would be in full bloom for the July wedding.

"Our wedding was in the garden," Diane says, "and we decided to dress up. Harv wore a white dinner jacket tux, and I wore a white brocade suit. We looked like a king and queen. It was so homemade, real, and cozy for all of the people who were genuinely happy for us. The intimacy came from the kind of people attending. It was perfect. We still get compliments from people about our wedding. It really set a standard for getting married the second time around."

Time to Clarify Your Values

Rev. Sally Gadd said it was her own wedding twenty years ago that woke her up to the idea of having a conscious, values-based ceremony. She says: "When I got married I didn't even think about the vows. We just focused on the when and where. We wanted to get married at a park near my folks' house and found a local minister. I didn't even *think* to look at the vows. At one point in the ceremony the officiant said to me, 'Will you love and obey your husband?' Everyone started laughing because they knew me and knew that wasn't at all my value!

"That's why I'm so adamant that people create their own vows, because for my own wedding, it wasn't a covenant that I had agreed to or believed in. It was just something out of a book. Now, as a minister, I really encourage my wedding clients to look at what they are agreeing to as they move into this marriage together, so they can keep their agreements.

"When you get married you're presenting your spiritual beliefs to the audience. Often when couples come to see me, they haven't given a thought to their spiritual beliefs. They look at me funny when I ask the question! I open the question because it's really setting the tone for their marriage and relationship. It also sets a tone if they plan to have children—frequently they have not talked about what kind of spiritual beliefs they want to instill in their children.

"You are making a covenant with each other that you will do certain things in the marriage. One example is a man who promised during his wedding to follow his spiritual path, and has done so over the years. It has helped him to be a calm, compassionate partner.

"When people stop and think about it, they do have values, but they need to look at how to blend that together into spiritual beliefs rather than just the religion they follow—it's up to them to decide what they want to present. It's an opportunity."

"When a couple is deciding what they want to present I encourage them to stop, get still and think about what their philosophy is for their life," Rev. Gadd says. "What do they believe and how are they guided through life? How will they be guided together as a couple? This also gives them an opportunity to talk about what they believe in, and that discussion creates a value system for them as a couple. As they go on this exploration together, it's a great opportunity to look at what each believes."

QUESTIONS TO HELP CLARIFY YOUR VALUES

From *Wedding Alternatives:**

If a desire to simply display wealth is not part of your value system, think about what you do believe in. During your preparation process, ask yourselves the following questions:

*See page 262 for publishing information.

- What will embrace our ritual giving of ourselves to each other?
- What religious or spiritual symbolism conveys our belief about marriage and our joining together as a couple?
- What will bring joy and love to this time we share with our community of support?
- How can we best and most fully celebrate this spirit-filled decision that we today announce?
- What are those things that are especially important to us as a couple that we want to share with the world?
- What beliefs, ideas, or philosophy do we have in common?
- What do we want to remember most from our wedding? Is it important that we have a solemn, prayerful experience, or would we rather have a joyous, upbeat affair?
- Is music a big part of who we are as a couple? What form might that music take?
- Are there friends, support groups, or faith communities whom we want to include in the wedding celebration?
- What traditions are part of our family histories? What traditions other than our own have become important to us?

From Rev. Sally Gadd:

1. How did you meet?
2. What do you value in your relationship?
3. What is your vision for your marriage? (This forces people to think about what they want, what they believe in, and how they'll bring that together as a couple.)
4. How does your spirituality play a role in your relationship, and how will you reflect that in the ceremony?
5. Then the particulars—the theme, mood, time, etc.

"Without exception, couples always tell me that they can't write their own vows, but I always insist that they do," says Rev. Dawn. "I'll help if needed, but I've found that they always return with incredible words. I

Creating Our Marriage Contract

❧

by Peter Sugarman and Kirstie Lewis

In 1983 the two of us found ourselves deeply involved in evaluating our relationship. We had known each other for more than two years and we felt it was time to take a step of deeper commitment, but the traditional cultural form of marriage both attracted and repelled us. We had both been married and divorced previously and were not eager to re-create what we felt were the limiting characteristics of marriage. For each of us, the years since divorce had entailed a spiritual search and we had separately begun to create lifestyles that reflected what we had learned. We wanted our spiritual beliefs to be reflected in our relationship and to be very clear about specific issues, such as parenting, livelihood and sexual commitment.

Because each state has its own set of legal dictates regarding issues of marriage like ownership, individual responsibility, property rights, dissolution, etc., signing a standard marriage license would entail the arduous task of finding out just what these dictates were. To simply sign the license, thus promising to adhere to a state-sanctioned contract, without knowing all the legal implications, seemed to us irresponsible. The idea of writing our own marriage contract was a positive alternative to this dilemma.

Drawing up the contract provided a structure within which we could discuss issues related to an anticipated lifetime commitment before the issues became problems. In the process we expressed and clarified our beliefs and values, reached consensus on each issue, and were able to state our agreements. A counselor helped facilitate exploration of interpersonal issues, such as sexuality, and helped us to clarify our common values and goals. Our lawyer then helped us create the contract as a legally binding partnership agreement that superseded governmental intervention in those matters which we specified (names, relationships with others, spiritual practice, children, careers and domicile, care and use of living space, property, debts and living expenses, termination of the contract, and decision making). We included in our contract a commitment to seek counseling/mediation if we could not agree on essential issues at any time in the future.

We are pleased with the final result. It gives us a way to make a public declaration of our love and commitment that reflects our particular needs and values. The contract is also, for us, a living document. We have pledged to reread it each year, to reaffirm our unity as we continue to grow, and to make changes as we agree upon their necessity.

NOTE: If you are interested in creating a legally binding alternative marriage contract, be sure to contact an attorney.

suggest to them, 'Look at what this person means to you, look at what your commitment means to yourself and look into the future. You don't want to think that your partner will become paraplegic, and some partners become so. Will you take care of this person? How far will your commitment go?' Then they write their own vows and rituals."

More Meaning for Less Money

The wedding business, like so many other parts of our lives, has fallen prey to Madison Avenue and is now a $32-billion-a-year industry. The average wedding today costs between $15,000 and $20,000. Many couples get so caught up in the material side of the wedding that they forget about its true meaning—as a reflection of the deep love between them that brought them to this point in their lives.

When the focus is taken off consumption, couples often create very heartfelt, unique, and special weddings. Take note of the following story and see how this couple managed to spend very little on the traditional wedding elements (clothes, food, entertainment, site) yet created a very moving ceremony: they were married before two hundred people at the groom's farm. Some friends provided the food, and others the music. The bride wore her mother's old-fashioned satin wedding gown, and the groom wore black cotton pants, a white shirt, and a Guatemalan vest. A creek ran through the farm, so the couple decided to make use of it as a symbol of letting go of some things in their pasts. They wrote these things on a piece of paper, tore it up, stood at the edge of the creek, and tossed the torn bits into the flowing water, watching as they drifted downstream and out of sight. They also decided to involve their parents in the ceremony by serving them cups of tea. That act symbolized the nourishment the parents had given them. The entire wedding had been so touching that when it was time for the parents to speak, the bride's father got up but was so moved to tears he was unable to continue.

In writing her book, *Green Weddings That Don't Cost the Earth*, Carol Reed-Jones researched everything from favors to flowers and food and discovered delightful ways to provide these things for less money. She also wanted the items to have as little environmental impact on the earth as possible.

Carol was moved to write the book when preparing for her own wedding. She says: "I just didn't want to buy a bunch of miniature plastic champagne glasses filled with stale candy to give away as favors, so I started looking for alternatives. My husband-to-be and I were very much into the environment, and live in a way that walks lightly on the planet . . . we wanted our wedding to reflect that. Also, this was a second wedding for both of us and we wanted something that wasn't a headache to prepare, such as making sure the candles matched the bridesmaids' dresses. Who cares!"

Carol wore a white brocade suit that she bought on sale for $69 and flat shoes that she could wear anywhere; she bought the cake at a local grocery store for $35. They ordered in-season flowers from the same store. Rather than a plastic bride and groom, the cake topper was a small glass flower holder that Carol found at a garage sale for a dime. She filled it with fresh flowers.

The most expensive item at Carol's wedding was the food—which she says she would do differently now. They wanted the reception to be at a favorite historic, antique-filled hotel in the town where they were married, and discovered that hotels insist that people use their in-house caterers to provide food. The tab for the brunch buffet was $2,500.

Since her wedding, Carol has been inspired by the potluck weddings of friends. Her lesson is: *Check to see what resources your friends have first!* Carol made a cake for one friend's wedding, and others have enlisted the talents of musician friends, cooks, gardeners, calligraphers. One friend was married in a public park wearing a $24 white cotton dress with white lace hosiery. Carol says the whole effect was lovely, with her hair French-braided and woven with flowers. They marked their area off from the rest of the park by trailing ribbon from tree to tree and tying bows in between. One friend played the flute and another barbecued salmon for the thirty to fifty people in attendance.

Here are a few ways you can save the environment and your pocketbook:

Flowers

✧ Rent live greenery. Look in the phone book under "Plants—Interior Design, Leasing and Maintenance" or "Plants—Retail."

✧ Buy live greenery that you can reuse in your own garden.

✧ Plan ahead and grow your own flowers or ask a gardener friend to grow them for you.

✧ Buy for less at your local farmers' market or directly from a grower.

✧ Have the wedding outdoors in a flower garden or other natural setting. Use the natural beauty in lieu of purchased flowers.

✧ To make bouquets, just tie a bunch of flowers with a ribbon.

✧ One couple took their closest friends and relatives to a local farmers' market and asked each one to pick out a favorite bouquet. They gathered together back home to make arrangements and had a great time getting acquainted with one another.

✧ Go beyond flowers and use whatever Mother Nature provides. For one October wedding, the couple used pumpkins, leaves, and candles rather than flowers. Another idea is to put potted trees in strategic spots (most nurseries sell small trees that you can later plant in your yard or a park), then hang a string of white twinkle lights, and you have created natural ambience.

Music. Consider acoustic (unplugged) music. Contact your local folklore society or music shop to get names of musicians if you don't have friends who could do the job for you.

Photography. Stay away from the disposable cameras that have become popular to hand out to wedding guests. Instead, ask a couple of photographer friends to take pictures for you, but make sure that these friends are capable and reliable. Otherwise, you can hire a professional photographer to take a few standard shots.

Invitations. Who says you need those fancy invitations with all the extra envelopes and tissue paper? If you or a friend is skilled at design or calligraphy, you can create your own. The most memorable invitations I've received are always of the noncommercial variety.

Gifts

✧ Two books that can give you ideas are *Gifts That Make a Difference*, and *Gifts that Save the Animals*, by Ellen Berry, Foxglove Publishing, (513) 293-5649.

❖ *Gift registry* is a good idea in that guests aren't left to buy things you don't need. Also consider alternative registries in catalogs like *Real Goods*, *Seventh Generation*, *Natural Choice*, or *Earth Care*.

❖ *Donations to charity*: Especially with second marriages, couples often don't need more housewares. Compile a list of perhaps three to five charitable organizations that you would like to help, and include with your invitation their names, addresses, and a short paragraph about what they do. Explain that you already have enough, and would like gifts to be given to one of these organizations. You can also set up a scholarship fund at a local college or university and ask guests to donate to it. Here are two ideas on how to make the request, from *Green Weddings*: 1. "At this time of great joy for us, we cannot help remembering others less fortunate. In lieu of gifts to us, a fund has been set up in our name with the Housing Authority (Salvation Army, etc.) to help a homeless family" (include address and account name). 2. "We are blessed to have everything we need. We would be honored by a donation to one of the following charities" (include a list of charities).

❖ *Other ideas*: Instead of gifts, ask guests to bring a favorite dish to share at the potluck, or ask them to bring the gift of time. One couple who asked for time gifts got an offer to take them to dinner at a later date, and another friend offered to send a favorite book or tape.

❖ *Recycled gifts*: I must admit I was taken aback when I first read about this idea but after I thought about it, I realized that for some people, it can be a fine idea. I was especially moved by this testimonial from a bride who wrote in *Wedding Alternatives*:

> When women in my home church of Aztec, New Mexico, said they wanted to give me a shower, I was apprehensive . . . imagining all sorts of electric frying pans, electric can openers, electric blankets, etc. So I wrote . . . expressing my concern about exploitation of natural resources and [saying] I would prefer it if items which were used but still good could be given as gifts—as a form of recycling. I

also included a list of items we needed, such as wooden clothes-drying racks, garden tools, trash cans. We didn't receive anything that was useless or wasteful, but we did receive practically everything on the list. The most wonderful part was that nearly everything was stuff people had had tucked away in closets for years and no longer used, or the gifts were handmade by the women.

Food. Many people are happy to contribute to a potluck wedding, as it makes them feel they are a part of it. You can ask everyone who comes to bring something, or delegate the job to your closest friends and family members. If you ask only close friends and family to provide food, you should make sure all food types are covered—hors d'oeuvres, salads, main course, etc. If you don't want to have a potluck, then consider hiring small caterers whose menus most match your own tastes. They will likely charge less than in-house hotel catering staff, and you are doing your part to support small, local businesses.

Cake toppers. For alternatives to plastic bride-and-groom cake toppers, consider edible flowers. A couple of good books are *Edible Flowers: From Garden to Palate*, by Cathy Wilkinson Barash, and *The Complete Herb Book*, by Maggie Stuckey. In Bermuda, the wedding cake is sometimes topped with a tiny cedar tree. After the wedding day, the couple plants the tree and watches it grow along with their love.

Candles. As a way to save money and also make the day more special, consider following one couple's example: "We asked people to bring a candle and holder (labeled with their name and phone number) from their home as symbolic of their role in bringing light and warmth to our relationship."

Wedding favors. If a value is living consciously and lightly on the earth, then why give your guests some plastic item they'll throw away after the wedding? First, you don't need to give favors out at all. Most people today do not expect a wedding favor, but if you want to give them out, do your best to make them meaningful. You can go as far as the idea in *Green Weddings*, which is to hand-write a haiku poem for each guest on homemade recycled paper, or simply hand out mints or chocolates.

Wedding clothes. There is no doubt that this is a special day, deserving of special clothing. But there are alternatives to traditional bridal gowns, which are expensive, often worn only once, and require dry cleaning and special storage. Consider borrowing or renting a gown. Wear an heirloom gown. Look for charming vintage gowns in antique shops. Have a gown made with washable fabric. Purchase or make a dress or suit that can be worn again. Rather than a wear-it-once veil, consider weaving flowers into your hair or wearing a hat.

Balloons and streamers. Balloons are a hazard to wild animals who may eat and choke on them. A good alternative is paper streamers—you can even find them made of recycled paper. You can use all sorts of patterns and colors in a very festive way. You can also use banners—either premade or made just for you.

Incorporate Your Heritage into the Ceremony

You can make your wedding unique and even more special, and in so doing take the emphasis away from commercialism, by incorporating your different ethnic, religious, or cultural backgrounds into the ceremony. One couple—she Christian, he Jewish—held a Christian/Jewish wedding in an outdoor arboretum. They said their vows beneath the huppah carried by the groom's siblings. It was made of over sixty unique squares, hand decorated by family and friends. The ceremony was a combination of the two religions, and also included elements of Native American tradition and a respect for the earth.

Michelle and Joel Levey wove together rituals from their Jewish roots and Tibetan Buddhist studies. Two hundred people came to the potluck wedding they held at a friend's house. After an initial one-hour meditation with the community gathered to "create a sacred space," Michelle walked down the aisle with Tibetan horns blowing and guests chanting *Om Mani Padme Hum*, the Tibetan mantra of Universal Compassion. The couple had a Buddha on their wedding cake, rather than the traditional bride and groom, because, they say, the Buddha represented that their relationship was about awakening to their true nature and potential, and helping others to do the same. They were married by a rabbi under the traditional Jewish wedding canopy, huppah, that symbolizes the four corners of the earth.

A Caucasian bride and Vietnamese groom had an Episcopal priest and a Disciples of Christ minister officiate at the ceremony, which started with the Vietnamese custom of having the couple enter the church arm in arm followed by a procession of their closest family members. In Vietnam, this symbolizes the solidarity of the families.

A few international customs are listed in *Wedding Alternatives*, and you can peruse books at the end of this chapter or in your local library for more ideas on how you can incorporate your own heritage and customs: Japanese couples take nine sips of sake, a Japanese wine made from rice, in the *san-san-kudo* ceremony, becoming husband and wife after the first sip. Family members repeat this at the reception. One Mexican tradition calls for a large loop of rosary beads, symbolizing unity, to be placed in a figure-eight shape around the necks of the couple after they say their vows. During a Native American wedding ceremony, the couple drinks from a two-spouted jug to symbolize the joining of two families. Crowns of orange blossoms (symbols of purity and loveliness) are placed on both partners' heads during a traditional Greek wedding ceremony. This symbolizes their entrance into the realm of marriage.

Sample Wedding Vows

When all is said and done, vows are the most important part of the wedding ceremony. When taken seriously, as they should be, they are the promises the bride and groom make to each other about how they will live together. They are the spiritually and emotionally binding part of the ceremony.

Vows are more than a string of poetic words spoken before your guests. They are promises of what you will do for each other as a married couple. As you speak your vows, you are making yourself accountable to each other under certain circumstances, and for a certain length of time.

The following are a few sample vows that exemplify the qualities of Simple Loving—being conscious, intentional, and heartfelt:

> I love you, Carolyn. I give you my love as a gift. You don't need to earn it; you don't need to question it; and you don't need to fear the loss of it. I commit myself to loving you for as long as we live.
>
> I commit myself to spending a lifetime building a relationship with you. I commit myself to being as open to change and growth when we are fifty as when we were dating. I want us to enjoy our relationship at every step of the way, even as we seek to grow.
>
> I commit myself to continue to grow by absorbing your strengths. I admire the person you are and have appreciated your influence in my life. I want to continue to learn from you about being honest in our relationship, about the willingness to openly express who we are, and about the value of silence and reflection in our lives. . . .
>
> I remember one rainy day when we came so close to not patching up a difference we had had. But we began to talk and then to share ideas of what we wanted life to be. That's when we realized how closely our dreams matched. I commit myself to resisting the death of our dreams, to resisting the pressure of compromise and dullness. I commit myself to keeping the hope of newness and growth alive.
>
> Carolyn, I love you, and because of that love, I will listen and talk to you; I will laugh and cry with you; I will go for walks with you and rub your back. I will live with you and grow old with you. I will be your partner, friend, confidant, and lover for a lifetime . . .
>
> —FROM *WEDDING ALTERNATIVES*

Joel and Michelle Levey wrote their own vows, which emerged effortlessly one day as they went for a walk in the woods together. Each one said:

From my heart
I make this promise to you:
To be honest,
To be true,
And to be here with you throughout all the changes.
I devote myself to learning, loving, and growing in Dharma and in
    service with you;
To nurture and support your spiritual awakening as I grow into my
    own wholeness,
For the benefit of all living beings.

Bev and Tom Feldman had spent six months preparing to marry by doing an intense engagement process, profiled on page 158. The following is their wedding vow to each other:

I give you my permission and my encouragement to walk on your path in life . . . to be, do and have all that there is for you in this life and to do so without wonder, concern or hesitation. I am a partner now in your adventure in this life.

You are the maker and creator of your experience, happiness, satisfaction and fulfillment. I am your resource and support. I am a safe place and haven. I am a source for you. I am a vessel to contain you and a mirror to reflect you. I am a place of renewal and friendship, of encouragement and power. I am here for you like the sun is for the earth. I shine in my heart for you every day.

You have my permission and blessing to be all that your soul requires. To visit faraway places. To study obscure subjects, to talk with me late at night when I'd rather sleep. You have my permission to love me and make me happy, to make me laugh, to have and nurture our children, to explore the universe with me and the universe without me.

I place no restrictions on your movement or being and I declare null and void any spoken or implied restriction which does not further you. I promise to care for you and our children, to be a guardian, a steward of your spirit, those of our children and of everything that nurtures you. For I am a universe without limitation. I am your meadow on which to graze and play.

Deborah Koff-Chapin and Ross Chapin wrote *Our Covenant* for their marriage:

I dedicate myself

To trust you, to be genuine with you
to be vulnerable with you, to reveal myself
with you
to be strong with you, to be gentle with you
to have faith in you, to love you
to allow you to change
to allow you to make mistakes, to fall—
as well as to succeed and to fly
to allow you the space to say no and to say yes

to be true to my own dance
to be a loving witness of your dance
to pursue the point of contact in our
dance together
to act from within the pulse, rather than
from impulse

to walk the edges with you
to be at home with you
to give you the freedom to explore
your edges
to give you the space in my heart to come home

to see our relationship as a mirror of my
own attunement
to see beyond the shell of outer appearances
to the seed of your essence
to be in the union beyond our differences
to remember always to give thanks

to assist your healing
to allow you to assist my healing
to assist our healing
to assist the healing of others and the earth

to harness our energies for consciousness
rather than to dissipate them
to resist becoming mesmerized by the habitual
patterns in life, by the mechanics of relationship
and marriage
to see and use all the circumstances of our
life as fuel for our growth, soul work and
spiritual journey
to align our hearts, minds, bodies and souls
with the Will of God

to embrace the unknown together, allowing for
deeper knowings to emerge
to allow the necessary deaths that bring new life
to share with you all the days that life may give us
together, and
to create the most beautiful life that we can

and, I invite the same from you.

Second Marriages

A second marriage is a reflection of the couple's individual histories as well as their collective future, of their losses and failures, as well as their achievements, hopes, and possibilities. Previously married people bring unique issues to their subsequent unions. For instance, often one or both parties has children—How will they be involved? Be prepared to handle resentments and jealousies. Involve the children in the plans by taking them along to help choose the location, and ask them to help make invitations or decorations. Often children are included in the vows, or in the prayers for the new family.

The entire ceremony for a second marriage is often less elaborate than for a first wedding, such as this example: The wedding was held outdoors in a relative's backyard, and guests sat in a circle (symbolically surrounding the couple with their love and support) on hay bales, which were rented for the day from a neighbor's farm.

Rev. Gadd remembers one second marriage ceremony where the couple thanked those who had helped them through their previous marriages, and supported them in coming together in this second wedding.

Second-marriage vows often include the idea of change—that marriage is a form in which you have chosen to express and live your loving relationship, and to serve its purpose your marriage must change as you change. Your unchanging commitment of love and devotion to each other will allow you both to experience and share the transformations of your life together.

Rev. Dawn says the actual celebration of a second marriage can be very similar to that of a first marriage, though often smaller, but the underlying personal issues can be very different. One common problem stems from Rev. Dawn's belief that once someone truly loves another person, that love never stops, even if there is a divorce. That recognition can be difficult for a second spouse—yet it is a fact of life in many second marriages. "I believe that love is constant," she says. "You may not be able to live together, but the love doesn't end. So the second spouse needs to recognize and accept that."

Rev. Dawn also finds that one or both partners often get into a second marriage in yet another attempt to make themselves whole. "People are trying to make themselves whole, and somewhere during a marriage some of them recognize that they still aren't whole, so they get divorced. Then they jump into another relationship because they're in the infatuation stage rather than the marriage stage and unconsciously say to themselves, This woman or this man will make me whole. Again they're missing the point that another person can't make them whole.

"I sometimes work with these people before I agree to marry them. We'll look at how they originally became unwhole. For instance, I had a mother who told me I'd never amount to anything. If I continued to believe that, I would have never amounted to anything—that affirmation was not only in my head, but the cells of my body and my soul foundation—so I needed to get to that level and believe that was not true for me. Then I could move beyond and look at my own value and reassess it.

"None of us are ever totally whole, but the difference is our ownership of the problem. You need to recognize that your partner can't make you feel better—only you can."

Renewal Ceremonies and Anniversaries

Vow renewal and anniversary celebrations can simply be an affirmation that, in the midst of high divorce rates, this union is still going strong. They can also celebrate major milestones or changes in the couple's life together. They can be regular reminders to continue living and loving consciously.

Recommitment ceremonies also recognize the value of ritual. Many of us no longer practice an organized religion, but in ceasing to do so, we've also given up the ritual that those religions offer. Rev. Dawn says: "In our culture we've thrown out ritual and celebration, which is an absolute need in human development. It keeps the myth alive—it's part of our heritage to pass on and we do that through ritual. One of the reasons that having a cup of coffee has become such a big deal is that there is a whole ritual around having a latte, and that demonstrates how hungry we are for ritual. People get a sense of renewal, a sense of themselves, and a sense of belonging when we do ritual, regardless of whether it's brushing your teeth, having a latte or getting married. The same aspects are there. When couples celebrate their anniversary every year, they are creating their own special family ritual. That doesn't need to cost money. Some people go somewhere, and others simply stay home, take the phone off the hook, unplug the TV and just be together for the entire day."

If you choose a more formalized recommitment ceremony, the following are a few sample vows from *Wedding Alternatives*:

> In our years of marriage times have been better, times have been worse, we have been richer, we have been poorer, we have been sick, we have been healthy. I stand here today, ten years and two daughters later, to tell you, our family and our friends, that I would do it all over again.

Another couple had more to say in these vows:

> Our life together had taken some unprecedented twists. In the face of those changes, it was important to remind ourselves of the constancy of the feelings we held for each other and the permanence of the promises we had made to each other. Five years also seemed to be a good time to reread our vows, assess our successes and failures in living up to them, and resolve to make improvements. Finally, we had found a strong faith community after our marriage and wanted to restate our commitments to each other before them . . .
>
> When we renew our vows at our tenth anniversary next year, I plan to expand on our original promises to include additional things I now believe to be important to a good marriage. I have learned so much about what it means to honor, trust, understand and respect, and how hard those promises can be to keep. So, I would not delete

any of those, but would add: a promise to listen more and argue less; to compromise; to support and encourage each other in work and community endeavors and in our spiritual journeys; to talk often about our feelings; to make time to have fun together . . . The next time around, I would also like to make promises to my children.

Betsy and Pete Smith re-created their wedding vows during an outdoor retreat to the Yukon. Betsy says, "I think the simplicity of being in such a remote place really allowed us to be our true selves, to pare down to our essence, to bask in the beauty of the wilderness, the quiet to hear ourselves think, the nowhere to rush to or be, the time to be totally in the present moment, to remember why we loved each other, and the time and structure to express that love. The trip was the best ever and both of us felt total contentment. The nice thing about the trip is that when things get tough, I can go to the memory and remember what it's like, what a perfect relationship can be, and it gives me encouragement.

"In our renewal of vows ceremony, each person in the group created his/her own piece as he/she wished. It was the last night of the week and we sat in the cabin around the table where we had eaten, talked, laughed and cried together, and had our reflection time all week. We had candles and flowers and it was a sacred time together, approached by all with reverence and joy.

"I found a unique rock on the beach and handed it to Pete. I said: 'Peter-my-rock—I give you this rock to symbolize my love for you. You have been Peter, the rock, from the time we were married. You have stood firm, even through rocky times. Your faithfulness to me and to our marriage has been like a rock in the winds, the rain, and the changing tides. I like the feel of this rock; it reminds me of your strong, smooth hands. Like this rock, our love will remain strong, and it will become smoother as it withstands the tests of time. It will remain unique and beautiful even as it stands on the shore among the thousands and thousands of rocks, each one different and unique, but part of the whole. I also give you my poem, "The Red, Red Rose," and I'll sing "The Rose" for you now.' Another woman in the group and I sang 'The Rose'—Bette Midler's version. Well, we weren't great, but it was heartfelt and we had fun!

"My love is like a red, red rose
Passionate, rich and deep.
In full bloom we inhale the fragrance,
Sweet or spicy
We go deep inside to its center—
sticky and full of honey
and envelop each other with love.
While there, there is nothing
but breezes and hummingbirds' wings
to match our hearts beating.
The thorns are there and they
have pierced and torn and festered.
But now, the leaves of green
which give renewal
year after year
protect us,
so this fragile beautiful rose
can bloom and grow again
forever."

Pete gave Betsy a set of nesting rocks to symbolize their marriage. He read a Baha'i marriage prayer which has these lines:

Wherefore, wed Thou in the heaven of Thy Mercy these two birds of the nest of Thy Love, and make them the means of attracting perpetual grace; that from the union of these two seas of love a wave of tenderness may surge and cast the pearls of pure and goodly issue on the shore of life.

—ABDU'L BAHA

Ideas for Vow Renewal Ceremonies
from *Wedding Alternatives*

1. A reaffirmation ceremony can be anything from a church service to a picnic. You can re-create your original wedding, including setting, music, readings, etc. Or you can create an entirely new celebration.

2. The reaffirmation can include just a few people, close friends and immediate family, or a larger group. Perhaps you may wish to restate your commitments before new friends or a new faith community.

3. You can restate your original vows or write new ones. Decide on what is most important to you. Review your original vows. Do they still cover the important promises you feel your marriage is based on? Would others more clearly state your feelings?

4. Include special music and readings, either those used in your original ceremony or others that have taken on special meaning.

5. Some couples wear clothing worn at the original service. Some choose other special outfits or everyday clothing. Would wearing your original wedding attire hold more meaning for you? Or would some other outfit better represent who you are today?

6. While some couples ask the original attendants to be a part of their vow renewal, others ask their children or new friends. Recognizing the importance of family, some couples with children choose to involve their children in some way. It can be quite meaningful to include children in the procession and/or to ask them to offer words of love and encouragement. Still others prefer to have no attendants. Perhaps entering alone arm in arm would be more appropriate in your situation.

7. Many couples choose to have a celebration after the vow renewal service. Choices include a potluck dinner, a barbecue picnic, a sitdown meal, dinner at a favorite restaurant, etc. Ask yourselves:

What kind of postceremony gathering do we want, if any? What is in keeping with our budget? Who will be invited?

8. Consider borrowing items you need for the celebration to keep costs at a minimum. When you must squeeze money out of the household budget to pay for celebration needs, money may be a big concern. Vow renewals don't have to cost a lot of money. Borrow items you need, such as clothing, chairs, eating utensils, tablecloths, candles, etc.

9. If you plan to send out invitations or to have a wedding bulletin, consider including an original wedding photograph or a photo of your family today. This can make the celebration even more personal and can offer guests a memento of the occasion.

❧ ❧ ❧

Resources

MINISTERS INTERVIEWED FOR THIS BOOK
Rev. Sally J. Gadd: (206) 362-7012
Rev. Diana B. Dawn: (360) 671-1884
Robbie Fahnestock: (206) 789-7989

BOOKS
The Art of Ritual: A Guide to Creating and Performing Your Own Ceremonies for Growth and Change, by Renee Beck and Sydney Barbara Metrick (Berkeley, Calif.: Celestial Arts, 1990).

The Cake Bible, by Rose Levy Beranbaum (New York: Morrow, 1988).

Creative Weddings: An Up-to-Date Guide for Making Your Wedding as Unique as You Are, by Laurie Levin and Laura Golden Bellotti (New York: Plume, 1994).

The Elegant Wedding and the Budget-Savvy Bride: How to Have the Wedding of Your Dreams for Half the Price, by Deborah McCoy (New York: Plume, 1999).

Green Weddings That Don't Cost the Earth, by Carol Reed-Jones (Paper Crane Press, 1996). 800-356-9315 or (360) 676-0226.

How to Have the Wedding You Want, by Danielle Claro (New York: Berkley Books, 1995).

I Do: A Guide to Creating Your Own Unique Wedding Ceremony, by Sydney Metrick (Berkeley, Calif.: Celestial Arts, 1995).

Love Sweeter Love: Creating Relationships of Simplicity and Spirit, by Jann Mitchell (Hillsboro, Ore.: Beyond Words Publishing, 1998).

New Traditions: Redefining Celebrations for Today's Family, by Susan Abel Lieberman (New York: The Noonday Press, 1991).

1001 Ways to Save Money . . . and Still Have a Dazzling Wedding, by Sharon Naylor (Chicago: Contemporary Books, 1994).

Wedding Alternatives, published by Alternatives for Simple Living, 5312 Morningside Ave., P.O. Box 2857, Sioux City, IA 51106. 800-821-6153.

Weddings from the Heart: Contemporary and Traditional Ceremonies for an Unforgettable Wedding, by Daphne Rose Kingma (Berkeley, Calif.: Conari Press, 1991).

If you would like a quarterly reminder about simplifying your life, you can subscribe to *Simple Living*, the newsletter published by Janet Luhrs. It is filled with real-life stories of people who have slowed down and created rich lives, as well as articles and tips by experts in the field. *Simple Living* also provides a forum for readers to connect with one another, through study circle and pen pal listings, as well as letters to the editor. Call (206) 464-4800 or write to Simple Living, 4509 Interlake Ave. N., PMB 149, Seattle, WA 98103. You can also visit the Web site, www.simpleliving.com.

INDEX